Sensory Capabilities of Hearing Impaired Children

Sensory Capabilities of Hearing-Impaired Children

Based on the proceedings of a workshop
Baltimore, Maryland • October 26-27, 1973

Conference Sponsor

Information Center for Hearing, Speech,
and Disorders of Human Communication,
The Johns Hopkins University School of Medicine

Rachel E. Stark, Ph.D.
editor

University Park Press

BALTIMORE • LONDON • TOKYO

University Park Press
International Publishers in Science and Medicine
Chamber of Commerce Building
Baltimore, Maryland 21202

Library of Congress Cataloging in Publication Data
Main entry under title:

Sensory capabilities of hearing-impaired children.

   "This workshop was the fourth to be organized by the Information Center
for Hearing, Speech, and Disorders of Human Communication."
   1. Hearing disorders in children—Congresses. I. Stark, Rachel E., ed. II.
Information Center for Hearing, Speech, and Disorders of Human Com-
munication. [DNLM: 1. Hearing disorders—In infancy and childhood—
Congresses. WV270 S478 1973]
RF122.5.C4S46   617.8'9   74-1413
ISBN 0-8391-0724-2

Contents

PREFACE

This workshop was the fourth to be organized by the Information Center for Hearing, Speech, and Disorders of Human Communication. The first dealt with the neuroanatomical bases of hearing, the second with the physiological bases of hearing (Sachs, 1972) and the third with vascular disorders and hearing defects (de Lorenzo, 1973). The topic for the fourth workshop, Sensory Capabilities of Hearing-Impaired Children, was proposed by Dr. S. Richard Silverman, its Chairman. With considerable energy and thoughtfulness, Dr. Silverman developed the program for the workshop. A number of conferences had dealt previously with the technical development of auditory and nonauditory aids for the deaf (Pickett, 1968; Levitt and Nye, 1971; Smith, 1972). He felt that it was time to consider the needs and capabilities of the deaf child for whom these aids were being designed. Accordingly a group of scientists working in the areas of speech science, hearing science, experimental psychology, linguistics, and education of the deaf were invited to share their thinking and experience with respect to the problems of deaf children. It was felt that their interaction would generate fresh ideas about features of technical aids and nontechnical aspects of training which would facilitate favorable development in the deaf child. With this in mind, Dr. Silverman suggested three questions to the participants: What do we know about sensory capabilities of the hearing-impaired child? What do we need to know? And how can we best find out those things we need to know?

Dr. Silverman made the decision with the concurrence of Dr. John E. Bordley, Director of the Information Center, and myself to experiment with a discussion format rather than one based upon contributed papers. Three topic areas were chosen as a basis for discussion, namely, Sensory Capabilities, Perceptual and Cognitive Strategies, and Language Processing. One half day was assigned to consideration of each of these topics. Each session was guided by a chairman who opened it with a fifteen minute State-of-the-Art report. Copies of these reports and of Dr. Hirsh's Keynote Address were made available to the participants immediately before the workshop began. Participants were invited to present their own recent work informally within this context.

The discussion was lively and the participants spoke their minds. It was also free-flowing and in no session did it stay within the designated topic area, partly as a result of the natural overlap of definition of sensory, perceptual, and cognitive processes. The major editorial task was that of reorganizing all that was said so that it formed a reasonable sequence within the framework of these topics. Also, it transpired that the discussion dealt (1) with the capabilities of the normal-hearing and of the deaf individual and the development of these capabilities and (2) with the implications of this information for treatment of the deaf child. The discussion falling naturally under each topic heading was therefore divided into two parts, one dealing with questions of capability and the other with considerations of treatment and training.

The participants' surnames have been used throughout without title for the greater ease of the reader. Both the discussion and the informal reports of experimental work have been presented in narrative form. Each participant was asked to read and correct those portions of the discussion in which he was quoted and also any accounts of recent experimental work which he had contributed. I accept final responsibility for interpretation of what was said and for the form in which it was cast.

The discussion continued unabated into what was intended as a final summary session. Dr. Silverman therefore contributed a summary chapter after the workshop was over. For the benefit of those readers who may be unfamiliar with some of the issues which were brought up, I have added a section dealing with these issues and with their relationship to special education for the deaf. In this section, I have also tried to indicate the directions for future research suggested by the Conference. I have received valuable help and advice in preparing this section from my colleagues, and in particular from Dr. Silverman. I have tried to reflect the concerns of the participants throughout, but inevitably I have conveyed some biases of my own as well. This should be kept in mind by the reader.

I would like to thank the Chairman for his dedication to the purpose of this workshop and the participants for their contributions to it and their usually prompt response to requests for revisions, figures, figure legends, references, and comments on specific aspects of the material presented here. I would also like to thank the staff of the Information Center for their efficient and supportive work behind the scenes and in particular, Mrs. Lyda Sanford, who has been involved in all aspects of preparation of the manuscript.

Rachel E. Stark, Ph.D.

REFERENCES

de Lorenzo, A.J.D.: Vascular Disorders and Hearing Defects. Baltimore: University Park Press, 1973.

Levitt, H., and Nye, P.W., eds.: Sensory Training Aids for the Hearing Impaired: Proceedings of a Conference, National Academy of Engineering, Washington, D.C., 1971.

Pickett, J.M., ed.: Proceedings of a conference on speech-analyzing aids for the deaf, Amer. Ann. Deaf. 13(2), 1968.

Sachs, M.B.: Physiology of the Auditory System. Baltimore: National Educational Consultants Inc., 1972.

Smith, C.P., ed.: Conference Record: Conference on Speech Communication and Processing, Special Report No. 131, Air Force Cambridge Research Laboratories, AFCRL-72-0120, 1972.

PARTICIPANTS

Chairman of the Conference:
S. Richard Silverman
Director, Central Institute for the Deaf
St. Louis, Missouri

Barry Blesser, Ph.D.
Department of Electrical Engineering
Massachusetts Institute of Technology
Cambridge, Massachusetts

Arthur Boothroyd, Ph.D.
Director of Research
Clarke School for the Deaf
Northampton, Massachusetts

Peter B. Denes, Ph.D.
Research Department
Bell Telephone Laboratories
Murray Hill, New Jersey

Rita B. Eisenberg, Sc.D.
Director, Bioacoustics Laboratory
St. Joseph's Hospital
Lancaster, Pennsylvania

Norman Erber, Ph.D.
Central Institute for the Deaf
St. Louis, Missouri

Hans Furth, Ph.D.
Department of Psychology
Catholic University
Washington, D.C.

Ira Hirsh, Ph.D.
Dean, Faculty of Arts and Sciences
Washington University
St. Louis, Missouri

Arthur S. House, Ph.D.
Institute for Defense Analysis
von Neumann Hall
Princeton, New Jersey

Harry Levitt, Ph.D.
Communication Science Laboratory
Graduate Center, CUNY
New York, New York

Alvin M. Liberman, Ph.D.
Department of Psychology
University of Connecticut
Storrs, Connecticut

Daniel Ling, Ph.D.
Project Director, Human Communi-
cation Disorders
McGill University
Montreal, Quebec, Canada

Paula Menyuk, Ed.D.
Research Laboratory of Electronics
Massachusetts Institute of Technology
Cambridge, Massachusetts

James D. Miller, Ph.D.
Central Institute for the Deaf
St. Louis, Missouri

James M. Pickett, Ph.D.
Hearing and Speech Center
Gallaudet College
Washington, D.C.

Irwin Pollack, Ph.D.
Mental Health Research Institute
University of Michigan
Ann Arbor, Michigan

Joseph Rosenstein, Ph.D.
Director of Research
Gallaudet College
Washington, D.C.

Carl E. Sherrick, Ph.D.
Department of Psychology
Princeton University
Princeton, New Jersey

Charles Watson, Ph.D.
Department of Psychology
Washington University
St. Louis, Missouri

THE INFORMATION CENTER CONCEPT

Information analysis centers have been developed to help the scientist and practitioner cope with the ever-increasing mass of published and unpublished information in a specific field. Their establishment resulted from a further extension of those pressures that had brought about the formation of the specialized primary journal and the abstracting services at the turn of the century. The information analysis center concept was greatly advanced by the 1963 report of the President's Science Advisory Committee Panel on Science Information. This report stated: ". . . scientific interpreters who can collect relevant data, review a field, and distill information in a manner that goes to the heart of a technical situation are more help to the overburdened specialist than is a mere pile of relevant documents." Such specialized information centers are operated in closest possible contact with working scientists in the field. These centers not only furnish information about ongoing research and disseminate and retrieve information but also create new information and develop new methods of information analysis, synthesis, and dissemination.

The continually expanding biomedical literature produced by scientists from the world's laboratories, research centers, and medical centers led the National Institute of Neurological Diseases and Stroke in 1964 to initiate a National Neurological Information Network of specialized centers for neurological information. The Centers are designed to bring under control and to promote ready access to important segments of the literature. The Network presently consists of the Brain Information Service at the University of California at Los Angeles, the Clinical Neurology Information Center at the University of Nebraska Medical Center, and the Information Center for Hearing, Speech, and Disorders of Human Communication at the Johns Hopkins Medical Institutions.

The mission of this Information Center is to identify, locate, store and retrieve, analyze, and disseminate information in hearing, language, speech, and communication disorders including reading disabilities. In the performance of its tasks, the Information Center has:

1. Developed a computer-based filing system containing information and references to articles published in journals, to the technical report literature, and to reports of research in progress;

2. Answered scientific questions;

3. Provided current awareness services, *Current Citations on Communication Disorders: Hearing and Balance* and *Current Citations on Communication Disorders: Language, Speech, and Voice,* computer-searched and printed lists of citations to recently published articles that incorporate relevant material from the MEDLARS tapes of the National Library of Medicine;

4. Written critical reviews, state-of-the-art reports, and biblio-profiles;

5. Translated material considered important to the subject area but not available in English;

6. Published two guides to sources of information: *Information Sources in Hearing, Speech, and Communication Disorders. Part 1. Publications. Part 2. Organizations;*

7. Produced a *Programmed Instruction on the Decibel in Clinical Audiology;*

8. Developed and prepared the *Index-Handbook of Ototoxic Agents, 1966–1971,* a computer-produced desk reference manual. A searchable data bank at the Information Center is part of this project;

9. Prepared bibliographies on many and varied subjects;

10. Sponsored workshops and produced the proceedings of these workshops.

The members of the Information Center will be well pleased if, through their most recent efforts, they have been able to help disseminate, quickly and effectively, the new knowledge derived from the Workshop on Sensory Capabilities of Hearing-Impaired Children to the scientists of the world.

Keynote Address
Information Processing and the Deaf Child

Ira J. Hirsh
Washington University
Central Institute for the Deaf

There are several fields of contemporary research—speech perception, psycholinguistics, the psychology of memory, the development of motor skills, and language acquisition—from which application might be made to those basic conceptions that lead to planning the special education of deaf children.

The conventional wisdom, at least with respect to oral education of deaf children, is that a child must be found and taught early lest his innate ability to acquire and use language become atrophied for lack of use and stimulation. It is assumed that a reliable audiogram will tell the educational planner what sound levels must be exceeded in order for sounds to be made available to auditory interpretation, or need to be supplemented by vision or by touch so as to enable a deaf child both to receive speech information and to utilize that information in developing his own speech. Particular ways of teaching, of presenting the speech information, and of providing the circumstances in which speech is produced and received and whether or not it should occur in the context of interpersonal communication are sources of argument and sometimes acrimonious debate.

PERCEPTION

Modern psychophysics not only continues to provide information on sensory scales and on the conditions necessary for detection of signals in noise, but also is beginning to include a much greater emphasis on the ways in which listeners process, discriminate, and recognize complicated acoustical patterns. Individuals differ with respect to complex auditory perceptual abilities and these differences are not well predicted by their performance in detection tasks. Thus we are forced to question the assumption that, if the signal is above the threshold for the deaf child, it can be processed in a normal way.

Another important aspect of perception and recognition is the relation between the coding or transformation that must take place when the signal enters the peripheral sensory system and storage, not only short-term storage but also that required to hold together long sequences of stimuli that comprise phrases and sentences of language.

Perhaps the most interesting and directly relevant aspect of this work is the suggestion that both verbal and nonverbal stimuli are somehow coded into a verbal form, and more particularly into a speechlike form. Are these short-term memory images to be thought of as acoustical or transformed auditory? Or are they proprioceptive or kinesthetic in form, representing some aspect of the speech act? If there is a motor component to a perceived and stored image, then it is clear that the receiving system must have become associated with the speaking system in order to function properly. Further, defective speech production may interfere with the perception process.

The connection between listening and speaking is not only a natural association, in the sense that a normally-hearing person's ears are never closed and he always hears himself talking, but also is related to the particular nature of those stimuli and responses that are members of the formal system of language. Recent work suggests that results of perceptual experiments on arbitrary or artificial complex sounds cannot predict precisely analogous performance when those sounds are events in a language sequence. In short, it appears that language communication involves both perceiving and producing in a fashion somewhat different from that adduced from nonlanguage experimentation.

LANGUAGE LEARNING

Recent work in language acquisition has imputed to the young child a tremendous amount of induction from language samples uttered by persons around him. The chief evidence for the inductive process appears to be the novel yet grammatically correct forms of his own utterances. Is such a learning model applicable only to children with normal hearing raised in a normal language environment or can the same model be used to fashion the educational and home program of the young deaf child?

At this point we must remind ourselves of concepts that emerge from learning theory, and in particular reinforcement theory. Its application to the education of the deaf child does in fact touch on virtually all aspects of human learning. The induction model of language acquisition emphasizes concept formation or the internalization of those principles that are the rules of one's language. At the same time, to recognize the speech of others involves learned discrimination and recognition. Again, to produce speech involves not only a very complicated series of speech acts with exquisitely fine control of complex motor patterns, but also the planning and enactment of long sequential patterns—a problem that has eluded psychologists for many years.

If we agree that such learnings are most effective when positively rewarded, we can make some deductions about what ought to be the circumstances under which a child learns his language. When the stimulus information is incomplete or when the speech production is defective, however, operant learning may be very time consuming, to say nothing of its taxing the patience of even the most devoted teacher. She wants to stop on that difficult word or group of words in the sentence in order to point out the relevant cues for recognition, or she wants to stop the child in the middle of his sentence to correct a particular aspect of speech production. The stopping itself may be a negative reinforcement, may discourage emitted speech production, and thus interfere with the interaction of communication that presumably contains both the rewards and the appropriate models for inductive language learning.

Suppose that we do identify a young deaf child before the end of his first year; what should we do? If we are convinced that acoustic input is absolutely essential for properly representing language, then our first efforts will be an appropriate amplifier that will produce sound levels for the speech spoken around him that are sufficiently high to be above his already high threshold. Such a plan is apparently feasible for the low frequencies for most profoundly deaf children, but does not, except under extraordinary circumstances, provide supra-threshold levels for the high frequencies. Some phonetics research has provided catalogues of the cues used by normal listeners for distinguishing among the sounds of speech and such catalogues might be used to predict which cues will be available for this defective listening system and which would not. The prediction, however, must be tested with young deaf subjects. In the light of such information, teachers can program the samples of language to which the child is exposed so as to maximize those discriminations that should be possible for him. You are familiar with the candidates most often supposed—number of syllables, stress pattern, certain vowel discriminations, tonal inflection, and duration cues of low-frequency spectra.

PROSTHETIC CODING

Contemporary research ought to provide us a guide for selecting crucial breaks along a continuum from genuine acoustic representation of language to acoustic information suitably transformed for the skin or the eye (on line) to stimulus transformations in which sound features may be presented graphically, to conventional signs or finger spelling, to the printed word.

Spectral features of speech sounds can be represented, as in the spectrogram, to either eye or different regions of the skin, and temporal or transitional information can similarly be represented. If machines were developed that could create such representations almost immediately and in an ongoing manner, could such patterns be used as the stimuli on the basis of which the deaf child would learn to perceive speech and gain models on the basis of which to produce speech? A question of great importance, at least to me, has been whether these temporal features need to remain temporal in form. That question has to do with the closeness of mapping of the stimulus form onto a kinesthetic form that would represent the motor speech act. It is the degree of remoteness of a particular signal transformation from the original that appears to be a crucial variable. The temporal form of an utterance that exists in the original acoustic signal can be appreciated, at least partially, by even the low-frequency region of a defective auditory system or perhaps also by the skin. A vibration pattern thus derived for the skin, however, may be less effective than a vibrational pattern that represents the speech act itself. Think for example of the difference between reception of the vibratory signal output from a special hearing aid with a vibrator attached, as contrasted with the vibratory signal available to the fingertips that are placed on the throat, the lips or the nose.

In this connection I wish to focus on several kinds of modality. We must choose the stimulus modality: whether the original acoustical pattern, a graphical transform available to eye or skin, or a complete symbolic translation as represented by phonetic characters or the traditional orthography. In addition there is the sensory modality through which these signals are perceived: whether the defective auditory system, the eye or the skin. An additional kind of modality that some of our experts in sensory and perceptual systems must address is that of the stimulus form, but now whether it is verbal or nonverbal. The special character of verbal percepts undoubtedly is related to the very special connection between the sound-producing mechanism and the hearing mechanism. We are beginning to learn something of the special nature of auditory perception of speech, as contrasted with more general aspects of auditory perception for nonspeech. Can such specialization also be counted on if speech information is to be presented to other sensory systems which are not so well connected to speech production?

Perhaps we can best summarize some of these introductory thoughts about prosthetic coding by asking you, representing your several specialties, to provide some reasonably specific instructions for the engineer who is perfectly willing to design a prosthetic system for deaf children. Does my emphasis on temporal form or does the emphasis of others on interactive communication require that the prosthesis deliver to the deaf child a stimulus pattern which features change in time in the same way that speech events change as they come from the talker? How many acoustical dimensions need thus to be represented? In fact, need they be acoustical, or can they be abstract features of the sort that characterize phonological systems common to a variety of languages? The use of such features implies that we would present through such a device some equivalences of phonemes or phoneme classes. Suppose then that we had the perfect speech recognizer with a phonetic-typewriter output. Would this serve as well? This machine would type letters or symbols standing for phoneme targets characteristic of a language and would contain within it the capacity to generalize or abstract such phoneme targets even from a great variety of talkers. The child's own speech production mechanism could also be trained with respect to those same phoneme targets. Even assuming immediacy of display and easy portability, does such a visual consequence serve our purpose? You will recognize that specific suggestions have been made with respect to such a device at different points along the continuum from a simple hearing aid or relatively simple schemes of transformation to such a device as a phonetic typewriter or even beyond to a representation of the message in another language. Can we not deduce from some of the kinds of knowledge represented at this conference at what stage we ought to focus the efforts of teachers and of those engineers who have shown a genuine interest in this problem?

THINKING

We must also move upward from these questions of perception, coding, storage and motor learning to those aspects of concept formation and thinking that have been held to be so closely allied with language. Very simply put, is the ability of the deaf child to think impaired seriously by this lack or deficiency of comprehension and use of this language system? Suppose it turns out that such children must be taught language as opposed to learning it through communicating experience; is conceptualization thus retarded until such time as a language system is internalized and subsequently made evident in their own productions?

By now we have gone quite far from perceptual processes mediated by peripheral systems to the interactions between language that is thus perceived and produced, and thought, a relation that has been a subject in psychology for many decades, even centuries. It brings us also farthest from some of the richest territories of empirical knowledge. On the other hand, much of what used to be called thinking is now called information processing and this latter term appears to imply a more manageable concept. I believe that some of our experts can help us focus on those aspects of thinking, of intelligence, and of creative activities that may be enhanced or treated with respect to specific emphases in the language-learning program that we would create for the deaf child.

CONCLUSIONS

I have attempted to sketch very briefly and crudely some of my suspicions about why you are all here. While scholars do pursue research in their own particular ways, there seem to be some important unifying threads that relate several separate enterprises. The problem presented by the deaf child who is to learn language seems to me to represent one of the most interesting of such threads and I hope that it provides an interesting focus for your discussions. Furthermore, I hope that those responsible for the education of the deaf children can profit from these same discussions.

Sensory Capabilities

1

Sensory Capabilities in Normal and Hearing-Impaired Children: State-of-the-Art Report

Carl E. Sherrick
Princeton University

INTRODUCTION

To avoid needless confusion it will be best to define at the outset what is meant by "sensory capabilities." For this report, the phrase is taken to mean the capacity of the organism to exhibit relatively simple behavioral or physiological responses to a set of simple and well-controlled stimulus conditions. The word "simple" does not imply that only topographically isolated "reflex" responses are included: a consistent and observable contingent change in some correlate of a complex activity, e.g., heart rate, EEG amplitude, or whole-body activity, may be the response examined. The stimulus may be defined in a similar manner.

A second constraint on the discussion in this paper, and one that follows from the definition given above, concerns the age of the children. Infants and early preschool children are the bulk of the population of concern, for two reasons: (a) older children are generally capable of participating in more sophisticated test situations involving perceptual tasks that may demand linguistic behavior; (b) an important area in need of concentrated research effort is that of neonatal and infant behavior, in view of both the difficulty of the subject matter and the importance of early diagnosis of problems.

Whereas the generally accepted goal of research in sensory evaluation is improved diagnosis, an important secondary goal is the development of aids for supplementation of deficient sensory inputs. Increasing knowledge of normal and deficient systems helps advance the design of devices and methods for the efficient use of alternative sense channels. Accordingly, a second objective of the present discussion should be the status of research on sensory aids for children.

PROBLEMS FOR RESEARCH IN SENSORY TESTING

The usefulness of the present report should be in suggesting gaps in the present research effort, rather than in hailing successes. A survey of research in sensory testing reveals a formidable list of methods and procedures, but they can be categorized roughly as follows:

A. Methods involving unlearned responses to stimuli.

1. Bioelectric potential changes, e.g., electrodermal responses, evoked potentials, EEGs, EKGs, electrocochleograms.

2. Behavioral responses, e.g., cochleo-palpebral reflex, Moro reflex, intra-aural reflexes, sucking response, orienting response.

B. Methods requiring learned responses.

1. Classically conditioned responses, e.g., conditioned electrodermal response, conditioned heart-rate response, pupillary response, etc.

2. Operant conditioning, e.g., "peep show" audiometry, orienting, object manipulation.

A number of tests that fall into one or another of the above categories have been devised to answer general questions concerning the nature of sensory processing in the infant, or the character of maturation of the nervous system, or have been applied as frankly diagnostic by pediatric neurologists. The process of standardization and normalization of the tests, as these terms are understood by biometricians, has most generally not been carefully followed or even attempted. The result has been that research findings may vary from laboratory to laboratory because of procedural changes or sampling variations. Other, equally significant sources of variance have been identified in a number of general issues that have emerged from such studies. Three that are of great current interest are: (a) the effect of the state of alertness of the infant on his responsiveness, (b) the problem of habituation, and (c) the problem of the detection of "true" responses by the experimenter from observations or recordings of weak or 'noisy' response patterns.

Problems of state of alertness

The graduate student in psychology who has spent the first five years of his professional life observing the behavior of a Wistar or Sprague-Dawley rat performing in an environmentally (and behaviorally) prophylactic Skinner box is amazed by the ethologist's description of the behavior of a battle-scarred, flea-bitten, wild Norway grey rat in his habitat. Similarly, the experience of the student of sensory processes with trained, normal, adult observers does not prepare him for the seeming vagaries of the young patient in the clinic. If you conclude that psychophysicists should appear more frequently in the clinic, and animal psychologists should spend some time in the sewers, I cannot refute your logic.

In the infant, a most outstanding feature of behavior is its shifting level of intensity, ranging through four more-or-less accepted stages: quiet sleep, active sleep, quiet waking, and active waking. The criteria for identification of the stages are based on observations with a variety of recording techniques, including stabilimetric records, heart rate, EEG, respiration, eye movements, and limb movements. A good review of the problems of state may be found in Hutt, Lenard, and Prechtl (1969), who point out that responsiveness is not necessarily correlated with increasing activity. Indeed, the authors note that some stimulus-response contingencies are enhanced in quiet sleep, others in active sleep, and some in two or more stages.

Davis (in preparation) has made similar observations in his studies of evoked response audiometry, and further has noted the necessity for a skilled attendant to manage the child's state. In studies of heart-rate change to auditory stimuli, Graham and Jackson (1970) reported that in neonates whose state went unmonitored, stimulation produced an average acceleration of heart rate, but for neonates stimulated only in the waking state, no significant change of heart rate was measured.

A general conclusion from critical reviews like that of Hutt et al. (1969) is that much of the earlier work on states, as well as both sensory and conditioning studies, should be reexamined. For the present discussion, the important question concerns the determination, if possible, of conditions that may produce and maintain the desired state of alertness in the child.

The problem of habituation

Interwoven with the problem of state is the question of the effect of the stimulus on the stage of wakefulness. Some stimuli, especially those with noxious elements, may arouse the child to undesirable levels of defensive activity, whereas others may appear to act as soporifics. The repetitive stimulus presentation required for sensory evaluation may lead to a decrement in frequency or magnitude of responses for other reasons. Two processes that are commonly held responsible for response decrement are adaptation and habituation. Both processes have common factors, e.g., greater decrement with increased frequency of repetition, and reappearance of response with prolonged interruption of the stimulus. Habituation, however, occurs more readily if the stimulus is weak; it will occur more rapidly with each additional trial series, and its effect will disappear if a novel stimulus is interpolated in the series. The last characteristic has proved useful in sensory studies, as Jeffrey and Cohen (1971) have noted in their review of the phenomenon. Investigators can habituate the child to a particular stimulus pattern, and insert in the series a probe pattern to determine whether the infant discriminates it. The fact that habituation shows generalization (but not in any well-understood manner) should be added to warn the reader that the technique is more complicated than it may first appear.

The interaction of habituation with state of alertness is particularly noticeable in experiments with neonates. Beyond the age of two months, however, habituation is readily obtained. Presumably this is due in part to the change in frequency of appearance of the various stages of wakefulness, and in part to the maturation of the habituation process itself. The need for study of the process, both for its utility in sensory research and for its role in obscuring desired results, is obvious.

The problem of response detection

Since the promulgation of the Theory of Signal Detection, psychologists, except for a few diehards, have been aware of the necessity for more rigorous monitoring of the O's behavior in psychophysical studies. When the O is the psychologist himself examining, say, an EEG or EDR write-out, or watching the behavior of another organism, the need for signal detection methods has been less readily apprehended. Several workers in the field of infant sensory evaluation have commented on the problem, however, e.g., Davis (in preparation), Goldstein (1963), Hutt et al. (1969), Ling, Ling, and Doehring (1970), and Weber (1969, 1970). Davis and Goldstein concerned themselves with evoked potential and EEG records, and the former has suggested the strategy of monitoring both visual and somesthetic evoked potentials in ERA tests, to ascertain the integrity of the central nervous system, as well as using the somesthetic evoked potentials as a template in examining the record for weak auditory evoked potentials. The review of Hutt et al., and the investigations of Ling et al., and of Weber deal with behavioral observations in real time. The reports of the latter two authors concern evaluations of a variant of the signal detection method in behavioral audiometry. Observers were paired to monitor simultaneously the behavior of a child being presented various sounds. In the Ling et al. procedure, one of the pair heard the sounds while the other received a masking noise. In Weber's procedure, both Os heard all the sounds through earphones, but only one could hear which were presented to the child. Weber's ignorant O gave no more false alarms than his informed O, but also had fewer hits, and thus appeared more conservative, therefore more likely to find hearing impairment. The Os of Ling et al., on the other hand, gave more false alarms, hence would find too few hearing-impaired children. The difference may be the result of the means of keeping the Os ignorant. The results of the two studies suggest that no great effect of knowledge of stimulus sequence can be shown, at least for relatively simple test situations. When, however, the Os report deals with more complex behavior, say interpretation of speech sounds, the effects of foreknowledge may be considerable.

PROBLEMS FOR RESEARCH IN SENSORY AIDS

It is possible to select only one or two topics from what has become a very large literature on sensory aids. I hope they will serve as exemplary illustrations of the problems encountered in the area, and of the potential for further work.

Auditory analogues for tactile communication of speech

The early work of Gault and his colleagues (1926) involved presentation of speech sounds to a single skin site by a mechanical vibrator. Dissatisfied with the poor showing by the skin, Gault (1936) modified the output of his system to provide several loci of vibrations on the fingertips, each having a restricted band of frequencies from low to high. The skin does not respond well to higher frequencies, however, and energy differences may have masked information from other bands, with the result that the modified device performed little better than the original. In succeeding decades, the Gault analogue of the Helmholtz place model was modified further, e.g., in the "Felix" project at Massachusetts Institute of Technology, and later tested more thoroughly by Pickett (1963). The major modification incorporated a Vocoder in the transmission system, and used the overall energy in a given filter band to modulate the amplitude of vibration of a 300 Hz signal. The various frequencies of the speech sounds were thus represented as loci on the skin, but the vibratory energy was always at a frequency to which the skin is highly sensitive. Pickett reported some success with his Tactual Vocoder, especially in conjunction with speech-reading in deaf children, when features of speech missed by the tactile system were captured visually, and vice versa.

Various modifications of the Teletactor design have since been made, but nearly all have applied the place principle in distributing speech frequencies over the skin. Recently, however, additional features were supplied by Keidel (1968), who applied von Bekesy's model of the cochlea to the task. In this apparatus, the speech frequencies are distributed over the skin according to the parameters of the model. In order to transpose the frequencies from 300 Hz to 3000 Hz down to 40 Hz to 400 Hz where they would be felt, Keidel played back recorded speech sounds at one-half to one-eighth normal speeds. He reported excellent recognition of new words after a 32-hour training period on phonetically balanced lists of words. The major problem with the system is in the sluggish transmission rates: the observer has difficulty retaining initial patterns over the duration of a word. A major additional feature provided by the Bekesy model is a time delay in the development of patterns of vibration over the skin (von Bekesy, 1967). All the previously cited tactile speech analyzers lacked this processing characteristic which separates the pitches of speech sounds in an orderly manner along a contiguous spatio-temporal surface. Thus the lateralization capacity of the skin, afforded by the inhibition of delay over very short times, is added to the localizing capacity of the skin over the longer times between phonemic and syllabic utterances. Whether the Keidel technique can be improved by more sophisticated (real time) frequency-transposing devices to allow tests at higher transmission rates remains to be seen.

Time, space, and the skin

The inability of the blind to process more than a single braille letter at a time has been reported by several investigators (Nolan and Kederis, 1969; Foulke, personal communication). Is this a deficiency of the cutaneous modality, or is braille itself an inadequate code, not designed to fuse into "chunks"? Fast reading may not have been Louis Braille's primary aim, of course. The demand for the talents of Evelyn Wood among sighted persons may have been very small in 1829, when Braille adapted his code from a military invention. In our research on cutaneous codes, we have been surprised by the results of what we thought were radical changes in stimulus conditions. For example, Geldard (1966) devised an alphabetic code involving the spatiotemporal display of nine vibrators on arms, legs, and trunk. When the code was well-learned, the connections to the vibrators were jumbled to disarrange the spatial cue. After the first trial, the subject was performing as well as previously. Shrinking the display to one arm had a similar effect. We concluded that the locus, which was designed to be a prominent feature of the code, was ignored in favor of a diffuse spatiotemporal pattern of stress or accentuation. In this as in other languages we have devised and tested, we have found the subjects unable to fuse letters into chunks. Again, the codes were designed as braille was, i.e., to represent the visual alphabet. The questions remain: Is there a display that permits fusion, or does the skin lack the capacity, or is fusion the product of either massive overlearning or very early experience?

REFERENCES

Bekesy, G. von: Sensory Inhibition, Princeton: Princeton University Press, 1967.

Davis, H.: Electric response audiometry, with special reference to the vertex potentials, In: Neff, W.D., and Keidel, W.D., eds.: Handbook of Sensory Physiology, (In preparation).

Gault, R.H.: Tactual interpretation of speech, Sci. Monthly 22:126–131, 1926.

Gault, R.H.: Recent developments in vibro-tactile research, J. Franklin Inst. 221:703–719, 1936.

Geldard, F.A.: Cutaneous coding of optical signals: The optohapt, Percept. Psychophys. 1:377–381, 1966.

Goldstein, R.: Electrophysiologic audiometry, In: Jerger, J., ed.: Modern Developments in Audiology, New York: Academic Press, 1963.

Graham, F.K., and Jackson, J.: Arousal systems and infant heart rate responses, In: Lipsitt, L.P., and Reese, H.W., eds.: Advances in Child Development and Behavior, New York: Academic Press, 1970, vol. V.

Hutt, S.J.; Lenard, H.G., and Prechtl, H.F.R.: Psychophysiological studies in newborn infants, In: Lipsitt, L.P., and Reese, H.W., eds.: Advances in Child Development and Behavior, New York: Academic Press, 1969, vol. IV.

Jeffrey, W.E., and Cohen, L.B.: Habituation in the human infant, In: Reese, H.W., ed.: Advances in Child Development and Behavior, New York: Academic Press, 1971, vol. VI.

Keidel, W.D.: Electrophysiology of vibratory perception, In: Neff, W.D., ed.: Contributions to Sensory Physiology, New York: Academic Press, 1968, vol. III.

Ling, D.; Ling, A.H., and Doehring, D.G.: Stimulus, response, and observer variables in the auditory screening of newborn infants, J.Speech Hearing Res. 13:9–18, 1970.

Nolan, C.Y., and Kederis, C.J.: Perceptual Factors in Braille Word Recognition (Research Series No. 20), New York: American Foundation for the Blind, 1969.

Pickett, J.M.: Tactual communication of speech sounds to the deaf: Comparison with lipreading, J. Speech Hearing Dis. 28:315–330, 1963.

Weber, B.A.: Validation of observer judgements in behavioral observation audiometry, J. Speech Hearing Dis. 34:351–355, 1969.

Weber, B.A.: Comparison of two approaches to behavioral observation audiometry, J. Speech Hearing Res. 13:823–825, 1970.

2

Sensory Capabilities
in Hearing-Impaired Children

DISCUSSION: SENSORY TESTING

Sherrick opened the discussion with the topic of research in sensory testing. He gave it as his impression that many tests, including some in clinical use, were poorly standardized. He felt that the most reliable diagnosis would come from a battery of relatively independent tests, and that a set of such tests should be tried out in a large survey of hearing-impaired children. These tests should be used predictively also, as in the studies of normal children conducted by Bayley (1965) and Graham et al. (1956). The problems of the multiply-handicapped should be tackled. These problems were a real challenge to sensory testing, involving a need to design a different test environment which dealt with the problems of controlling an unmanageable child. Sherrick was also concerned about the interaction between the states of the infant, the effect of these states upon his responding, and the response bias in the observers.

Sensory testing

Menyuk felt that development of a battery of tests to evaluate the status of the organism and its neural maturity, and to predict later deviancy, was of vital importance. This goal had not been accomplished in spite of the work of the massive Collaborative Perinatal Project (1957). It was necessary to our understanding of the normal development of sensory capabilities, auditory, visual and tactile; and our understanding of the deficited child who may deal with all of these sensory modalities quite differently from the normal child. If prosthetic devices are to be developed, they have to conform to the capacities of the organism. For example, it has been suggested that a tactile device might be better than other kinds of devices for use with infants (Stratton and Lee, 1972). It is one which could be made wearable, which could be used to present a spectral display, but we do not know how the infant will deal with this kind of input, or whether or not he will pay attention to it.

Testing and prostheses

Sherrick replied that he was very much concerned about this issue of what might be called developmental prosthetics, and found it a difficult and interesting problem. He thought it would be very appropriate if we could provide different groups of hearing-impaired children with different devices in order to see how these children improved as compared with control subjects, but, he felt that this approach posed very great design problems. It would be possible instead to deprive animals of sight or hearing, for example, by maceration of the cochlea, and to provide some of them with prosthetic devices designed to compensate for the loss of sensory input. The performance of those receiving the devices could then be compared with that of a control group which did not. Again, this presented problems of experimental design. He did like the idea, however, of tying together the questions of sensory testing and sensory aids in a kind of bootstrap operation. Testing has an older more set tradition. Having determined by testing that there is a hearing deficit, it is appropriate to ask when and how one should begin to provide a substitute environment. Should the child's crib have a vibrotactile device responding to the mother's voice and to ambient sounds in the house in order to give the child input which he would not otherwise have?

Developmental prosthetics

Eisenberg thought that the use of the nonspecific word, "deficit," lies at the crux of our problems with the pediatric-aged, both from a diagnostic and a treatment standpoint. Until that word can be defined operationally, in terms of something more than peripheral sensation, she said, prosthetic devices cannot be expected to meet all auditory deficits, however well they may meet standards for quality control and the like. Hearing aids, as currently designed, relate largely to threshold measures that tell us what a subject *cannot* hear with respect to population norms. This leads to an assumption that one merely has to make sounds louder in order to improve hearing when, in fact, a given problem may have less to do with loudness per se than it has to do with the manner in which auditory inputs are coded. We are faced today with a large number of important questions respecting how subjects *can* hear and/or listen: few of these have been approached and none of them presently are answerable. How does the auditory system operate to distinguish between speech sounds and nonspeech sounds (Eisenberg, 1970, in press)? Do coding processes that underlie this kind of differentiation change during the course of development and if so, how? Does the defective eighth nerve system differ from the normal in processing different kinds of input signals and if so, how? For example, what response does a "deaf" infant give to a 40-msec tone burst (the approximate time of an onset transient) presented at different intensities?

Defining the deficit

Another set of questions which should concern us, having to do with the organism's adaptation to the world about him and his ability to deal with it, are implied in the word "state." The answers to these questions have enormous predictive value. Neglect of them leaves us unable to say why one child with a speech hearing threshold of 50 to 60 dB SPL learns and another with the same threshold does not. Eisenberg felt that one sensory system could not be substituted for another until (a) the ways in which each system functions normally are understood and (b) there is some reasonable body of information on how the auditory system is affected in the hearing-impaired child who is to receive the substitute.

Substitution of one sense for another

Sherrick pointed out that if such a stand were taken, no progress would be made. Nothing would be done about maladaptive behavior until the underlying physiology was understood nor about physiological malfunction until the underlying anatomy and biochemistry were understood. His inclination was that of the engineer, namely, to start somewhere, to proceed by trial and assessment of the effects of that trial, iterating the process as often as was necessary to progress.

Problems of state of the subject

Sherrick returned to the problems of state, in particular to degree of alertness and habituation. It is desirable to maximize responsiveness to stimuli and also the stability of the child's performance, he said. Yet, the study of habituation can be useful in itself. If it disappears upon introduction of a novel stimulus, the organism has been made to show that it differentiates the familiar and the novel stimulus. Also, habituation may provide an index as to the level of maturity of the central nervous system (see, for example, Kessen et al., 1970).

Pickett felt that the study of habituation and adaptation and their development in children was just as important as the application of tests taken from the psychophysics laboratory, and more exciting. How does one test, for example, whether an organism's adaptation is normal or abnormal? There must be functional reasons for adaptation and these deserve to be stated in their own right.

Habituation and adaptation

Eisenberg said it was quite impossible to keep an organism, especially an infant organism, in the same state throughout testing. She felt that tests of young infants especially (a) should require no cooperation on the part of the subject, (b) should not depend upon the maintenance of a proven state but should be so designed that they separate out the effects of different states from the ability to respond, and (c) should not be age-dependent. The absence of need for instruction or any attentional set on the part of the subject would then make it possible to look at functions on a developmental scale and in terms of their expressions in different kinds of states.

Test requirements

Pollack reported that on a recent visit to Stanford University he had observed a testing situation which would meet some of these demands. Blair Simmons (personal communication) had set up a system which permitted him to monitor an infant's physiological state and his behavior around the clock. By means of this system, the experimenter could control the infant's acoustic environment and select the optimum time for testing his responses. This

Monitoring of state of infant

system did not get around the problem of definition of "state," but at least yielded greatly increased opportunities to observe the infant's behavior and thus to recognize recurring patterns in that behavior. The continuous naturalistic observation of large numbers of infants has an advantage over episodic testing for the early identification of defects. It should also aid us in interpreting measures of heart rate and evoked cortical potentials.

Use of electrophysiologic measures in the assessment of auditory functions

Eisenberg then was asked to describe her experiences in assessing sensory function in infants. She stated that the aim of her work was not to measure auditory thresholds; rather, it was to find out (a) how the young organism operates when test signals are at levels of average conversational loudness and (b) whether certain kinds of operational measures might be applied to the design of *predictive* auditory study procedures for the pediatric-aged.

Her original work, undertaken solely with neonates, was begun more than ten years ago, at which time even the fact that newborns could hear had not been established unequivocally. Since then, a variety of studies have shown not only that neonates can hear, but also that they respond differentially to parameter and envelope variables (Eisenberg, in press). Current work involves a wide age range of subjects (12 hours to 27 years), both normal and aberrant, and the types of dysfunction under study range from "at risk" infants to older subjects with clearly defined neurological deficits, autism, or other complex problems.

Three indices of stimulus-bound auditory behavior are employed: overt behavior, which is defined by a standardized coding system referable to system(s)-specific response modes (Eisenberg, 1965); heart rate, measured by cardiotachometry; and EEG (Eisenberg, in press). In evaluating the relative utility of these indices, Eisenberg felt (a) that behavioral measures, having already served the purpose of providing broadly useful basic information (Eisenberg, 1965; Eisenberg et al., 1964), had prime value in terms of their correlation with electrophysiologic measures; (b) that heart-rate measures, now in the "refining" stage at her laboratory, have potential as measures of hearing loss in infancy which may turn out to be foolproof; and (c) that EEG, though past the stage of preliminary exploration, would require considerably more basic research before it could serve as a widely useful and reliable clinical tool.

In discussing cardiac measures, Eisenberg noted that attempts to define *the* heart-rate response to a given signal had served largely to delay progress in dealing with methodologic problems (Lewis, in press). She showed some typical raw data on one 13-day-old infant (Figures 1.1 through 1.4) to indicate that successive presentations of the same signal to a given subject can elicit quite different patterns of response. As shown by the correlative data provided in Table I, such disparate response patterns cannot be related to state, gross movements, or artifacts.

A basic problem in applying cardiac measures, then, is to find some way of dealing with response variability in a meaningful fashion. Another problem is to deal with age-related differences in cardiac function. For instance, resting heart rates during the first two and a half months or so of life range between roughly 150 and 180 bpm and, even in the absence of any external stimulation, instantaneous changes on the order of twenty to thirty beats are not uncommon; after this period, on the other hand, resting heart rates range between about 60 and 90 bpm, and instantaneous changes in excess of three to six beats are rare. In addition, when one is using regular and very potent stimulation, even at intervals in excess of one minute between successive trials, temporal conditioning tends to manifest itself within the initial five trials of a schedule.

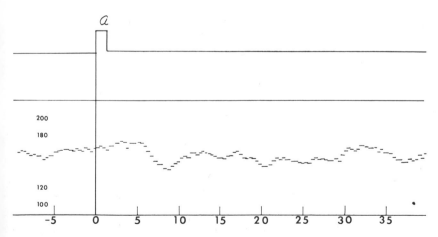

Fig. 1.1 Cardiotachometer stripchart tracings of individual responses to a 60 dB synthetic vowel ("ah") in one 13-day-old subject. Heart-rate levels in bpm are shown on the ordinate while the abscissa represents time in seconds over 40-second epochs commencing at stimulus-onset minus 5 seconds. Trial 1.

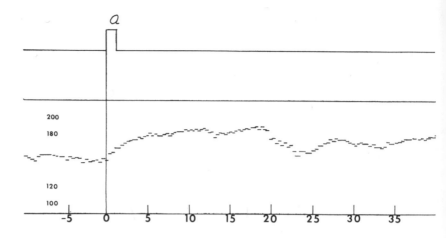

Fig. 1.2 Cardiotachometer stripchart tracings of individual responses to a 60 dB synthetic vowel ("ah") in one 13-day-old subject. Heart-rate levels in bpm are shown on the ordinate while the abscissa represents time in seconds over 40-second epochs commencing at stimulus-onset minus 5 seconds. Trial 2.

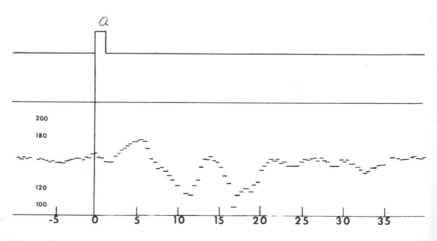

Fig. 1.3 Cardiotachometer stripchart tracings of individual responses to a 60 dB synthetic vowel ("ah") in one 13-day-old subject. Heart-rate levels in bpm are shown on the ordinate while the abscissa represents time in seconds over 40-second epochs commencing at stimulus-onset minus 5 seconds. Trial 3.

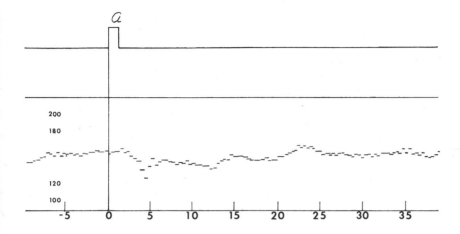

Fig. 1.4 Cardiotachometer stripchart tracings of individual responses to a 60 dB synthetic vowel ("ah") in one 13-day-old subject. Heart-rate levels in bpm are shown on the ordinate while the abscissa represents time in seconds over 40-second epochs commencing at stimulus-onset minus 5 seconds. Trial 30 (final presentation, showing no evidence of habituation).

In order to illustrate an approach now under investigation at her laboratory, Eisenberg described an ongoing study involving a 30-trial sequence in which a synthetic vowel /a/, was presented at fixed 90-sec intervals (onset-to-onset). The vowel was 1.16 sec in duration and its intensity level was 60 dB SPL. Eisenberg presented data on one 43-day-old control infant from this study.

When initial attempts to analyze study data by averaging procedures of one kind or another proved unsatisfactory (because significant differences did not emerge consistently even when individual responses could be discerned easily), parametric techniques were abandoned in favor of a nonparametric approach. In that approach, 40 selected seconds of a complete 30-trial experiment in matched time-units were compared as follows:

1. A 10-sec stimulus-bound sample, T_0 (stimulus-onset) to T_0 plus 10 sec, with the 10-sec sample immediately preceding it in time, T_0 to T_0 minus 10 sec;

2. Another 10-sec nonstimulus sample, T_0 minus 5 to 15 sec with the like sample immediately contiguous to it, T_0 minus 15 to 25 sec.

The distribution of taus, or heartbeat durations in seconds (HR = 60/tau), during these various periods then were obtained and converted to equivalent heart rates.

Both sets of data, i.e., those related to the two 10-sec periods around

Table I. Correlative data showing the behavioral and EEG ratings made at the time of the recording of heart-rate measurement trials. The output from the cardiotach strip-chart during trials 1 through 3 is shown in Figures 1.1 through 1.3, and for trial 30 in Figure 1.4.

Correlative Data

Behavioral Ratings		EEG Ratings
Trial 1 (Figure 1.1)		
State	III	III
Response	Minimal body movement	K(1) - Forehead movement
Trial 2 (Figure 1.2)		
State	III	III
Response	Visual and motor arousal	K (all leads)
Trial 3 (Figure 1.3)		
State	III	III
Response	Visual and motor arousal	K(2) - Diffuse K - movement
Trial 30 (Figure 1.4)		
State	II	III
Response	Undifferentiated attentive behavior	K(2)

stimulus onset and those related to the two 10-sec periods remote from stimulus onset were accumulated in three-trial blocks over the entire 30-stimulus schedule. These cumulative distributions (for trials 1-3, 1-6, 1-9, etc.) then were subjected individually to the Kolmogorov-Smirnov Two-Sample Test (Siegel, 1956, pp. 47–52) in order to quantify the significance of observed differences between them.

Several suggestive trends were observed.

1. There seemed to be significant differences between heart rates characterizing the 10-sec period preceding stimulus onset and those characterizing the like period beginning with stimulus onset. *These differences were systematic* and essentially decelerative in nature, that is, there was a consistent one-interval shift (on the order of five to eight beats). (This in itself is interesting, since it is commonly assumed that decelerative heart-rate responses, presumably associated with an orienting system (Sokolov, 1964), are not present in the neonatal period.) Although such differences showed a declining statistical value, from .001 to .05, as more and more trials were accumulated, they *never* reached a point of no significance.

2. For both samples, i.e., that preceding and that beginning with stimulus onset, the distribution in heart rates shifted considerably over the course of the 30-trial schedule. The nature of the differences between these samples varied according to the dispersion of heart values along some dynamic continuum. Thus, when the pre-stimulus distribution was concentrated near the middle of this continuum, the sole indicator was deceleration. On the other hand, where the pre-stimulus rates were dispersed in more or less bimodal fashion, there seem to be relatively fewer low heart rates during the period beginning with stimulus onset.

3. For the 20-sec period occurring well before stimulus onset, only one of these trends could be found. There was no strong evidence of significant differences between heart rates characterizing the period T_0 minus 5 to 15 sec and those characterizing an immediately preceding 10-sec period. Differences that were statistically significant at the .05 and .01 levels were found during the time encompassing trials 9 through 21, but these dwindled as further samples were accumulated. *Differences between nonstimulus samples,* then, *were not systematic.* In effect, the data indicated that infant heart rates tended to be similarly unstable under both stimulus and nonstimulus conditions. It seemed entirely likely, therefore, that *occasional* findings of statistically significant differences between nonstimulus samples of equal duration reflect nothing more than changes in physiologic state over time that occur (a) as a matter of chance or (b) as a consequence of some particular small sample.

Given these encouraging findings, a number of extremely useful new avenues for exploration open up. First of all, given a consistent and statistically significant trend over accumulated-trial blocks, it is possible (a) that the existence of response can be defined unequivocally, (b) that response onset for single trials can be defined with reference to statistically significant changes in heart-rate distributions, (c) that response time for single trials similarly can be defined by changes in heart-rate distributions; and (d) that the potency of given test signals can be measured with reference to the number of trials required before significance is lost. Secondly, given particular distributions of heart rate that relate to particular physiological states, it is possible (a) that variations in state over time can be defined with reference to interval histograms for individual trials and (b) that the nature of response can be related, at least generally, to pre-stimulus state.

Eisenberg felt that these data indicated (1) that responses were occurring and could be detected regardless of the state of the organism; thus an unequivocal indication of ability to hear could be derived without controlling state; (2) the approach could also be used to derive possible measures of state.

At this point, House asked what the responses would look like if no stimulus had been applied in any of the trials. Eisenberg replied that the data would be relatively flat, somewhat like the distribution for the pre-stimulus interval although at a different average level. Levitt was not happy about the cumulative treatment of the data. Spurious responses occurring early in a trial sequence would have an undue weight in this case. The drop-off in significance after the twenty-first trial which Eisenberg reported might be the first point in time at which the effect of such responses disappeared. Eisenberg replied that if one examined the data carefully and systematically, it was clear that the drop-off in significance reflected an increased variability of response, i.e., the fact that an increasing number of responses were not decelerative but accelerative or multi-phasic. She felt, however, that if the first twenty-one trials continued to show significance at the .0001 level, then it would not be necessary to run so many trials in a screening test situation. On a mass level the approach might be used with perhaps as few as six trials and the response measurements automated. Such a screening device would have the advantage of being entirely free of bias.

Cumulative treatment of heart-rate data

Heart-rate responses to different types of auditory signals

Eisenberg went on to discuss the second question of interest to her, namely, how one might characterize heart-rate responses in order to detect ways in which the auditory system is dealing with different kinds of signals. In this work, she felt, the major problems were not in designing the experiment but in handling the data. After stressing that her approach towards characterizing heart-rate responses to sound was not yet firm, she briefly outlined the method being used at the Bioacoustic Laboratory as follows:

1. Treatment of stimulus-bound cardiac behavior derives from two initial sets of heart-rate distributions, each of which is obtained by histogram analyses. The first set of two distributions, permitting one to define basal conditions and to determine whether a given stimulus battery exerts any long-term effects on cardiac levels, refers to *steady-state* data obtained during

rest periods before and after presentation of a study schedule. (The size of these samples is a matter of preference and, depending on study purposes, intervals as short as two minutes may be adequate.) The second set of distributions, which varies according to the size of an experimental schedule, permits one to group all trials according to cardiac boundary conditions. Since it is assumed that a response, if it occurs, takes place within these boundary conditions, the existence of a response event is irrelevant at this point. *Dynamic,* or stimulus-bound, equilibrium is defined on a trial-by-trial basis, according to individual histograms for the full inter-stimulus interval encompassing each trial. For example, given current study conditions, which involve 30 signals presented at fixed 90-sec intervals, 30 histograms are derived, each of which covers a period from T_0 minus 30 sec through T_0 plus 60 sec. These 90-sec interval histograms for individual trials, sorted into homogeneous groups according to boundary conditions, become the basis for scaling procedures.

2. The occurrence of a response event and the nature of that event are defined by statistically significant shifts in heart-rate distributions during periods associated with stimulus presentation. These distributions are obtained by segmenting each of the initial 90-sec epochs into smaller units. (a) The histogram distribution for an initial 10-sec epoch (T_0 minus 30 to minus 20 sec), assumed to be uncontaminated by stimulus effects, is used as a "window," or comparator, to be shifted along the time axis in selected steps. The *existence of a response event* then is defined on the basis of statistically significant differences between the nonstimulus window and one or more 10-sec epochs in the immediate vicinity of T_0. (b) *Response-time boundaries* are defined by contiguous intervals of statistically significant shift, and *response peak(s)* by the period(s) of maximum shift within these boundaries. (c) *Mode of response,* defined by the direction of heart-rate shifts during peak periods, accordingly may be characterized broadly as accelerative, decelerative, or some permutation of the two.

In effect, the purpose of nonparametric treatments is to provide a logical and orderly basis for parametric analysis. If one can define response events unequivocally, group them according to response modes, and line them up with reference to response onset as well as stimulus onset, it seems likely that conventional measures of central tendency and variance can begin to yield more useful and valid information.

Eisenberg went on to state her conviction that measures of dynamic equilibrium over time may attain considerable diagnostic significance as further electrophysiological studies are pursued. As a case in point, she showed some further data obtained from the ongoing 30-trial study with a synthetic vowel (Figure 1.5). These data derive from the initial 90-sec epoch and, as used, they have three specific advantages. They take into account

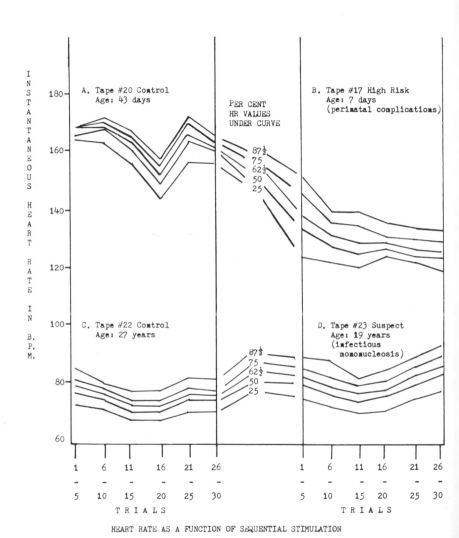

HEART RATE AS A FUNCTION OF SEQUENTIAL STIMULATION

Fig. 1.5 Heart rate as a function of slowly repeated stimulation with a synthetic vowel ("ah").

individual levels of somatic function; they permit correlation with behavioral state or other indices of physiological equilibrium; and they provide a common denominator for comparison across age groups, stimulus conditions, and so on.

Figure 1.5 shows pilot data relative to changing cardiac dynamics as a function of regular stimulation with a potent signal. Two infants and two adults were selected as experimental "prototypes" and the thirty 90-sec histogram printouts for each subject were treated manually to disclose dynamic changes during the test run. Specifically, in order to compress the mass of 120 histograms, each of the thirty 90-sec printouts for each of the four subjects was reduced to a set of five percentile points referable to individual heart-rate boundaries. The choice of these points was dictated by the contents of the 90-sec interval histograms: each of them contained values that referred in unequal part to nonstimulus and stimulus conditions; each of them was weighted in the direction of lower heart rates (because responses to synthetic vowels tend mainly to be decelerative). It accordingly was assumed that the most representative region for looking at cardiac dynamics was that lying between the 25th and 87th percentiles. Thus, the lower boundary of the cardiac range was defined as that heart rate below which 15% of the heart-rate values fell; the higher boundary as that above which 12.5% of the heart-rate values fell; and the intervening points (50%, 62.5%, and 75% respectively) were included to provide some slight degree of refinement. Then, to compress the data still further, the thirty trials per subject were segmented into six consecutive five-trial blocks and the mean heart-rate value for each block was plotted. Figure 1.5, then, is designed to yield information on whether or not, and in what way, sequential stimulation affects cardiac dynamics. It affords a number of provocative trends.

First of all, it immediately is apparent that cardiac boundaries change over trials and, for the three out of four subjects, in much the same way, that is, heart-rate levels tend to fall during middle trials (11-20) and then to return towards the initial range. Since analysis of behavioral and EEG state rating yields essentially the same results, it seems likely the trend is real.

Secondly, since the normal infant, despite differences in cardiac function that are reflected in higher heart-rate levels and greater lability over time, behaves similarly to the normal adult, it seems likely that similar control mechanisms in the nervous system (which presumably relate to attentive behavior) are operating in both age groups.

Thirdly, since the high-risk infant is the only subject to show a systematic decline in heart-rate level over trials, it seems possible that measures of cardiac dynamics under defined stimulus conditions may afford useful diagnostic information. (The trend is not related to age since eyeballed data on control infants in the age range between 28 hours and 11 days shows them to behave similarly to the older control shown in Figure 1.5.)

Fourthly, while the significance of differences between the control and suspect adults cannot be evaluated adequately at present, it is of interest simply because the tendency towards a wide dynamic range and increased lability also was noted for a few suspect infants on whom 90-sec histogram data sets were available.

Pollack and Watson wanted to know if the infant's behavioral response resembled a startle response or a curiosity response. Eisenberg assured them that at 60 dB SPL, she was not eliciting a startle or Moro response. Pollack commented that if the stimuli were presented on some kind of random schedule so that intervening base line intervals might be sampled, sharper discrimination between response and nonresponse might be found, and temporal conditioning and habituation would no longer have to be taken into account. Eisenberg agreed that it would be desirable to eliminate habituation. She had at one time been very interested in the possible predictive value of measures of habituation (Eisenberg et al., 1966). It seemed that infants who showed habituation later turned out to be normal in every respect. The converse was not true, however. Many infants who failed to show habituation (about 40%) also showed normal development. Thus, the tests of habituation which she had administered yielded many false positives and were, in addition, time consuming, at least as they were conducted in her laboratory.

Comments on temporal conditioning, habituation

Hirsh commented that as far as the work with evoked response audiometry in very young children, i.e., down to the age of several months, was concerned, Hallowell Davis' group were reasonably comfortable about its use in estimating auditory threshold (Davis, 1968; 1971). The percentage of preschool children from whom they got a technically unsatisfactory result was very small if a sedative was used for those under three years of age. He mentioned this in view of Eisenberg's reservations about the use of heart rate for the purpose of audiometric testing. Davis' group were frankly using evoked cortical responses as a physiological indicator, i.e., as a technique for exploring threshold where this is difficult to do by other means. They had found that where indications of threshold have also been obtained by behavioral measures, these agree very closely with thresholds indicated by EEG audiometry (Davis et al., 1967; Davis and Niemoeller, 1968; Davis, 1970).

Eisenberg agreed that EEG audiometry could be used to provide a reliable index of threshold, but she felt it was more apt to be misused as a technique if put in the wrong hands than heart-rate measures would be. Evoked response audiometry was being badly managed and badly interpreted in some places and it was also very expensive. One of the practical problems involved was the need to have a quiescent subject. Heart rate, on the other hand, could be measured while the subject was free to move around, especially if telemetry was used. It was cheap and she believed it could be mechanized. She was not suggesting that the use of EEG be completely preempted by heart-rate measurement in studies of hearing. Basic information about the functioning of the auditory system would not be answered by cardiotachometry, but by sophisticated studies employing EEG. However, as far as threshold measurement was concerned, the faster and the cheaper this could be done, the better. Where the need was merely to determine the presence or absence of hearing loss and if it were present, its extent, these measures could be made more reliably and cheaply and by more clinics by means of heart-rate measures.

Interpretation of amplitude of EEG response

Watson commented that a major effort was underway at the Central Institute for the Deaf to develop systematic procedures for conducting and interpreting evoked response audiometry (ERA) on *anesthetized patients*. This work, under the direction of Hallowell Davis, has been in progress for several years. Tests on anesthetized infants have sufficient reliability and validity, in comparison with ERA measures obtained from subjects who are awake, to reduce the concern that subjects be "quiescent" for ERA to be a useful procedure.

Watson also described an evoked-response study on which Davis, Hirsh, Wier, and he (1973) had recently collaborated. It illustrated the need for considerable caution in drawing inferences about *perception* from cortical evoked responses.

An adult subject was found for whom it was not necessary to sum responses over a number of trials in order to average out the random components in the EEG waveform. Instead, each individual trial yielded a healthy response which could easily be seen without averaging. In studying this subject, the investigators first presented an electric shock to the median nerve at low-level constant amplitude. The responses were recorded from both hemispheres with reference to the usual vertex point. Davis et al. were interested in the relative latencies and also in the relative variance at the two points, i.e., over the right and the left cerebral cortex, as a source of information about the generator. If the processing operation is a sequential one, there should be more variance of the second point in the processing sequence; if it is a parallel system, the variance of both should be roughly the same. In fact, the variance was approximately the same, and there was essentially no difference between right and left in response. The very small difference which did exist was in the latency opposite in direction from that which would be predicted by theories of cerebral dominance.

Trial-by-trial variance in response amplitude was large, varying from 30 microvolts to about 7 microvolts. It was therefore of interest to the investigators to find out if the shocks were subjectively different in strength from one trial to another, even though they were physically constant in amplitude. The subject assured the experimenters that the shocks appeared to be different in strength from trial to trial. In a second part of the experiment, the stimulus duration was varied from 5 to 40 msec. The subject was asked to rate the magnitude of the shocks on a five point scale. The N_1-P_2 responses to each stimulus shock were again measured. Correlation measures were then calculated between stimulus magnitude, subjective intensity, and response amplitude. The correlation between stimulus magnitude and the size of the response was essentially zero. The correlation between the subject's rating and the size of the response was low, about .25. Only the correlation between stimulus magnitude and subjective rating was significant; it was about .8. These correlations imply that, for such a narrow range of stimuli, differences in evoked responses may be essentially meaningless when compared to an observer's subjective judgment, even though those judgments are closely tied to the levels of stimulation.

REFERENCES

Bayley, N.: Comparison of mental and motor test scores for ages 1–15 months by sex, birth order, race, geographical location, and education of parents, Child Develop. 36:379–411, 1965.

Davis, H.: Averaged-evoked-response EEG audiometry in North America, Acta Otolaryng. 65:79–85, 1968.

Davis, H.: Evoked response audiometry, Trans. Amer. Acad. Ophthal. Otolaryng. 74:1236–1237 (Nov.-Dec.) 1970.

Davis, H.: Is ERA ready for routine clinical use? Arch. Klin. Exp. Ohr. Nas. Kehlkopfheilk. 198(2):2–8, 1971.

Davis, H.; Hirsh, S.K.; Shelnutt, J., et al.: Further validation of evoked response audiometry (ERA), J. Speech Hearing Res. 10(4):717–732, 1967.

Davis, H.; Hirsh, S.K.; Wier, C., et al.: Individual responses to somatosensory stimuli, In: Periodic Progress Report No. 16, Research Department, St. Louis: Central Institute for the Deaf, June, 1973.

Davis, H., and Niemoeller, A.F.: A system for clinical evoked response audiometry, J. Speech Hearing Dis. 33:33–37, 1968.

Eisenberg, R.B.: Auditory behavior in the human neonate: I. Methodological problems and the logical design of research procedures, J. Aud. Res. 5:159–177, 1965.

Eisenberg, R.B.: The organization of auditory behavior, J. Speech Hearing Res. 13:453–471, 1970.

Eisenberg, R.B.: Auditory Competence in Early Life: The Roots of Communicative Behavior, Baltimore: University Park Press (In press).

Eisenberg, R.B.; Coursin, D.B., and Rupp, N.R.: Habituation to an acoustic pattern as an index of differences among human neonates, J. Aud. Res. 6:239–248, 1966.

Eisenberg, R.B.; Griffin, E.J.; Coursin, D.B., et al.: Auditory behavior in the human neonate: A preliminary report, J. Speech Hearing Res. 7:245–269, 1964.

Graham, F.K.; Matarazzo, R.G., and Caldwell, B.M.: Behavioral differences between normal and traumatized newborns: II. Standardization, reliability, and validity, Psychol. Monogr. 70(22, Whole No. 428):17–23, 1956.

Kessen, W.; Haith, M.M., and Salapatek, P.H.: Human infancy: A bibliography and guide, In: Carmichael, L., and Mussen, P.H., eds.: Manual of Child Psychology, 3d. ed., New York: Wiley, 1970.

Lewis, M.: The cardiac response during infancy, In: Thompson, R.F., and Peterson, M.M., eds.: Methods in Physiological Psychology, New York: Academic Press (In press).

National Institute of Neurological Diseases and Blindness: Collaborative Project for the Study of Cerebral Palsy, Mental Retardation, and Other Neurological and Sensory Disorders of Infancy and Childhood, Bethesda: National Institute of Neurological Diseases and Blindness, 1957.

Siegel, S.: Nonparametric Statistics for the Behavioral Sciences, New York: McGraw-Hill, 1956.

Sokolov, Y.N.: Perception and the Conditioned Reflex, Elmsford: Pergamon, 1964.

Stratton, D., and Lee, F.: Pitch feedback for the deaf through the tactile sense, Paper presented at Hearing Loss in Children: A Multidisciplinary Symposium, Children's Hospital Medical Center, Boston. October, 1972.

3

Sensory Capabilities
in Normal and
Hearing-Impaired Children

**DISCUSSION: RELATION OF SPEECH PERCEPTION AND PRODUC-
TION TO ASSESSMENTS OF AUDITORY FUNCTION**

The participants agreed that the auditory function of the child with significant hearing impairment should be studied in detail and the nature of his
deficit more fully understood. They were not in agreement, however, about
the usefulness of the audiogram as a predictor of the child's ability to learn,
or to understand and produce speech.

Boothroyd pointed out that the potential value of residual hearing is
often overlooked in the excitement of the search for tactile or visual sensory
aids. He further felt that much could be gained by investigating the relationship between hearing level and other aspects of function in the deaf. For
example, in the population of students at the Clarke School for the Deaf,
whose hearing level distribution is shown in Figure 1.6 (Boothroyd, 1970), he
had found a clear and interesting relationship between hearing level and
speech intelligibility. From his own work he felt that while the audiogram
does not describe the hearing of a child completely, it is, statistically speaking, a very powerful predictor.

*Effects of
level of hear-
ing loss*

Eisenberg replied that it seemed powerful mainly because it was the *only*
predictor (Eisenberg, 1971). Boothroyd said he had looked at others but had
found the audiogram to be much superior to them. The reason, he thought,
was simple: If the child is measured on some ability which requires hearing,
then hearing is going to affect that measurement; if he is measured on some
ability which does not require hearing, hearing will not affect that measurement.

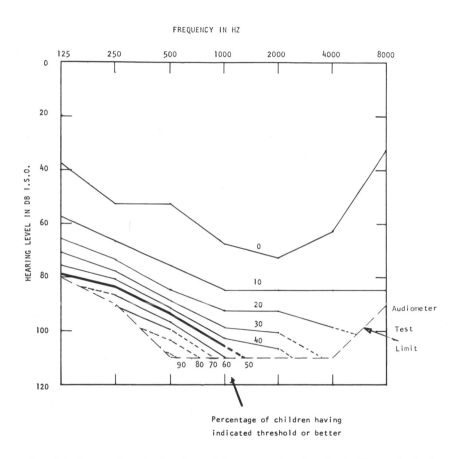

Fig. 1.6 Percentile distribution of better ear hearing level (ISO) of Clarke School students, 1969.

Effect of level of hearing loss upon speech intelligibility

The particular ability Boothroyd was interested in measuring was that of speech production in a group of deaf children, a capability which is often the subject of question and debate in terms of the issue of oral education.

Figure 1.7 shows the distribution of intelligibility scores from the speech of a population of deaf children from Clarke School for the Deaf. All of these children had been in an oral education program with exposure to amplifica-

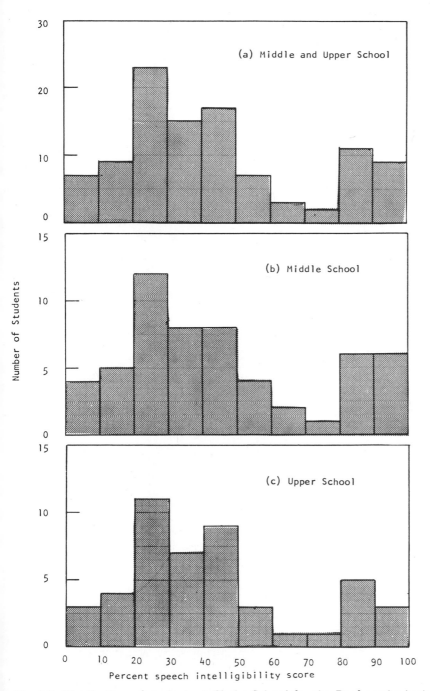

Fig. 1.7 Distribution of students at Clarke School for the Deaf on the basis of the intelligibility of their speech. Intelligibility was measured by having each student record six sentences and then measuring the percentage of words understood by a group of six naive listeners.

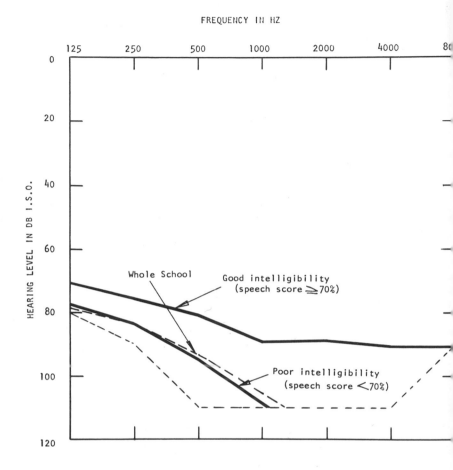

Fig. 1.8 Median thresholds for two groups of Clarke School for the Deaf students. Grouping is based on the speech intelligibility scores of the previous figure (1.7).

tion for a considerable time. Their ages were twelve to eighteen years. The children in the study were asked to read a ten-syllable sentence and their attempts were recorded on tape. Percent intelligibility scores were derived from transcriptions of the sentence made by relatively naive listeners (Magner, 1972). The scores are displayed in the form of simple histograms for the younger and older students and also for both combined. Clearly, these scores show a bimodal distribution. It was a matter of interest, then, to find out how this distribution related to level of hearing loss. Figures 1.8 through

1.10 show that there is a correlation between the percent intelligibility scores and hearing level at all frequencies but especially at 1 KHz and at 2 KHz. The correlation is not perfect. At least one child with very little residual hearing is making an 80% score. In general, however, the children with good speech intelligibility have considerable residual hearing; those with poor speech intelligibility have little hearing (see Figure 1.7). In addition, it is clear that this is not a continuous function. The median scores are fairly constant up to about 90 dB and then there is a very marked transition or drop-off in intelligibility. The step function is found with respect to hearing level at both 1 KHz and 2 KHz.

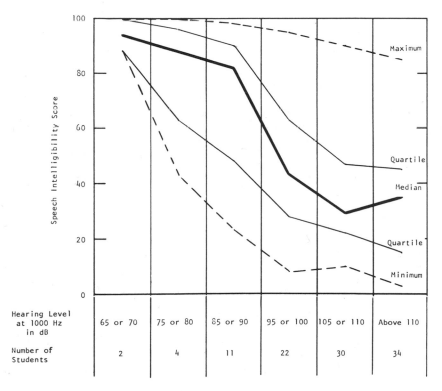

Fig. 1.9 Distribution of speech intelligibility scores of Clarke School students as a function of hearing level at 1000 Hz. It will be seen that the function relating median speech intelligibility to pure-tone hearing loss shows a marked drop around 90 dB (ISO).

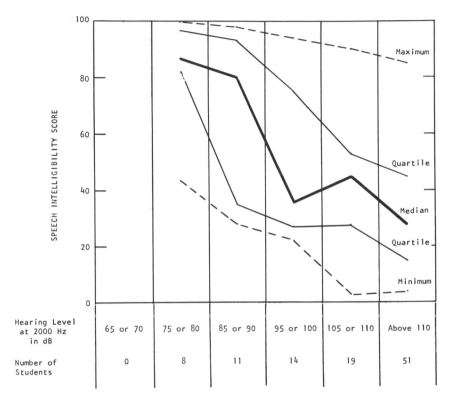

Fig. 1.10 Distribution of speech intelligibility scores of Clarke School students as a function of hearing level at 2000 Hz. The sharp drop in median speech intelligibility for hearing losses greater than 90 dB (I.S.O.) is again apparent.

Furth pointed out that the findings could not be generalized to all deaf children. Boothroyd agreed. He felt, however, that it was interesting to find this step function even in an ideal environment from the point of view of speech learning. This led him to ask whether or not children with losses greater than 90 dB obtained so little help from hearing that its use might perhaps be de-emphasized in training.

Use of amplification with profoundly deaf children

Effect of residual hearing upon outcome of visual pitch matching experiment

Boothroyd stated that the results of a quite different experiment had convinced him that this was not a proper conclusion (Boothroyd, 1971; in press).

The experiment was concerned with pitch control acquisition in a group of subjects whose hearing levels are illustrated in Figure 1.11.

These subjects were trying to match a simple visual display of pitch by varying their own fundamental frequency. They had simultaneous feedback from their own hearing aids as well as visual feedback. Subsequently, the hearing levels of these students were examined in relation to their performance on the pitch matching task. The subjects were divided into two groups as a function first of hearing level at 125 Hz, then of hearing level at 250 Hz, and finally at 500 Hz. The pitch-matching scores of these groups are shown in Figure 1.12 for a pre-test (A), a mid-training test (B), an immediate post-training test (C), and a test given six weeks post-training (D). The groups that were formed in the manner described did not differ when the grouping was

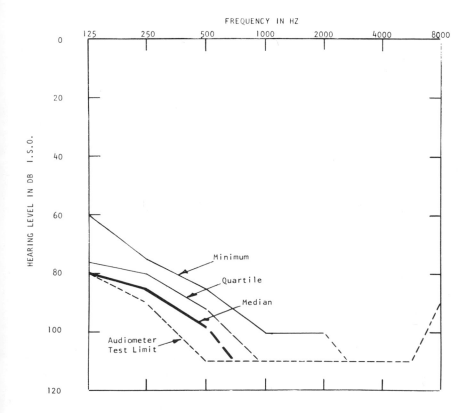

Fig. 1.11 Distribution of hearing levels in a group of students used in a pitch training experiment. From Boothroyd, in press.

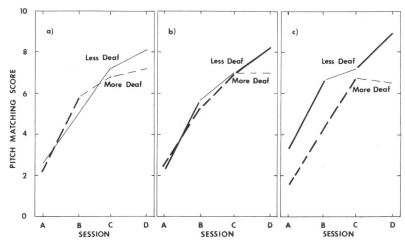

Fig. 1.12 Performance on a pitch matching task of students whose hearing losses are illustrated in Fig. 1.11. Test session A was before special training, sessions B and C after 4 and 8 weeks of training respectively, and session D after a further 6 weeks without training. Although all students were profoundly deaf, it is interesting to note that students with more hearing at 250 and 500 Hz showed significant improvements in the 6 weeks following training. From Boothroyd, in press.

based on the hearing level at 125 Hz or 250 Hz. When grouping was a function of hearing level at 500 Hz, their scores began to differ, but not at a statistically different level. During the six weeks following training, however, the less deaf group, with respect to levels measured at 250 Hz and at 500 Hz, showed a continuous improvement on this task, while the more deaf group did not. It was almost as though in the case of the less deaf, visual training had attuned them to auditory feedback cues which had later taken over the role of controlling pitch, although no attempt had been made in training to ensure this transfer of control. This was mere speculation but suggested that it is necessary to consider how poor hearing must be before deciding it is not of use to the child and that visual and tactile input should be presented as a substitute. On the basis of these findings, it would obviously be wrong to ignore the hearing channels just because the loss exceeds 90 dB.

Effect of level of hearing loss upon speech intelligibility and speech reception

Levitt presented some data obtained from a different sample of deaf children; that is, forty children attending Lexington School for the Deaf, which had yielded highly similar findings. The data were from a doctoral dissertation of one of his students, Clarissa Smith (1972, 1973).

Two groups of children had been studied, one of eight to ten years, the other of thirteen to fifteen years. In the case of these children, average pure-tone thresholds were reported for the frequencies of 125 Hz, 500 Hz, and 1 KHz, rather than 500 Hz, 1 KHz, and 2 KHz. This was because many children did not respond at the limits of the audiometer at 2 KHz. The correlation between the two three-frequency averages was very close.

Speech reception and speech intelligibility were measured in these children. Speech intelligibility was measured by having the children read twenty sentences. One hundred and twenty naive listeners transcribed these sentences. Each sentence was listened to by three listeners so that inter-listener differences might be stabilized. No listener heard the same sentence twice. The percent scores are plotted against average hearing levels in Figure 1.13a. It can be seen that there is a sharp drop-off in intelligibility scores as hearing levels reach about 90 dB.

Levitt stated that neither he nor Smith believed that there was a unitary relationship between intelligibility score and hearing level. They had carried out an extensive factor analysis in which all possible frequency averages were used, including the conventional one of 500 Hz, 1 KHz, and 2 KHz.

The correlation of intelligibility scores with hearing level was slightly higher for the hearing levels shown, namely 125 Hz, 500 Hz, and 1 KHz, than for the conventional average. The investigators felt that an L-shaped curve with a sharp transition in the 90 dB region would fit these data very well.

A group of children, however, clearly showed deviant results. These were eight children with hearing levels better than 90 dB, who had, nevertheless, very poor intelligibility scores. These particular children came predominantly from homes in which the parents were also deaf, whereas the remainder of the children came from homes where the parents were normal hearing (see Figure 1.13a). Therefore, they felt the hearing and thus the speech skills of the parents might be another factor of importance. The finding is to be checked by examining a further twenty children, this time from Clarke School for the Deaf, and additional children from the New York City area. The effect of language environment, i.e., of American sign language versus American English, upon speech intelligibility will be explored further.

The same children were also given a speech reception test, which was very much like a modified rhyme test. In responding, they were required to select from a closed set of pictured words on the basis of phoneme recognition. The word stimuli were presented in the form of tape-recorded natural speech samples. The results obtained for speech reception are plotted against the three frequency average hearing loss in Figure 1.14. This shows a greater scatter of scores than was found in the case of speech intelligibility (see

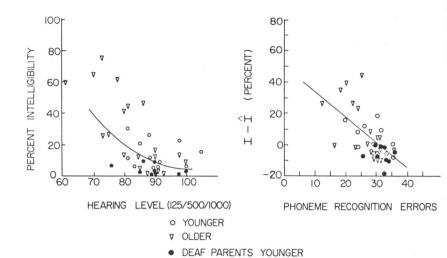

Fig. 1.13a Scatterplot showing speech intelligibility in percent as a function of average hearing level at 125/500/1K Hz. A relatively good approximation to the average trend is given by the quadratic regression line shown. Children of hearing and of deaf parents are identified as shown in the key.

Fig. 1.13b Deviations of intelligibility scores from estimations based upon the quadratic regression line of Fig. 1.13a are plotted against percent errors on the phoneme recognition test.

Figure 1.13a). There was no sharp drop in phoneme recognition scores at 90 dB comparable to that found for the speech intelligibility scores. It was also found that the phoneme recognition score was the measure of hearing most closely correlated with speech intelligibility (see Figure 1.13b).

Menyuk asked if any measures of intelligibility of spontaneous speech had been obtained. Levitt said they had, but the data had as yet not been analyzed. Samples of spontaneous speech had been obtained by asking the children to discuss their favorite television shows, their favorite teachers, and so on, but it had not been possible to control for the length, content, or complexity of the samples of speech obtained in this way. Menyuk asked if listeners had rated the intelligibility of the children's spontaneous speech or attempted to transcribe it. Levitt said that they had not, but that he believed it would be possible to use intelligibility ratings with spontaneous speech. The naive listeners who had transcribed the sentences spoken by the deaf children had also rated the intelligibility of these sentences. The correlations between intelligibility scores based on word counts from the transcriptions and intelligibility ratings made by the transcribers was very high. This approach could

Questions of intelligibility of spontaneous vs. read speech

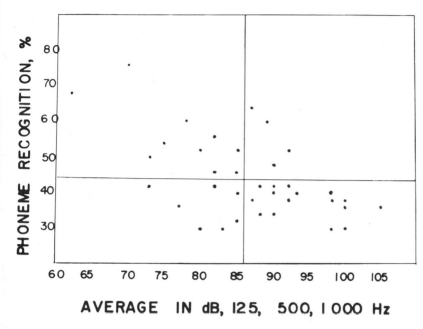

Fig. 1.14 Scatterplot showing percent phoneme recognition scores as a function of average hearing level at 125/500/1 K Hz.

also be used with spontaneous speech. Menyuk thought that it should. She felt that the magic number of 90 dB hearing level might not show the same relation to intelligibility of spontaneous speech as to that of the reading of an isolated sentence. Levitt did not accept the representation of 90 dB as a "magic number" and reiterated his statement that there was a very sharp drop-off in intelligibility with hearing loss at 90 dB. Menyuk still expressed a question about general intelligibility and hearing loss.

Pickett recalled the findings of a study carried out in the Swedish schools for the deaf by Ahlstrom (1970). In that study, a number of different measures of the language achievements of deaf children were made, such as the reading of single words and phrases, various kinds of language reception tests, tests of the intelligibility of the children's speech, and so on. High correlations were found between degree of hearing loss, speech intelligibility, and auditory reception but there was no correlation between degree of hearing loss and other linguistic skills such as reading, lipreading, and use of grammar.

Correlation of language measures and hearing loss

Vibrotactile responses to acoustic stimuli

Erber then reported a series of careful studies which had led him to the conclusion that the audiogram is an inadequate predictor of speech recognition in the case of some profoundly deaf children. Many of these are children who give responses to pure-tone signals on the basis of vibrotactile sensation and not hearing.

Effect of level of loss on word recognition

First, he reported a study that he had conducted in which the Manchester University Monosyllabic Word List was presented to forty deaf children at the Central Institute for the Deaf. This is a phonetically balanced word list employing a vocabulary appropriate for the age range of the children in the study. The words were presented monaurally through a high-quality amplification system at comfortable listening levels. Figure 1.15, in which data from four investigations are shown, suggests that an average hearing level greater than 95 dB is quite predictive of poor performance on this test.

Furth objected; the data did not clearly indicate a relation between hearing level and the word-recognition score. However, Erber assured him

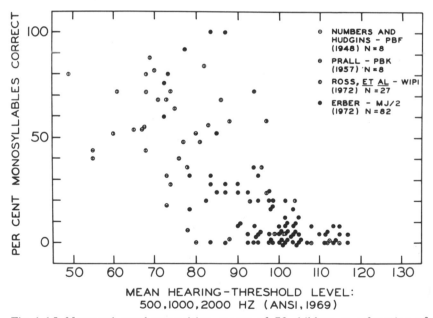

Fig. 1.15 Monaural word-recognition scores of 72 children as a function of average hearing threshold level for 500/1000/2000 Hz. The results of four different investigations are shown. The stimuli in each case were monosyllabic words.

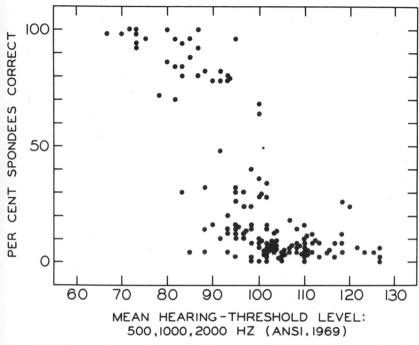

Fig. 1.16 Monaural spondee-recognition scores of 72 children as a function of average hearing threshold for 500/1000/2000 Hz (N=144 ears). The subjects chose their responses from a printed list of the 25 alternatives in the set.

that, while the spread of scores reflected the characteristics of hearing of the children in the school at that time, he had himself concluded that monosyllabic words were not the most suitable items for testing the speech reception of severely hearing-impaired children, since many of these children found them too difficult.

Instead, Erber had constructed a list of twenty-five spondaic words. These were carefully recorded to provide similar patterning and stress within each word; that is, test items were accepted only when the syllables appeared to be equal in amplitude and duration on an oscilloscope screen. These stimuli were presented in a closed-set word-recognition test. The twelve children who were tested had the list of words in front of them, and they selected from that set the spondaic word which they perceived. Interestingly, the distribution of scores was now a more striking one, revealing a dichotomy between high scores (70-100%) and low scores (0-30%). However, the data points of the high scores and of the low scores do show some overlap when they are plotted, as in Figure 1.16, against the three-frequency average hearing threshold for 500 Hz, 1 KHz, and 2 KHz, and also many other average hearing thresholds that were examined. The finding suggests that the pure-tone audiogram is not a perfect predictor of the group into which children's monaural responses to spondees will fall.

Erber said he regarded the high-scoring group as severely hearing-impaired; most of them would be similarly classified on the basis of the pure-tone audiogram. The low-scoring group, he regarded as profoundly deaf; many of these children would not be so classified on the basis of their pure-tone audiograms. In short, Erber used the word-recognition score as a means of classifying children as severely and profoundly hearing-impaired. The children in the severely-impaired group, he believed, are those who possess true residual hearing. They have nearly normal ability to discriminate between frequencies, at least in the low frequency ranges. The profoundly deaf group of children perceive acoustic stimuli vibrotactually, with their ears. They have the ability to perceive time and intensity cues in speech but not to discriminate small differences in frequencies or rapid frequency changes, that is, the spectral changes which are characteristic of speech.

In order to study more closely the ability of these two groups of hearing-impaired children to make basic perceptual distinctions among speech sounds, Erber carried out the following experiment (Erber, 1972b).

Eight consonant sounds, /p/,/b/,/m/,/t/,/d/,/n/,/k/, and /g/, were presented to a group of subjects in the context, /a/-C-/a/. The consonants were chosen from the set used by Miller and Nicely (1955) because they occur frequently in English and because they represent three different places of articulation in the mouth, bilabial, alveolar, and velar; also, different manners of articulation, namely nasal and nonnasal, and voiced and unvoiced sounds. A speaker whose face was ideally illuminated was videotaped as she produced these eight consonants in random order. The stimuli were presented to five normal-hearing, five severely hearing-impaired, and five profoundly deaf children of ten to fifteen years, in three different ways. These were (1) visually, that is, through lipreading alone, the sound turned off, (2) auditorially, that is, with the videomonitor turned off, and (3) visually and auditorially combined.

The results are shown in Figure 1.17 in the form of confusion matrices. Erber said, for the normal children under the auditory and auditory-visual conditions, as one would expect, the responses are mostly correct and fall along the main diagonal. For the visual-only condition, however, the normal children confuse consonants mainly within each place of articulation category. The confusions among items in each place cluster do not seem to be the result of experience with lipreading, since hearing-impaired subjects make these confusions as well as normal children. Notice, however, that the normal-hearing children made a greater number of random errors which fall outside these clusters.

The stimulus/response items have been reordered in the second row of matrices in order to illustrate more clearly typical error patterns under the auditory reception-only condition. In this condition, the severely hearing-impaired group (that is, those children who make good scores on the spondee recognition test) now show a different pattern of errors. They can discriminate nasal from nonnasal and voiced from voiceless sounds on the basis of their low-frequency residual hearing. However, they cannot discriminate within nasal and nonnasal voiced categories or nonnasal voiceless categories on the basis of listening alone. When they are given combined visual and auditory information, that is, low-frequency auditory cues to voicing/nasality and visual place cues, they are able to identify the eight consonants in the matrix quite well.

These results probably could be extrapolated to the perception of other phoneme classes such as fricatives, Erber said. Thus, the predictions that have been made on the basis of the Miller and Nicely (1955) data about the responses of hearing-impaired persons are borne out in the case of the severely hearing-impaired. As a result, when both residual hearing and lipreading are available to the severely impaired child, he may do reasonably well on a communication task. In fact, this group of children could carry on a conversation without too much difficulty. This is not true of the profoundly deaf group. When provided with acoustic information alone, they do not have the ability to classify on the basis of low-frequency voicing and nasality cues, and their errors appear to be quite random.

Also, when visual and acoustic cues are combined, these children do no better than under the visual-only condition; that is, they are able to make little use of acoustic cues. There is a small increment in the amount of information received by them under this condition, but it is not impressive. This would suggest that conventional hearing aids, that is, simple amplifiers, should be adequate for the severely hearing-impaired group; but, the profoundly deaf children need to have voicing and nasality information made clearly available to them, through some other sensory modality as an aid to lipreading. These are the primary cues that they are unable to perceive with their existing sensory systems through conventional hearing aids.

Pickett pointed out that there was some resolution of voicing and nasality under the auditory-visual condition as compared to the visual-alone condition for the profoundly deaf children. He wanted to know if this was attributable to an individual subject. He suspected that if a profoundly deaf child could hear the voiced/voiceless distinction or even feel it, then he would be able to make the distinction all the time. Perhaps one or two subjects consistently showed this ability while others did not. Erber replied that this was not the case. The subjects in the profoundly deaf group, who had been chosen because they were very homogeneous with respect to their pure-tone audio-

Resolution of voicing and nasality by profoundly deaf

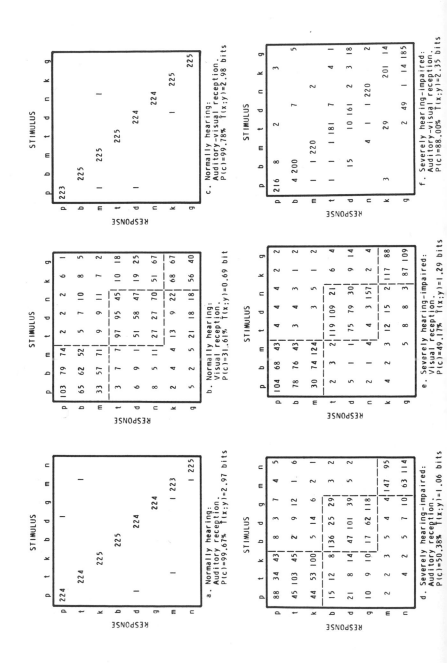

a. Normally hearing:
Auditory reception.
P(c)=99.67% T(x;y)=2.97 bits

b. Normally hearing:
Visual reception.
P(c)=31.61% T(x;y)=0.69 bit

c. Normally hearing:
Auditory-visual reception.
P(c)=99.78% T(x;y)=2.98 bits

d. Severely hearing-impaired:
Auditory reception.
P(c)=50.38% T(x;y)=1.06 bits

e. Severely hearing-impaired:
Visual reception.
P(c)=49.17% T(x;y)=1.29 bits

f. Severely hearing-impaired:
Auditory-visual reception.
P(c)=88.00% T(x;y)=2.35 bits

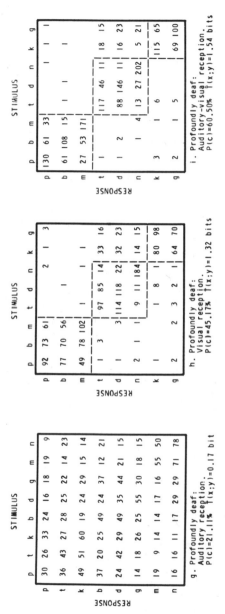

Fig. 1.17 Auditory, visual, and auditory-visual recognition of eight plosive and nasal consonants by 5 normally-hearing children, 5 severely hearing-impaired children, and 5 profoundly deaf children. The data are presented as confusion matrices. From Erber, 1972b.

grams, all showed some degree of difficulty in making distinctions on the basis of voicing and nasality cues; and all were much poorer in this respect than the subjects in the severely hearing-impaired group.

Etiology of hearing impairment in Erber's subjects

Eisenberg asked if the severely hearing-impaired children had etiologies similar to those with which the profoundly deaf children presented, as well as similar audiograms. Erber replied that etiology for most of the hearing-impaired children in his study was unknown and that the audiograms of children in the severely and profoundly deaf groups were dissimilar.

Effect of training upon resolution of voicing and nasality

Ling then described an experiment which he and his graduate student, Corletta Aston, had conducted with a group of ten hearing-impaired children, ten to sixteen years of age, whose average hearing loss for the frequencies 125 Hz to 1 KHz was 79 dB (Aston, 1971). Half of these children had no measurable hearing above 1 KHz. The investigators had presented similar VCV stimuli to these children auditorially under the conditions of no filtering and of low-pass filtering at 1 KHz. There were no differences in the phoneme recognition scores attained by the deaf children under these two conditions at first. Thus, whatever cues the profoundly deaf children were using were in the region below 1 KHz. Figure 1.18 shows, however, that after about eighteen sessions of training, there were large increments in the scores of the children, reflecting an increased ability to discriminate manner and nasality cues. There was no significant improvement with training in the ability of the children to discriminate place cues.

Ling suggested to Erber that he too might have found increments in scores based on classification by voicing or nasality after a period of training.

Use of supplementary cues in lipreading

Erber maintained that the children he had designated as profoundly deaf perceived vibrotactual and not auditory cues. The vibrotactual cues carried information primarily about time and intensity, that is, the wave form envelope of speech, provided that preliminary analysis of the speech signal by means of a vocoder had not first been carried out. Erber originally began to suspect that this was the case upon examining data on supplementary cues from a number of investigators (see Erber, 1972a). These data showed that when lipreading was supplemented by information from another sense, profoundly deaf subjects consistently showed a modest improvement in their word-recognition scores (see Figure 1.19). Usually the supplementary information was in the form of a signal presented to the ears, but in one case it was in the form of vibratory cues presented to the hand (Gault, 1928). The mean increment in word recognition ranged from 1% to 15%. In no case was it as great as that shown by the severely hearing-impaired in response to

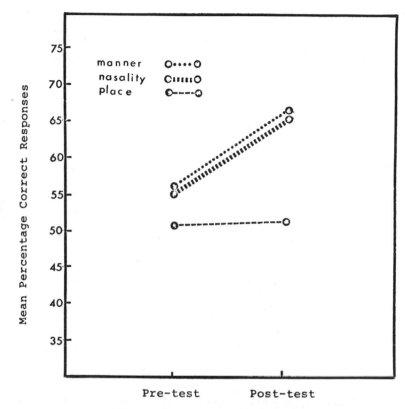

Fig. 1.18 Mean percentage correct responses on pre- and post-training tests for the features: manner, nasality, and place of articulation.

supplementary auditory information (see Figure 1.17). Also, the increment resulting from the additional vibratory cues was approximately the same as that resulting from additional acoustic cues.

Nature of supplementary cues received by profoundly deaf

Erber then described an experiment (Erber, 1972a) designed to test the hypothesis that only time and intensity cues are received through the auditory system by children designated as profoundly deaf in his system.

In this experiment, stimuli were prepared as follows. Recordings of words produced by a female speaker were low-pass filtered at 2 KHz to eliminate energy not received by the profoundly deaf subjects in the study. The resulting signal was then passed to a multiplier which effectively took the

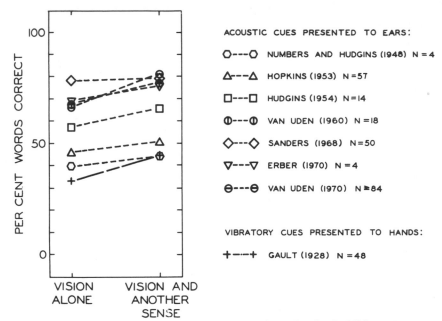

Fig. 1.19 Mean recognition of words by profoundly deaf children through vision alone (lipreading) and through vision plus another sensory system. From Erber, 1972a.

waveform envelope of the signal and filled it with low-frequency noise. In this way, the spectral cues in the signal were eliminated and only its time-intensity pattern was preserved.

Examples are shown in Figure 1.20. These stimuli were presented to six normal-hearing adults aged twenty-three to thirty-one years, six normal-hearing children aged ten to fifteen years, and six profoundly deaf children aged fourteen to fifteen years. Word recognition for a large number of items was then tested under three conditions.

In the first condition, the subject had to respond to a videotaped presentation of the speaker saying each word; that is, by lipreading alone. In the second, he was given this lip-reading information and also supplementary acoustic information in the form of either conventional amplification of the unfiltered speech signal in the case of the profoundly deaf group or in the form of amplified speech-modulated noise. The results of the experiment are summarized in Figure 1.21. First, it can be seen that the six profoundly deaf children performed in a highly similar way, regardless of whether they were presented with the visual signal plus conventionally amplified speech, or were presented with the visual signal plus speech-modulated noise. What was more,

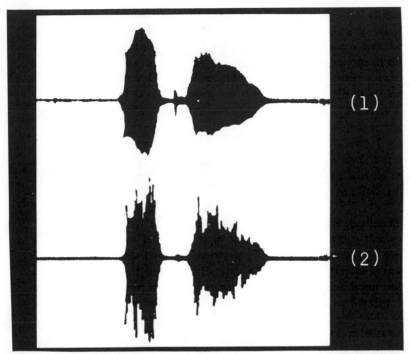

Fig. 1.20 Waveforms illustrating the similarity in envelope between: (1) the speech input to the modulator (after low-pass filtering at 2000 Hz); and (2) the modulated-noise output. The stimulus word is "airplane." From Erber, 1972a.

the profoundly deaf children receiving the speech-modulated noise in the second condition did not comment that it sounded unspeechlike to them, but only that the speaker in this latter condition sounded hoarse. In other words, they were not aware of the fact that they were not receiving speech. The performance of the six normally-hearing adults and of the six normally-hearing children who received speech-modulated noise in the second condition also is shown in Figure 1.21. The slopes showing the improvement from the visual alone to the visual plus speech-modulated noise condition for these two subject groups, were very similar to those obtained from the profoundly deaf children under both visual plus amplified real speech and visual plus speech-modulated noise conditions.

The finding suggested that the information from lipreading was being supplemented by the information presented to the ear, but that the supplementary cues were those present in the time-intensity envelope of the speech signal in every case. Even when the profoundly deaf child was given spectral

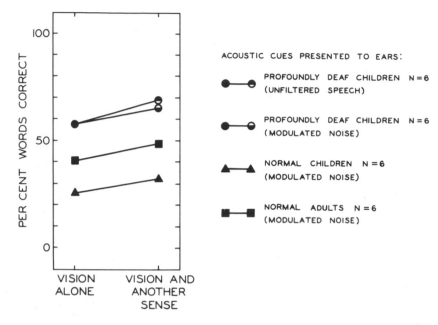

Fig. 1.21 Mean recognition of 240 words by several groups of subjects through vision alone (lipreading) and through vision plus acoustic reception. Two acoustic signals were used: (1) linearly amplified speech; and (2) thermal noise that first was passed through a 500 Hz octave band filter and then was amplitude-modified by the envelope of the speech signal.

cues in addition to lipreading, that is, in the conventionally amplified speech signal condition, his performance was no better than under the speech-modulated noise condition. Erber felt that the technique he described provided a valuable means of discovering the nature of the speech signal which the profoundly deaf child must deal with in communicating receptively.

Ling agreed that modulated noise could supplement lip-read information much as speech information which was not discriminable by audition alone could supplement it, a fact which had been known for years (Ewing, 1944). However, in his experience, amplified real speech was more effective as a signal supplementing lipreading than speech-modulated noise, at least for some profoundly deaf children (Birtles, 1970). He felt that the use of a 95 dB pure-tone average threshold as a means of classifying groups of deaf children had a built-in artifact. It did not take into account the slope of the loss, that is, whether the child had hearing at frequencies above 1 KHz, or at 4 KHz. The speech reception of hard-of-hearing and of profoundly deaf children was frequency dependent and this could be lost sight of in a pure-tone average assessment of threshold.

Significance of slope of hearing loss

Hirsh restated the question being considered as follows. Is there a real dichotomy between deaf children who are easy and those who are hard to teach? If so, is this correlated with the hearing loss scale? He wished to answer the points raised by Furth and Menyuk. First of all, there was no new magic number of 90 to 95 dB. The notion of a threshold of 90 dB re normal hearing as a cut-off point from the point of view of educational planning had been around for a long time. It was first proposed at the Pedo-Audiology Congress in the Netherlands in 1956. Hirsh himself, at the Congress on Education for the Deaf in 1963, had reported on some planning in Western European countries which, in fact, set up two basically different kinds of programs depending on whether the child had hearing levels that were greater or less than 90 dB. As far as the choice between 90 and 95 dB was concerned, he drew the attention of the participants to the fact that Erber used 2 KHz in his pure-tone average while others did not. The relation between 2-frequency and 3-frequency averages was easily dealt with arithmetically, as Elliott (1967) had shown in her audiometric description of the children at the Central Institute for the Deaf. Hirsh said that at one time he believed that the dichotomy between difficult and easy children had to do with the child's ability to respond at the higher frequencies. He was no longer convinced of this. He would like to see evidence from audiometric tests where the higher frequencies were presented at sufficiently high levels of amplification, that is, beyond the limits of present-day commercial audiometers. In other words, he would like to see the actual thresholds for profoundly deaf subjects at high frequencies before accepting this concept. He felt that the evidence was particularly strong in favor of a dichotomy based upon an average threshold for lower frequencies and upon a predominance of vibrotactile responders among the more profoundly deaf, those children who are difficult to teach.

Nature of dichotomy in speech scores of deaf children

Lip-reading skills

In further discussion, it was stated that scores for lipreading must also be considered as predicting the deaf child's ability to acquire language skills.

The contribution of lipreading to speech perception was further elaborated by Erber who reported a detailed study of the discrimination of consonants by six profoundly deaf children (age range nine to fourteen years) by means of lipreading alone. The consonant sounds were presented in a VCV context in which the vowels /i/,/a/,/u/ were employed. The experiment was carried out under ideal illumination. The teacher faced the windows of the classroom; in addition, her mouth was illuminated by two 200-watt light bulbs which were placed at a 30 degree angle to the mouth and at mouth level. The teacher was a good speaker but did not articulate in an exaggerated

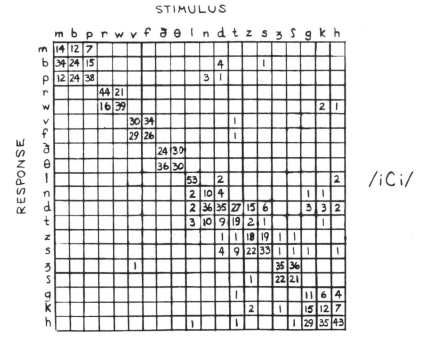

Fig. 1.22 Visual recognition of 20 consonants by 6 profoundly deaf children. Intense, shadow-free illumination was provided at mouth level for the speaker, who spoke clearly but without exaggeration. The stimuli were presented in the following context: /i/-C-/i/.

way. Under these conditions, it was possible to see the placement of alveolar and velar consonants. No acoustic cues were given to the children in this study. The results are shown in Figures 1.22 through 1.24. It may be seen that, as before, profoundly deaf subjects perceived the twenty consonant sounds categorically with respect to place of articulation. There are small blocks of consonants with the same place of articulation (for example, /m/, /b/, and /p/) which were confused. These patterns of reception occurred in all vowel contexts but the alveolar consonants, /n/, /d/, /t/, /s/, and /z/, were more frequently confused with one another in vowel contexts, for example, /u/-C-/u/, where the size of the mouth opening is reduced. This confusion presented a real problem since consonants with an alveolar place of articulation have a high frequency of occurrence in English. Within each place category, the distinction between items is in most cases on the basis of voicing or nasality, the cues which profoundly deaf children do not receive.

STIMULUS

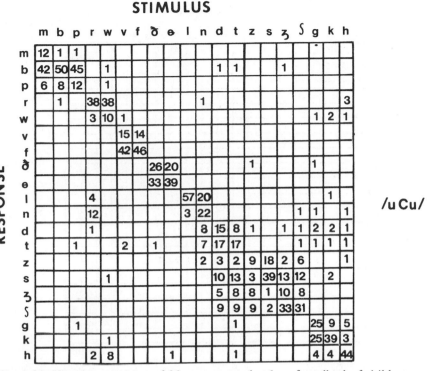

RESPONSE

	m	b	p	r	w	v	f	ð	e	l	n	d	t	z	s	ʒ	ʃ	g	k	h
m	12	1	1																	
b	42	50	45		1						1	1			1					
p	6	8	12		1															
r		1		38	38						1									3
w				3	10	1												1	2	1
v						15	14													
f						42	46													
ð								26	20					1				1		
e								33	39											
l				4						57	20							1		
n				12						3	22			1	1					1
d				1							8	15	8	1	1	1		2	2	1
t		1		2			1				7	17	17				1	1	1	1
z											2	3	2	9	18	2	6			1
s					1						10	13	3	39	13	12		2		
ʒ												5	8	8	1	10	8			
ʃ												9	9	9	2	33	31			
g		1											1					25	9	5
k				1														25	39	3
h				2	8		1				1							4	4	44

/uCu/

Fig. 1.23 Visual recognition of 20 consonants by 6 profoundly deaf children. Intense, shadow-free illumination was provided at mouth level for the speaker, who spoke clearly but without exaggeration. The stimuli were presented in the following context: /u/-C-/u/.

Other cues, however, are involved in the case of the fricatives (/s/ and /z/ in these figures) and glides (/r/ and /w/ in these figures). In addition, the data indicated a distinct bias, within place categories, to perceive one item rather than another. There was a bias, for example, toward the perception of /f/ rather than /v/ in the /v-f/ block, in the /a/-C-/a/ vowel context. This bias is not found in other vowel contexts. Erber was not sure whether this reflected differences in articulation on the part of the teacher, or biases on the part of the subjects; but, in either case, he felt that such effects should be taken into account in training.

Erber contrasted his findings with respect to lipreading of consonants with those of Berger (1970) on the lipreading of vowels by normal-hearing adults. These data are shown in Figure 1.25.

Lipreading of vowels

Studies of the lip-reading skills of deaf children, Erber said, had yielded comparable data (Heider and Heider, 1940). He pointed out that while

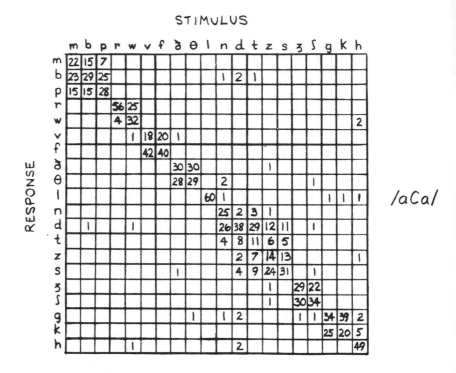

STIMULUS

RESPONSE

/aCa/

Fig. 1.24 Visual recognition of 20 consonants by 6 profoundly deaf children. Intense, shadow-free illumination was provided at mouth level for the speaker, who spoke clearly but without exaggeration. The stimuli were presented in the following context: /a/-C-/a/.

consonants were perceived categorically as far as place of articulation was concerned, vowels were not perceived categorically, but rather on a continuum. Vowels tended to be confused primarily with other vowels, articulated in neighboring positions within the mouth. There tended to be a general smear in the vowel confusion matrix rather than distinct clustering.

Silverman thought that deaf children also tended to produce vowels that were slightly off target with respect to tongue position. In his experience, this was particularly true for front vowels. Levitt pointed out that there was clustering in Berger's confusion matrix on the tense/lax dimension. The heavy preponderance of responses near the diagonal together with the system which had been used to order the vowels reflected the tense/lax confusions, as for example /i/ as in beet and /I/ as in bit. Erber agreed that this was the case and stated that he thought this confusion could be resolved for the deaf child by use of information in the time-intensity envelope received by him. In other

Relation of lipreading to speech production

Response*

Stimulus	i	ɪ	e	ɛ	æ	ɑ	ɔ	o	ʊ	u	ʌ	ɝ
i	63.7 (82.2)	27.4 (5.9)										
ɪ	23.0 (38.5)	37.8 (18.5)	12.0 (18.5)	17.8 (6.7)	(5.9)							(5.2)
e		9.6	23.0 (39.3)	14.8	34.1 (29.6)	5.9 (15.6)						(7.4)
ɛ		12.0	32.6 (25.2)	22.2 (13.3)	14.1 (20.7)	5.2 (22.2)						
æ			11.9 (7.4)	8.9 (5.9)	60.7 (63.7)	10.4 (15.6)						5.9 (12.0)
ɑ					12.0	67.4 (73.3)	7.4 (13.3)					10.4 (8.9)
ɔ						(6.7)	59.3 (74.8)	25.9 (17.0)				
o								74.1 (92.6)	5.9	11.9 (6.7)		
ʊ									36.3 (35.6)	42.2 (34.1)		12.0 (25.2)
u									20.0 (12.0)	68.1 (80.0)		5.2
ʌ				5.9 (8.9)		10.4	7.4		12.6	5.2	27.4 (46.7)	17.8
ɝ	7.4	15.6 (14.8)					7.4		13.3 (20.7)	15.6 (15.6)		61.5 (54.1)

*Initial vowel scores are shown in the upper part of each square. Final vowel scores are shown in parenthesis in the lower part of each square.

Fig. 1.25 Visual recognition of 12 vowels in initial and final position by 45 normally-hearing adults. From Berger, 1970.

words, the differences in intensity and duration between tense and lax vowels probably could be perceived vibrotactually, although the deaf child might have to be trained to make use of this supplementary information.

Pollack asked if proficient lip-readers also were good speakers. Silverman answered that there was a reasonably good correlation between ability to speak well and ability to lip-read in congenitally deaf children. This might have to do with the children's language capabilities and the frequency with which lipreading is used in school, as well as other factors.

Levitt observed that the speech production errors documented in Smith's thesis (1972; 1973) showed confusions very similar to those Erber had shown in lipreading. For example, Figure 1.26 shows that there were confusions between the tense/lax cognates, /i/ and /I/ in vowel production. Also, with respect to consonant production, patterns of confusions were found which were very similar to those in Erber's data on visual reception of consonants. Figure 1.27 shows that, among plosives of the same place of articulation, there was a tendency for deaf children to respond with a voiced plosive both receptively when the voiceless cognate was a stimulus and productively when a voiceless cognate was the target. The substitution of a voiceless for a voiced plosive at the same place of articulation was less common, both receptively and productively. This bias also was present in Erber's lip-reading data (see Figures 1.22 through 1.24).

Sherrick commented that there did not seem to be agreement with respect to questions of some kind of fixed sensory task or system of evaluation to use with hearing-impaired children of more than three or four years. In addition, it seemed that it was necessary to introduce description of relatively complex receptive and motor skills in order to establish external criteria and to make any kind of sense out of the evaluation. It was his impression that the whole area was in a state of flux and in spite of the fact that ideas of substance had been expressed, it would be difficult at present to give them any particular form.

Testing of nonauditory perceptual skills in the deaf child

Relation of speech skills to nonauditory skills

Bordley stated that as a clinician, he felt some concern that tests were being used in evaluating the deaf child's capabilities which tapped nonauditory skills. How much was known about the deaf child's nonauditory sensory and perceptual capabilities, which he must use in responding on these tests; for example, for how many of the children whose performance had been described thus far had information been gathered about nonauditory sensation and perception? How many of them had been carefully studied with respect to their total mental capacity? Bordley felt that a complete evaluation of this

TARGET

PRODUCED \	i	I	ɑ	ɛ	æ	ɔ	ʊ	u	ʌ	ə	ɝ	ɚ
i	57	8		2						1		
I	20	71		2						4	2	
ɑ			80		3		1			6		
ɛ	2	3		72	5					2		
æ		1	2	6	74					1		
ɔ						61	2					
ʊ		1				2	69	8				
u						2	3	74	4			
ʌ	1	2	3	2	2	4	3	1	84	3	33	1
ə	4	4	2	2	4	6		2	2	71	10	47
ɝ											33	
ɚ										3	3	15

Fig. 1.26 Confusion matrix of vowel phonemes for hearing-impaired children. The sum of proportions (percentages) across columns is always less than 100% because diphthongs, unrecognizable substitutions, omissions, and non-English phonemes have been omitted.

TARGET

PRODUCED

target \ produced	m	b	p	r	w	v	f	ð	θ	l	n	d	t	z	s	ʒ	ʃ	dʒ	g	k	h	ŋ
m	70.2	3.3	3.9	1.7	2.8	2.1	.8	.4	1.0	.4	.6	.5	.5	.2	1.8			.6		.3		.8
b	17.5	85.0	17.0	13.0	5.0	7.9	4.4		.5	.2	.1	.5	.4	.2	.2					.5	1.0	
p	2.7	4.0	70.0		.5		1.9			.2	.1	.2	.2									
r	.2		54.7		.5	.4					.1	.2										
w	.2			11.9	82.8	62.9	.4			.2	.1	.3		1.2						.6		
v		.3		1.9	2.8	9.7		.4				.3		1.0	1.4					.2	.5	
f	.4	.5		.6		8.3	69.7	1.4	1.0		.3	.3	.2	1.0	1.1	1.7				.3	.5	
ð								37.1	5.0													
θ							.3	3.8	38.2	70.6		.3	.2	.5	.4	2.5				.2		
l	.2		.6	.6		.4	.3	1.7	1.0	2.9	58.8	1.2	.5	.2	.7						.5	
n		.7	.7	.3		.8	.3	39.6	17.1	1.7	2.5	38.2	1.3	2.0	1.1	5.0	1.3	1.9	1.1	.3	6.7	
d	.4	.4	.4	.3	.3	.4	1.1	.5	17.6		1.2	6.2	7.3	5.8	7.9	17.5	1.9	1.4	1.5	.3		
t							.3			.2	1.2	36.8	36.8	1.3	14.3		.3				.8	
z											.5	.5		17.5	2.5	1.7						
s										.1	.3	.3	.7	4.5	22.9	7.5			.5			
ʃ													.2	.2		.8				.3		
dʒ				.3		.4	.3			.1	.3	.4			.7	21.7			.2			
g	.3									.1	1.0	.7	.5	.4	.8	.8	33.8	5.0	5.5	.5		
k											.1	.3	1.8	.2	.8	.8	5.0	1.9	39.1	1.5		
h					1.0			.8		.3	.3	.2	.9	.7	1.1	.8	1.9	1.4	4.2	36.8		
ŋ											1.3		.2	.7	1.7	1.3	.2	.3	30			

Fig. 1.27 Confusion matrix of consonant phonemes for hearing-impaired children. The sum of proportions (percentages) across columns is always less than 100% because /m/, /tʃ/, and /dʒ/; also glottal stops, unrecognizable substitutions, and non-English phonemes, have been omitted.

kind should go along with studies of speech perception and speech production and he was alarmed not to hear this brought out in discussion.

Elliott (observer) said that such data were available on children admitted to the Central Institute for the Deaf (CID) although these had not been thoroughly studied. She looked at the IQ scores of children when first admitted to the school's Division for the Deaf over a ten year period beginning in the early 1940's. She divided the children into three groups according to the outcome of their education, that is, (1) children who stayed in school less than two years, (2) children who stayed in school for more than two years but did not graduate, and (3) children who did graduate (and in consequence were given a certificate permitting them to attend high school with normal-hearing children). The average IQ's of these three groups at the time of initial testing was approximately 109, 113, and 128.

IQ scores and educational outcome

Bordley asked if these were the children whose speech-perception and speech-production scores had been discussed earlier in the session and if so, what their nonauditory capabilities were. Elliott indicated that data could be pulled from the records of the children participating in studies of speech reception at CID which would help to answer Bordley's question.

Relation between speech skills and intelligence

Levitt presented data on children studied at Lexington School for the Deaf, which he felt were relevant to Bordley's question. These were in the form of a proximity plot shown in Figure 1.28. In it were displayed (1) average pure-tone threshold (L-1 and L-2); (2) speech intelligibility to naive listeners (I); (3) D-1, phoneme discrimination score from a modified rhyme test; (4) D-2, a score reflecting ability to perceive prosodic aspects of speech; (5) P-1, the speech-production score for individual phonemes; (6) P-2, the speech production score deriving from rating of prosodic features in the children's speech; and (7) IQ. The data were arranged so that the spacing of the points indicated the degree of correlation between each of these measures; that is, close spacing reflected a very high correlation and conversely, a divergence reflected low correlation. There was, for example, a close spacing between the two measures of average pure-tone threshold; also, between percent intelligibility of the child's speech, and his phoneme-reception and his phoneme-production scores. The intelligibility of his speech also correlated moderately well with average pure-tone thresholds. The rating of prosodic features in the child's speech and his ability to perceive prosodic features showed only a moderate degree of correlation with one another, but this was perhaps because they were measured in ways that were not comparable. In addition, the ratings of prosodic features were not thought to be very reliable. With reference to

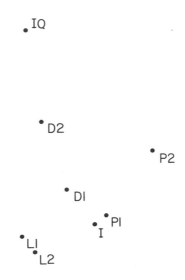

Fig. 1.28 Proximity plot in which the degree of correlation between measures is indicated by spacing of the points. Key: L1, L2 = average pure-tone
thresholds; I = speech intelligibility score; D-1 = phoneme reception score;
D-2 = score for reception of prosodic features; P-1 = phoneme production
score; and P-2 = score for production of prosodic features.

Bordley's question, however, it was clear that intelligibility of speech was
correlated only moderately if at all with IQ score.

Pickett thought that these were very interesting data; he pointed out,
however, that they did not answer Bordley's question, which was, Were there
studies relating amount of hearing loss, or the fact of deafness per se, to
nonauditory perceptual skills? This was an important question, but one with
few answers. Bordley said that his concern was with the child who had a high
IQ score, but a perceptual deficit which would nevertheless prevent him from
acquiring language. Furth referred to studies of other aspects of visual
functioning in deaf children which had been conducted in New Mexico
(Marshall, 1967). Sherrick felt that it would be important to study somesthesis and especially oral stereognosis in deaf children utilizing the approaches
cited by Bosma (1969).

*Studies of
visual and
somesthetic
capabilities in
deaf children*

Study of oral and manual stereognosis in deaf children

House stated that a study of this kind had been carried out by Bishop et al.
(1972). The aim was to compare oral stereognosis in normal-hearing and deaf

high school students. Eighteen students from a predominantly manual training program and eighteen normal high school students were studied. The investigators found that two-point discrimination in the mouth was approximately the same in the normal and deaf high school students. On the other hand, oral stereognosis, i.e., the recognition of different forms held in the mouth, was not the same for deaf children who use sign language and normal school children. In this study, three-dimensional forms were placed on the tongue and the subject was allowed to manipulate them in the mouth. He then had to make a same/different judgment for a given pair of test items. Curiously enough, the normal and the deaf students made highly similar judgments when the two forms of a pair were the same. Hearing students with articulation defects did not do as well as normally-hearing or deaf students in this situation. On the other hand, on those test items where the two forms presented were in fact different, the deaf students had the highest error rates and the normal and articulation-defective students performed at about the same level.

In order to make sure that the deaf students did not perform poorly on the different pair because of some cognitive difficulty, i.e., in classifying squares, stars, triangles, etc., a control experiment was run in which manual form discrimination was tested. The subjects were now asked to make same/different judgments with respect to pairs of test items presented successively to the hand. In this situation there was no difference in performance between the normal-hearing and the deaf subjects.

Pollack wanted to know if this implied that deaf speech was defective because of an oral sensory deficit. Furth assumed it was the other way around; that is, the deaf child manifested an oral sensory deficit because he spoke so much less than the normal child. The investigators' conclusions, House said, were that either oral sensory discrimination abilities and speech development exist in a cause-effect relationship or both are related to a more general factor such as neurological maturation and/or perceptual skill development. House added that the study had subsequently been extended. The oral form-discrimination abilities of a group of orally educated and oriented deaf high school students were subsequently determined and compared to those of the manual deaf group and to those of normal-hearing students (Bishop et al., in press). In general, the discrimination scores separated the manual deaf from the other two groups, particularly when differences in form shapes were involved in the task. The results led to the postulation that, while a failure in oroperceptual functioning may lead to disorders of articulation, a failure to use the oral mechanisms for speech activities, even in persons with normal orosensory capabilities, may result in poor performance on oroperceptual tasks.

Orosensory deficit as cause or effect

Use of nonauditory senses other than hearing in speech acquisition of the hearing-impaired

Implications of orosensory deficits

It was clear that more information about sensory processing in the hearing-impaired child was required in order that effective plans might be made for treatment. For example, if it is true that there is a cause-effect relationship between orosensory discrimination deficit and speech development in deaf children, ways of compensating for disrupted orosensory input should be sought. If, on the other hand, impaired orosensory discrimination skills in deaf children are related to a more general problem such as delay in perceptual skill development, then a more global approach such as that recommended for use for brain-injured or perceptually-disturbed children by Ringel et al. (1970) would be indicated. However, if poor performance on oroperceptual tasks results from a failure to use the oral mechanism in speaking, that might indicate a primary need to intensify the efforts to improve speech.

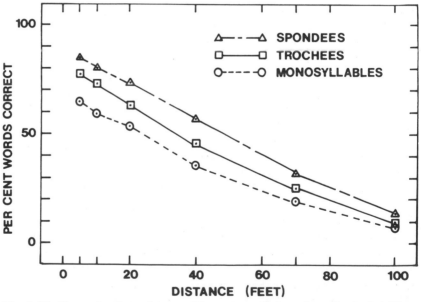

Fig. 1.29 Mean visual word-recognition scores of 6 profoundly deaf children as a function of distance for words with different syllabic structure. Intense, shadow-free illumination was provided at mouth level for each of two speakers. Data are pooled across speakers. Total vocabulary = 240 words (80 monosyllables, 80 trochees, 80 spondees). From Erber, 1971.

MONOSYLLABIC

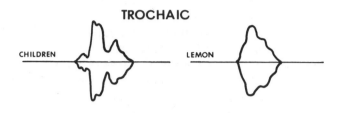

TROCHAIC

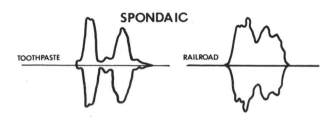

SPONDAIC

ENVELOPES OF STIMULUS WORDS - TRACED FROM SCREEN OF
STORAGE OSCILLOSCOPE

Fig. 1.30 Examples of typical speech envelope patterns for words with different syllabic structure. The stimuli were passed through a 2000 Hz low-pass
filter prior to display on the screen of a storage oscilloscope. Note that some
trochaic words (e.g., lemon) appear as one-syllable words, and that some
spondaic words (e.g., railroad) are not clearly bi-syllabic. From Erber, 1971.

Lipreading

It was also clear that in acquiring speech, the deaf child made use of
information from senses other than hearing. The visual sense was used
primarily in lipreading, and lipreading contributed not only to the reception
of speech but also to speech production. This raised questions as to how best
help the child make maximum use of lipreading.

Erber referred to a relevant study (Erber, 1971) designed to determine
the relative ease of lipreading (1) monosyllables, (2) words of two syllables
with a trochaic (strong-weak) stress pattern such as 'paper,' and (3) spondees.
At all reasonable distances between sender and receiver, he found that

*Length of
unit in lip-
reading*

spondees were more often perceived correctly by lipreading than were monosyllables (see Figures 1.29 and 1.30). This suggests that training in lipreading should begin with easier spondees and with other multisyllabic words, rather than with monosyllables.

Another factor of importance, Erber said, was suggested by a study of lipreading conducted by Heider and Heider (1940) at Clarke School for the Deaf. These investigators found that ability to discriminate consonants visually was not highly correlated with skill in lipreading as measured by a sentence recognition test. They speculated that this was because nearly everyone, even poor lip-readers, can discriminate between consonants on the basis of place of articulation; but some individuals are much better than others at difficult vowel discriminations. The latter should be superior lip-readers. Accordingly, Heider and Heider trained a group of deaf children on vowel discrimination and found that these children improved in their overall lip-reading performance as they improved in vowel discrimination. Unfortunately, they did not include an untrained control group so that it was not possible to estimate the effects of training reliably. It might be worth considering this further.

Lipreading of vowel sounds

House stated that he had never seen data on lipreading that were comparable to Erber's in accuracy of consonant discrimination. He asked if this was due simply to the illumination used; if so, that was not a natural situation. Erber replied that it was due primarily to illumination and that it was approximately a natural situation. His implication was that the teacher should face the windows while speaking. In many classrooms he had visited, the side of the teacher's face was to the window so that her mouth received strong side-lighting and somewhat weaker overhead lighting. This produced deep shadows within the mouth; lip-reading confusions which occur under poor lighting do not occur under good lighting conditions, that is, where the light is at mouth level. House observed that he had been watching people's mouths all his life, but even on television, where strong lighting is used, he had never been able to extract the amount of information reflected in Erber's data. Erber replied that lighting at mouth level generally was not used in television. The lights typically were so strong that this would be very annoying to participants in a TV program. Miller intervened to say that if hearing aids were accepted as an important part of training for the deaf, special illumination should be also. Erber then demonstrated the visibility of velar articulation in front of extremely bright lights.

Use of illumination in lipreading training

House stated that he did not object to the use of illumination, but to the exaggerated articulation used by teachers of the deaf. No one outside of schools for the deaf articulated as Erber had done in his demonstration. Erber acknowledged the fact that teachers of the deaf do not speak to deaf children whom they are instructing in the same manner as hearing people speak to one another. The classroom environment of the deaf child was not a normal one, but this was intentional. He claimed that if profoundly deaf children could learn in a normal environment, it would not be necessary to set up special education programs for them. House still expressed concern over the stylized articulation used by teachers of the deaf. He thought that one of the reasons that deaf children spoke as they did was because they were presented with these exaggerated models. Erber, on the other hand, felt that one way of teaching perceptual distinctions was to present a maximal difference between items at first and then to gradually reduce the difference, that is, the number of cues available for making a discrimination to a realistic level. For example, if one wished to teach a child to distinguish between /ga/ and /da/, one could do this first under a high level of illumination and then gradually reduce the level so that the child came to depend on jaw height, for example, rather than tongue position in making this discrimination.

Exaggerated articulatory gestures used in training deaf children

Erber added that it was important to be as precise as possible in thinking about the kinds of information in the speech signal which the profoundly deaf child receives. The normal-hearing teacher who speaks to him experiences feedback from her own utterance which is very different in nature from the signal which the deaf child receives. When the teacher is not understood, she tries to modify her utterance so as to make it more intelligible, but in doing so, she is not able to monitor her output in the deaf child's terms. For example, the normal-hearing person has no difficulty in identifying the trochee 'lemon' as a two-syllable word (see Figure 1.30). He probably does so on the basis of the number of vocalic segments in the word. For the profoundly deaf child who receives only the time and intensity information, the low-frequency continuant /m/ which is relatively high in energy in this word, may mask the clear break between syllables and cause him to hear the word as a monosyllable.

Monitoring of own speech by deaf children

This kind of finding emphasized the fact that the profoundly deaf child, the child who presents the greatest educational problem, depends very heavily on lipreading for the reception of speech. Studies of auditory reception will not be very helpful in planning for the training of such a child. Erber felt that further study of lipreading is necessary for this purpose.

Other systems

Sherrick referred to the Tadoma (Alcorn, 1945) vibration method in which the blind-deaf subject feels the throat, lips, nose and cheeks of the speaker. By means of this method, such individuals as Helen Keller, Robert Smithdas and others learned to speak. The method, like lipreading, made use of input from articulatory gestures rather than acoustic cues, and was used to develop both reception and production of speech.

Prosthetic
devices

Supplementary speech information has also been presented to both the visual and the tactile sense with the aid of sensory devices (Upton, 1968; Risberg, 1968; Kringlebotn, 1968; Willemain and Lee, 1972; Kirman, 1973). Some time was spent discussing the merit of these approaches. Erber referred to the modest improvement in speech recognition reported by Gault (1928) for subjects using his Teletactor. Essentially, the profoundly deaf subject showed the same degree of improvement when receiving vibrotactile time/intensity cues from his hearing aid. Recent attempts to analyze the speech signal in some way before presenting it to the visual or tactile sense were more ambitious. The discussion of such prosthetic devices is reported in Chapter 9.

REFERENCES

Alcorn, S.: Development of the Tadoma method for the deaf-blind child, Exceptional Child. 11(2):117–119, 1945.

Ahlstrom, K.G.: On evaluating the effects of schooling, In: Proceedings of the International Congress on Education of the Deaf, vol. I. Stockholm, 1970. (Proceedings available from A.G. Bell Association, Volta Place N.W., Washington, D.C. 20008).

Aston, C.: Hearing-impaired children's discrimination of filtered speech, Master's thesis, McGill University, 1971.

Berger, K.W.: Vowel confusions in speechreading, Ohio J. Speech Hearing 5(2):123–128, 1970.

Birtles, G.J.: Auditory and visual speech discrimination by hearing-impaired children, Master's thesis, McGill University, 1970.

Bishop, M.E.; Ringel, R.L., and House, A.S.: Orosensory perception in the deaf. Volta Rev. 74(5):289–298, 1972.

Bishop, M.E.; Ringel, R.L., and House, A.S.: Orosensory perception, speech production, and deafness, J. Speech Hearing Res. 16(2):257–266, 1973.

Boothroyd, A.: Distribution of hearing levels in the student population of the Clarke School for the Deaf (SARP Report #3), Northampton: Clarke School for the Deaf, 1970.

Boothroyd, A.: An experiment on the learning of pitch control by profoundly deaf children (SARP Report #5), Northampton: Clarke School for the Deaf, 1971.

Boothroyd, A.: Some experiments on the control of voice in the profoundly deaf using a pitch extractor and storage oscilloscope display, IEEE Trans. Audio Electroacoust. (In press).

Bosma, J.F., ed.: Oral Sensation and Perception: Second Symposium, Springfield: Charles C Thomas, 1970.

Eisenberg, R.B.: Pediatric audiology: shadow or substance? J. Aud. Res. 11(2):148–153, 1971.

Elliott, L.L.: Descriptive analysis of audiometric and psychometric scores of students at a school for the deaf, J. Speech Hearing Res. 10:21–40, 1967.

Erber, N.P.: Effects of distance on the visual reception of speech, J. Speech Hearing Res. 14(4):848–857, 1971.

Erber, N.P.: Speech-envelope cues as an acoustic aid to lipreading for profoundly deaf children, J. Acoust. Soc. Amer. 51:1224–1227, 1972a.

Erber, N.P.: Auditory, visual and auditory-visual recognition of consonants by children with normal and impaired hearing, J. Speech Hearing Res. 15:413–422, 1972b.

Ewing, I.R.: Lipreading and Hearing Aids, Manchester: Manchester University Press, 1944.

Gault, R.H.: Interpretation of spoken language when the feel of speech supplements vision of the speaking face, Volta Rev. 30:379–386, 1928.

Heider, F., and Heider, G.: An experimental investigation of lipreading, Psychol. Monogr. 52:124–153, 1940.

Kirman, J.H.: Tactile communication of speech: A review and analysis, Psychol. Bull. 80:54–74, 1973.

Kringlebotn, M.: Experiments with some visual and vibrotactile aids for the deaf, Amer. Ann. Deaf 113:311–317, 1968.

Magner, M.: A Speech Intelligibility Test for Deaf Children, Northampton: Clarke School for the Deaf, 1972.

Marshall, H.: Strengthening the visual perception of deaf children, Final report OEC-4-7-00269, U.S.Dept. of HEW, Office of Education, Bureau of Education of the Handicapped, Los Crues, N.M.: University of New Mexico, 1967.

Miller, G.A., and Nicely, P.A.: Analysis of perceptual confusions among some English consonants, J. Acoust. Soc. Amer. 27:338–352, 1955.

Ringel, R.L.; House, A.S., Burk, K.W., et al.: Some relations between orosensory discrimination and articulatory aspects of speech production, J. Speech Hearing Dis. 35:3–11, 1970.

Risberg, A.: Visual aids for speech correction, Amer. Ann. Deaf 113:178–194, 1968.

Smith, C.: Residual hearing and speech production in deaf children, Doctoral dissertation, City University of New York, 1972.

Smith, C.: Residual hearing and speech production in deaf children, Communication Sciences Laboratory Report #4, CUNY Graduate Center, New York, 1973.

Upton, H.W.: Wearable eyeglass speechreading aid, Amer. Ann. Deaf 113:222–229, 1968.

Willemain, T.R., and Lee, F.F.: Tactile pitch displays for the deaf, IEEE Trans. Audio Electroacoust. AU-20(1):9–16, 1972.

Perceptual and
Cognitive Strategies

4

Perceptual and Cognitive Strategies: State-of-the-Art Report

Irwin Pollack
University of Michigan

In recent years, the distinction between perceptual processes and cognitive processes has been blurred by a steady stream of brilliant theorists and empiricists. Some of these developments will be reviewed in the next few pages. We shall also consider an approach which attempts to finesse the distinction between perceptual and cognitive processes. Despite the preponderance of argument and evidence for blurring the distinction, my personal bias is to preserve the distinction as a useful heuristic for sharpening our theories.

A. THE BLURRING OF THE DISTINCTION BETWEEN PERCEPTUAL AND COGNITIVE PROCESSES

The ordering of sampling of developments which have blurred the distinctions is personal—not reflecting the order of evidence, but rather my own personal biases from the point of view of sensory psychology.

1. Pure measures of sensory discriminability

The theory of signal detectability represents one of the most important recent milestones in sensory psychology (Green and Swets, 1966). The d' measure of this theory attempts to achieve a pure measure of sensory discriminability apart from bias and other response factors, usually labelled cognitive. Indeed, this measure had an enormous and successful impact on the study of sensory and perceptual response processes in the dissection of stimulus and response factors. But, even in the prototype task of detection of narrow-band signals in noise, certain factors emerge which detract from the apparent factoring of sensory discriminability and response factors. The theory beautifully handles the case of the attentive subject with a consistent response bias in one direction. The theory—and perhaps any theory based on the stationarity of statistical processes—has trouble with inconsistent biases. The theory—and perhaps any theory of discriminability—has difficulty in discriminating sensory factors from motivational or attentive factors which are not reflected in a consistent response bias.

More importantly, even in the simplest forced-choice detection task, the observer engages in problem-solving activities. All of the strictures employed by William James about the dullness of psychophysics apply many-fold to the detection experiment. Yet in this apparently dull task, subjects may be adopting entirely different modes of listening behaviors; in many cases, these cannot be verbalized.

For example, Leshowitz and Wightman (1971) have reinterpreted the masking of brief signals by narrow-band noise in terms of detection of signal energy at auditory frequencies different from the signal. This off-center listening plays havoc for an auditory theory based upon critical bands for masking, but may be extremely successful for the enterprising listener in solving a signal detection task.

2. Interest in attention processes

Spurred by Broadbent's (1958) *Perception and Communication* the study of attention emerged from mysterious forces of ideation and vital force to the respectability of the laboratory. A series of ingenious experimental paradigms were developed. Yet, without fully understanding that set of variables identified as attentional, workers quickly saw parallels between perception and cognition in terms of attentional demands. Visual search tasks easily lend themselves to modelling as tasks of 'focal attention.' It may well be that, anatomically, only the central retina possesses the neural structures for the resolution of fine detail. The parallel anatomical basis for cognitive focusing is unknown, but the behavioral comparison is too compelling to ignore. Most cognitive tasks suffer under competing activities. Neisser's (1963) ingenious notion of focal cognitive stream and a cognitive background stream preserves the flavor of a perceptual focus and a perceptual background.

3. Pattern recognition and constructive views of perception

One of the most influential views of pattern perception is that we recognize patterns by constructing a model against which we test the to-be-recognized pattern. Because the list of features which enter the construction are 'known' to the observer, the unknown pattern may be recognized. This view is stated explicitly by many theorists. Garner (1966) for example argues:

To perceive is an active process, one in which the perceiver participates fully. The perceiver does not passively *receive* information about his environment; rather, he actively *per*ceives his environment. Nor does he simply impose his organization on an otherwise unstructured world— the world is structured. But he does select the structure to which he will attend and react, and he even provides the missing structure on occasion. (p. 11)

The 'analysis-by-synthesis' procedure has been put forward as a tool for speech recognition (Stevens, 1960; Liberman et al., 1967). The special problem of speech recognition is that successful recognition depends heavily upon context. The same targeted sound will have different acoustical characteristics in different speech contexts; different targeted sounds may have nearly identical acoustical characteristics. F.C. Frick has aptly described the problem of speech recognition as 'deciphering the speaker's intentions.' Analysis of the given stimulus, without running context, has been successfully applied only to carefully spoken isolated words. To decipher the running stream of grunts and groans, speech theorists have been forced to take a broader view of speech recognition. Perception and cognition are not clearly separated in this task.

Perhaps the most vigorous and persuasive exponent of the unity of perception and cognition is Ulric Neisser. His influential book, *Cognitive Psychology* (1967), is used in undergraduate courses in perception at the University of Michigan. Let him explain it in his own words:

As used here, the term 'cognition' refers to all the processes by which the sensory input is transformed, reduced, elaborated, stored, recovered, and used. It is concerned with these processes even when they operate in the absence of relevant stimulation, as in images and hallucinations. Such terms as *sensation, perception, imagery, retention, recall, problem solving,* and *thinking,* among many others, refer to hypothetical stages or aspects of cognition. (p. 4)

This broad view of cognition probably stemmed from Neisser's approach to cognition. Drawing a parallel between attention and thinking, Neisser argues for a distinction for a focalized detailed, restricted main 'stream of consciousness' and a fuzzy, diffuse, outlined peripheral stream. He could not help being impressed by a similarly restricted 'searchlight' probing of the control visual environment for detailed viewing and a broader diffuse examination of the peripheral visual environment for nondetailed viewing. This duplex view of visual perception, of attention, of thinking—it is my guess—contributed strongly to the unitary view.

4. To perceive is to know

An intriguing title of a paper by W.R. Garner is "To perceive is to know"

(1966). In that paper, he shows that performance in tasks, typically considered to be perceptual, depends strongly upon the structural properties of sets of stimuli not just properties which are immediately relevant to the discrimination—in short, upon the subject's understanding of the class of possible stimuli with which he must deal. Garner's work is probably the best vindication of the technique of information measurement which does not measure the proximal properties of a particular stimulus, but rather, measures the properties of the set from which that stimulus could have been chosen. To the extent to which perception is identified with the proximal stimulus and cognition is identified with the set of possible stimuli, Garner was arguing for the unity of perception and cognition—in short—to perceive is to know.

B. FINESSING THE DISTINCTION BETWEEN PERCEPTUAL AND COGNITIVE PROCESSES

1. The work of W.R. Garner and associates

In a brilliant series of publications on the identification of repeated auditory temporal patterns, Garner and his associates have examined the identification of temporal binary patterns as a function of their internal structure (e.g., 1968). In addition to the internal structure which distinguishes easy from difficult patterns, the rate of presentation was an important variable. At slow rates of presentation, subjects identify the individual elements, intellectualize the sequential contingencies, employ elaborate hypotheses about the sequences—in short—they go through a set of behaviors which typically qualify as 'cognitive.' At higher rates of presentation, there is insufficient time to isolate the individual items and to spin elaborate hypotheses, and subjects report they seek out repeated patterns—they go through a set of behaviors which typically qualify as 'perceptual.' That is, within the same task requirements, with the same set of stimuli, observers act cognitively at slow rates of presentation and perceptually at high rates of presentation.

Garner and Gottwald (1968) express it better than my paraphrasing:

> (the) consistently different effects of starting position and modality at low and high rates require a distinction between *pattern perception* at higher rates, which is phenomenally integrated, immediate, compelling and passive, and *pattern learning* at lower rates, which is unintegrated, derived, intellectualized and active. Even though a distinction between perception and learning is necessary, similar principles of pattern organization operate for both. (p. 97)

2. 'Perceptualization' of cognitive information

The military services are quick to exploit technology to improve the efficiency of their operations. In 1949, I served as a laboratory observer at the U.S. Navy Electronics Laboratory attempting to detect moving aircraft by means of radar. I quickly discovered that I wasn't very good at this task, but under the conditions of observation, neither were more experienced operators. The experienced operators knew the directions for the most probable targets, the characteristics of targets, and had lots more savvy than untrained observers, but still performed poorly under the conditions of testing. The sweep rate of the radar was one sweep every ten seconds and the operator had to remember the positions of blips over successive sweep periods. Lund, Cheatem, and White (White, 1956) quickly discerned that they had to convert this intellectual task into a perceptual task. They did this by simply photographing the slowly developing display and replaying their films back at motion picture speed. In the 240-to-1 time compression, the moving aircraft literally 'popped out' of the screen. The inexperienced observer, like myself, performed as well as the experienced observer, presumably because we came to the demonstration with the same set of perceptual processing machinery.

The use of time-compression of slowly developing information has become a standard tool in human factors engineering. A related auditory example is the discrimination of earthquakes from explosions from seismic signals (Speeth, 1968). I have belabored this technological development because I believe it may be useful in the study of perceptual and cognitive processes in children. Wier and his associates (personal communication) have employed the Humphrey's probability guessing game with children and have developed important useful information. Such experiments typically proceed at the rate of one trial every ten seconds. We can gain an order of magnitude in efficiency by converting the guessing sequences to a choice-reaction time paradigm, in which trials proceed at the rate of one per second.

If we drop the requirement that the observer respond to each item of the sequence, we can gain several orders of magnitude in the efficiency of presentation by converting the same probabilistic sequences into visual and auditory displays. I have employed auditory displays at rates of nearly 10,000 pulses per second, a 10^5 improvement over the original guessing game, or visual displays with thousands of items in a fraction of a second (Pollack, 1971a,b).

Clearly, the task requirements differ in the presentation of visual displays for perceptual processing from those in the presentation of sequential displays for cognitive processing. The time scale available for perceptual processing simply does not admit the rich cognitive structures available to the guessing game task. Depending upon your point of view, the speed-up either has distorted the original materials so that the connection between the cognitive and perceptual tasks is only incidental, or has preserved the original materials to reveal the essential continuity between cognition and perception. I favor the latter view but am sympathetic to the arguments of the opposite side.

C. THE EMPLOYMENT OF CHILDREN TO REVEAL PSYCHOLOGICAL PROCESSES

To a naive investigator who has never worked with children, such as myself, there is the temptation to think that working with children may explicate basic psychological processes. I have always admired the skill of E. Gibson in handling such materials (e.g., Gibson, 1965). My hang-up is that I cannot distinguish failures in performance which are due to failure to understand instruction from failures due to competence factors. In visual acuity tests, where the task is to report the direction of a spatial gap, children are, if anything, superior to adults. My guess is that on matters perceptual, their competence is fully developed at an early age. And even their competence on cognitive matters may be seriously underestimated by inadequate understanding of the task environment.

I am reminded of Herbert Simon's (1969) admonition which may be paraphrased: Human behavior appears complicated to the experimental psychologist because the tasks to which we submit our subjects are complicated. It may well be that we need only a small list of about a dozen parameters or functions to describe human behavior, but we cannot discern this order as long as we do not fully understand the task environment. Perhaps we must embark upon a theory of tasks before we can embark upon a theory of behavior.

REFERENCES

Broadbent, D.: Perception and Communications, New York: Pergamon Press, 1958.

Garner, W.R.: To perceive is to know, Amer. Psychol. 21:11—19, 1966.

Garner, W.R., and Gottwald, R.L.: The perception and learning of temporal patterns, Quart. J. Exp. Psychol. 20:97—109, 1968.

Gibson, E.J.: Learning to read, Science 148:1066—1072, 1965.

Green, D.M., and Swets, J.A.: Signal Detection Theory and Psychophysics, New York: Wiley, 1966.

Leshowitz, B., and Wightman, F.L.: On frequency masking with continuous sinusoids, J. Acoust. Soc. Amer. 49:1180—1190, 1971.

Liberman, A.M.; Cooper, F.S., Shankweiler, D.P., et al.: Perception of the speech code, Psychol. Rev. 74:431—461, 1967.

Neisser, U.: The multiplicity of thought, Brit. J. Psychol. 54:1—14, 1963.

Neisser, U.: Cognitive Psychology, New York: Appleton Century Crofts, 1967.

Pollack, I.: Depth of sequential auditory information processing: III. J. Acoust. Soc. Amer. 50:549–554, 1971a.

Pollack, I.: Perception of two-dimensional Markov constraints within visual displays, Percept. Psychophys. 9:461–464, 1971b.

Simon, H.: The Sciences of the Artificial, Cambridge: M.I.T. Press, 1969.

Speeth, D.D.: Seismometer sounds, J. Acoust. Soc. Amer. 33:909–916, 1961.

Stevens, K.: Toward a model for speech recognition, J. Acoust. Soc. Amer. 32:47–55, 1960.

White, C.T.: Time compression of radar and sonar displays, Report 671 San Diego: Naval Electronics Laboratory, 1956.

5

Perceptual and Cognitive Strategies

DISCUSSION: PERCEPTION OF SPEECH AND NONSPEECH STIMULI

Pollack opened the discussion by pointing out that, although conventional wisdom distinguished among sensory capabilities, perceptual strategies, and cognitive function, these distinctions became blurred as soon as one began to devise tests of performance. Any performance test, he said, involves several levels of function. For example, a speech intelligibility test where the set of responses permitted is an open one, is a test of sensory capability, but even more, of higher intellectual functions. EEG audiometry and heart-rate audiometry, on the other hand, are more clearly tests of sensory capabilities per se, although the results on these tests, as Eisenberg suggested, seem to be affected by the overall functioning of the central nervous system.

Boundaries of sensory, perceptual, and cognitive functions

It seemed to Pollack that the deaf child has an important role to play in adding to the understanding of sensory and perceptual processes. Studies of his responses might contribute to understanding the link between auditory and articulatory theories of speech perception. He was thinking particularly of the work of Conrad (1970), who has utilized responses of congenitally deaf children on conventional short-term memory tests in exploring the role of auditory, visual and articulatory processes. On the other hand, a clinical orientation toward evaluation of such congenitally deaf subjects was relevant to the therapeutic approach but not to the investigation of a crucial link in information processing.

Understanding these functions through studying deaf child

Pollack added that when tests of perceptual and cognitive function are considered, it is clear that the tasks involved are often identical in structure. The only difference between them is in the rate of processing required for successful completion of the task. Any arbitrary intellectual transformation can be set up as a perceptual processing task, for example, paired-associate learning. All that is required is that the subject learns to process the information rapidly either (1) by means of a natural code, that is, something akin to hard-wired or unlearned transformations upon sensory input, (2) or, as a result of sufficient practice in handling an arbitrary code, that is, by means of soft-wired or learned transformations so that the task becomes semi-automatic. Pollack thought that in the session on perceptual and cognitive strategies it would be useful to examine research which breaks in upon the confounding of sensory and perceptual processing and then to proceed to consider perceptual and cognitive functions. He called first upon Watson to discuss the methodology of sensory and perceptual experiments, matters to which he, Watson, had devoted some hard thinking (Watson, 1973).

Sensory capability and response proclivity

Watson drew the attention of the group to a distinction which can help to avoid certain fundamental errors in psychophysical measurement. He described it as more primitive than the related dichotomies of sensation vs. perception, direct vs. indirect measures of sensation (Stevens, 1955), or bias vs. sensitivity.

The most primitive distinction of all is that between aspects of sensory processing that a scientist can deal with objectively and those that are out of reach of his methods. That is to say, between aspects of consciousness, or conscious experience on the one hand and behavioral variables on the other. Restricting his attention to behavioral measures, Watson proposed that the major concerns of psychophysics are with what we are capable of doing with our senses on the one hand, and what we actually do with them on the other. He referred to the first aspect as *sensory capability,* i.e., the limits of sensitivity, resolving power, and channel capacity of sensory systems, and to the second, for want of a better term, as *response proclivity.* Response proclivity is defined as a systematic tendency to respond to a particular sensory stimulus or sequence of stimuli in a particular way, even though a variety of other responses are clearly within the capability of the organism. The two aspects and the appropriate experimental methods for measuring them are shown in Table II.

Sensory capability has become a matter for concern since theories and ideas about signal detection began to find expression (Green and Swets, 1966). It includes such factors as resolving power, storage capacity, channel capacity, and even aspects of memory. Methods of measurement are mainly correlational in the sense that we demonstrate capability by presenting a sequence of at least two types of stimuli in random order. If the capability is present, we may show a significant correlation between the stimulus sequence and a behavioral response sequence. The methods are also forced-choice in nature. An important feature of such measurements is that the nature of the response is irrelevant and so is the direction of the correlation, i.e., whether positive or negative. The measure of sensory capability is always a boundary measurement. That is, the subject is *at least* as sensitive along whatever stimulus dimension is explored as the test which has been used for the purpose. This also implies an evaluation of the methods used. Whichever method produces the most sensitive result is the best method.

Response proclivity on the other hand is concerned with stimulus values which are called "equal" along some instructionally-defined continuum, or pairs of stimuli called "equally different" or standing in "equal ratio" to one another. Thus it involves experimental semantics, since the common element in such experiments is that the continuum or dimension of interest is defined for the observer through instructions. The methods are mostly those of classical psychophysics, although this need not be so; the most valid of all is probably the method of adjustment. It is disturbing to modern psycho-physicists to realize that, when dealing with relations between stimulus events on instructionally-defined continua, the most valid and direct method is to let the subject manipulate the stimulus until he has satisfied the condition specified in his instructions. Since the experimenter is interested in the *proclivities* of the subject, the subject must *not* be led to respond in any particular way, by the use of feedback for example. The response proclivity measurement is not a boundary measure, but rather an unbiased estimate of the proclivity in question. The limitations on that class of measures are the generality of the conditions under which they are obtained, and how well they relate to the conditions in the world for which the predictions are made. A measure of response proclivity is thus valid by definition. If a subject is asked to make a loudness comparison 1000 times, all one can say is that the right answer is the central tendency of those judgments. This is not a measure of sensory capability, even though the variability of the judgments is certainly capability-limited.

The kinds of models which are built upon these two aspects of psycho-physics might seem to suggest that nature is represented in capability and nurture in proclivity. This is not the case. The effects of both nature and nurture are present in both. It is typically necessary to seek more peripheral effects and to include more theorizing with respect to physical attributes in the case of sensory capability and to seek more central effects in the case of response proclivity, but exceptions to these rules of thumb are not hard to find.

Watson then described an experiment on the perception of temporal sequence which illustrated the sensory capability—response proclivity dichot-omy he had outlined. The experiment was conducted by Divenyi and Hirsh (1973). These investigators presented subjects with a sequence of three very

Table II Classes of Psychophysical Problems and Some Appropriate Experimental Methods

Class	Problems
SENSORY CAPABILITY (The measurement of the sensitivity and resolving power of an organism.)	Absolute sensitivity. Ability to discriminate between presence and absence of some stimulus, or more accurately, between stimulus-plus-ambient background and only that (specified) background. When background is parametrically manipulated this is the special case called *masking*.
	Sensitivity to differences. Ability to discriminate between stimuli, each of which is discriminable from the ambient background.
	Stimulus identification. Ability to sign a different response to each stimulus from a set of n = 2. A special case of differential sensitivity, in which the ability to make all possible pairwise discriminations, and the absolute sensitivity for each stimulus must be considered.
	Effective stimulus magnitude. The magnitude of a stimulus, scaled in units derived from measurement of a sensory capability.
RESPONSE PROCLIVITIES (The measurement of characteristic responses to particular stimuli, or stimulus sequences, when the stimuli are clearly discriminable from each other and from the ambient background.)	Equality. The determination of those stimuli called equal along some instructionally defined continuum, as distinct from a determination of the ability to discriminate between the stimuli.
	Equality of differences. The determination of those stimuli pairs reported to have the same differences along an instructionally defined continuum, as distinct from the determination of the ability to discriminate between the differences.
	Sense ratio. The determination of those stimuli that are reported to stand in particular ratios to one another along an instructionally defined continuum.
	Stimulus ranking. The determination of rank order into which stimuli are placed on an instructionally defined continuum.

Examples of some appropriate methods	Measures
Forced-choice (spatial or temporal), with m-alternatives. Single-interval methods, with binary decisions (yes-no), or with confidence ratings.	Per cent correct. d' or other index of detectability. P(C) max.
Paired comparisons.	Per cent correct. d' or other index of discriminability.
Rating, or binary decisions of the sameness or differentness of stimuli pairs, AA, AB, or BB. Identification of third stimulus in sequence ABX.	Per cent correct.
Identification, generally using a pre-learned response associated with each stimulus, thus providing the data for a confusion matrix (n-stimuli-by-n-responses).	Constant error. Standard error or other measure of dispersion. Information transmitted. d' matrix.
Measurement of effective stimulus intensity in terms of equidiscriminable units.	Stimulus values (range) called equal on some specified per cent of the judgments.
Method of adjustment. Paired comparison, with "equal" judgment allowed. Constant method. Limits.	Average and dispersion of stimuli called equal on specified per cent of the judgments.
Method of adjustment. Paired comparison, with "equal" judgment allowed. Constant method.	Average and dispersion of stimulus differences called equal on specified per cent of the judgments.
Method of adjustment. Magnitude estimation.	Average and dispersion of stimulus ratios reported as standing in ratio required by instructions.
Rating, ranking, or sorting of individual stimuli. Paired comparison.	Means and dispersions of ranks. Separation between ranks in terms of stimulus confusability. Mean stimulus values in various classes.

brief pure tones and asked the subjects to identify each sequence as high-medium-low, low-medium-high, and so on. There were six possible sequences and they were presented in random order. Now, the *perception of temporal order* should really be approached by methods appropriate to assessment of response proclivity, since it involves a semantic relation, not a capability determination. However, Divenyi and Hirsh thought it would be interesting to approach the question as one of sensory capability. Accordingly, they had the subjects respond by means of a computer-controlled keyboard. The keys were inscribed with diagrams illustrating each of the six possible temporal sequences. The subject's instructions were merely to be right in his choice as to which key should have been pushed.

The pure tones making up each sequence were so short, the shortest only being 2 msec, that even when presented in groups of three tones they sounded like a click or a birdlike chirp. Yet the subjects performed quite accurately, at least if the pure-tone components were 6 msec long or longer and if the separation in frequency between the tones was about 200 Hz. The frequency ratio from the highest to lowest of the three tones was about 20%. Thus, the subjects were listening to three notes on a diatonic scale which happened to differ in physical order but which were perceived as a unitary sound, i.e., as a chirp. In responding, the subjects pressed a button which implied that they actually heard three separate notes. Of course, when one asked them if they did perceive the stimulus as three tones in sequence they replied unanimously, "No!"

The experiment as described measured only sensory capability, specifically the ability to discriminate between certain sounds which happen to have differences in physical order built into them, that and no more. The conscious experience of the subjects is beside the point as far as this experiment is concerned. Yet, in fact, this latter issue can be perfectly well investigated by giving the listener control over the duration of the pulses, and having them adjust them to the minimal duration at which they "hear the tones as a sequence." When the investigators tried this, they found that listeners in fact require durations of 100 to 200 msec.

House commented that many similar experiments had been misinterpreted time and again. Good examples were Helmhotz's experiment on vowel perception and Peterson's thesis on vowels (Peterson, 1939). Watson agreed, and said he and his colleagues wished to develop a vocabulary and a way of looking at problems which would help to avoid such misinterpretations in the future.

The participants were nevertheless very interested in the substantive results and the way in which the subjects of the Divenyi-Hirsh experiment did perceive the chirps. Watson said that Divenyi was a musician and described the chirps in terms of color and timbre. Hirsh stated that the primary differences between them were of pitch. He believed that the pitch was associated with the last of the three pure-tone components of the blend. Levitt thought that since very short duration stimuli were used it would be worthwhile looking at the waveforms of the stimuli on an artificial ear to check for possible ringing of the headphones. Liberman pointed out that the opposite kind of phenomenon could be found in speech, where subjects believe they hear a temporal ordering of elements when in fact they are responding to acoustic shape (Liberman et al., 1967).

Perception of complex stimuli by normal-hearing adults

Watson then went on to describe an experiment of his own. It was intended to close a gap between experiments concerned with speech perception, where description of the physical characteristics of the stimuli presented an overwhelming problem until quite recently, and psychoacoustics, which has mainly investigated the hearing of pure tones, clicks, and noise bursts. The experiment illustrated an attempt in psychophysics to present complex stimuli in such a way as to improve our understanding of the capability of the ear to deal with them, and ultimately, to deal with speech. In common with other investigators, he was impressed with the very precise temporal capabilities of the human auditory system. Pollack (1968), for example, had reported temporal discrimination capabilities in the microsecond range obtained with complex stimuli. Patterson and Green (1970) had shown that the energy detector model of the auditory system fails miserably to account for such results as the ability to discriminate between a click, only a few milliseconds long, played backward and forward. In this case, the two clicks have the same spectrum, thus the subject must respond to differences in temporal resolution, utilizing the so-called time constants of the ear.

Watson worked with the stimuli shown in Figure 2.1. These stimuli were sequences of ten 40-msec tone bursts whose frequency was in the range of 200 Hz to 1 KHz. They were presented at 70 dB SPL. They were intended to resemble words in duration and the frequency range of the higher formants. The stimuli were presented in pairs. The comparison stimulus differed from the standard stimulus in the frequency of one of its elements, and the amount of the difference in hertz was varied. Sometimes the listeners were instructed that only a given member of the set of ten elements could change (the seventh). At other times, they were told that one of two, four, or eight elements was subject to change. Their task was to respond "same" or "different" after each pair of patterns.

The primary results of the experiment are shown in Figure 2.2. The tonal components are shown on the abscissa and df/f on the ordinate. Notice that

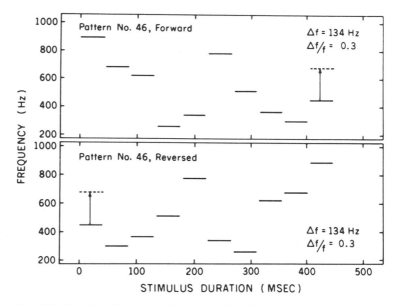

Fig. 2.1 Sample stimulus pattern in which there is a sequence of ten 40-msec tonal elements ranging in frequency from 200 Hz to 1 KHz. One element in the sequence differs in frequency from the standard to the comparison stimulus pattern.

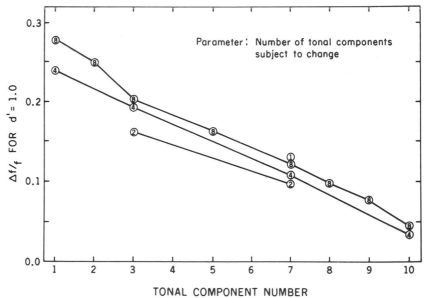

Fig. 2.2 Detectability of Δf as a function of the ordinal number of the tonal components changed.

the just-noticeable-difference (jnd) for frequency is smallest for the tenth 40-msec component; it may be as small as 10 or 15 Hz, i.e., about the same as it would be for that component presented in isolation. All the contextual information in the pattern does not disturb the subject's ability to deal with the tenth component. However, as the subject has to deal with differences occurring earlier in the pattern, the information becomes progressively degraded; that is, the frequency change has to be larger before it can be detected. Also, the subject finds it just as difficult to detect the frequency change when he knows on which component it will occur, as when he does not. Apparently this says that he can do as well when he has to store the whole pattern as when he has to try to ignore everything except component seven. A logical inference would be that listeners always store an entire sound (of such duration), whether the task requires it or not.

These data have also been analyzed with respect to the effect of the frequency of the element of the standard pattern which is to be changed upon the size of the jnd. This effect upon tonal component seven is shown in Figure 2.3. Notice that there appears to be a downward spread of the interference effects, with resolution of medium- and low-frequency components much more degraded than that for high-frequency components.

Finally, Figure 2.4 illustrates the effect of length of interval between presentation of the standard and comparison patterns. In a first experiment

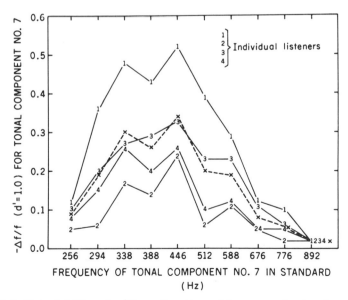

Fig. 2.3 Detectability of $-\Delta f$ as a function of frequency for tonal component number 7.

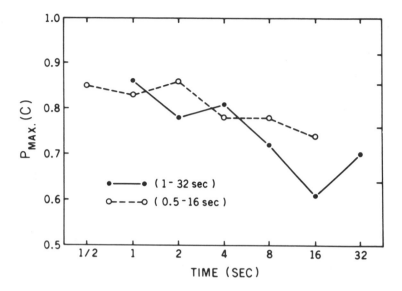

Fig. 2.4 Detectability of Δf as a function of interval between standard and comparison patterns.

very little effect of interval duration was found for intervals up to 16 seconds. The study was replicated, with the shortest interval omitted and a longer interval (32 seconds) added. For the 32-second interval fewer trials were accumulated than for the other intervals because of the tedium which this long delay imposed upon the subjects. The 16-second point is one in which a good deal of variability is present. Df/f is no longer shown on the ordinate since this measure failed to show any clear effect of length of delay interval, and a more sensitive measure (C) was used instead. The investigators concluded that, although the pattern might have decayed more rapidly if the subject had been required to perform some task in the interval, he can store the pattern extremely well in the absence of such competing information and for periods of up to 32 seconds.

In summary, Watson felt that more empirical results of this kind should be sought; and that we should be cautious in drawing premature conclusions that fine grained perception of complex sounds is restricted to speech sounds.

In reply to a question from Liberman, Watson stated that his subjects were well able to say on which element in the sequence a change had occurred. What the subject did in this case was to divide the sequence into thirds and to try first to decide in which third the change had occurred. The subjects have experience of changes in known components, i.e., the fifth, the seventh, and so on, and know exactly what to listen for. It is as if they try to match two notes in a selected third of the stimulus using an attentional filter which rolls off at about 12 dB per octave. Watson compared this to the Bregman streaming results (Bregman and Campbell, 1971).

Perception of complex stimuli by children

Ling reported an experiment conducted by his wife (A.H. Ling, 1973) in which the recall of temporal sequences of speech and nonspeech stimuli were compared. Previous experiments (Warren et al., 1969; Thomas et al., 1970) indicated that normal adult listeners perceived the order of speech sounds more readily than nonspeech sounds, especially at rapid presentation rates. The present experiment was designed to answer the question: Can preferential processing of speech sequences be documented in normal-hearing children, and if so, is it also present in hearing-impaired children? Studies of auditory sequencing involve not only perceptual processes, Ling pointed out, but also memory processes such as coding and rehearsal strategies (Aaronson, 1968). Thus, if differences exist between normal-hearing and hearing-impaired listeners on auditory sequencing tasks, they may be related to differences in any one of these processes. Certainly as long ago as 1917, Pintner and Paterson had shown that visual short-term memory for digit sequences was defective in deaf subjects.

The sounds used by A.H. Ling were (1) five CV syllables differing in initial consonant, /pa/, /ta/, /ma/, /sha/, and /ga/; (2) five CV syllables differing in the final vowel sound, /pi/, /pe/, /pa/, /po/, and /pu/. These syllables, recorded by a male speaker, were all very close to 200 msec in duration; (3) five nonverbal sounds, namely, the bark of a dog, the hoot of a car horn, the bleat of a sheep, a gun shot and a high-pitched whistle. Only the first 200 msec of these sounds was used so that they were comparable in duration to the syllables. Ling commented that it was difficult to find environmental sounds which could be identified when their duration was as brief as this. A rifle shot, for example, was not recognizable as such unless it was about 500 msec in duration. The five elements were recorded in sequences of two, three, and four elements and at rates of one, two, and four per second; the interval between each element was a function of the rate. For example, at a rate of four per second, there was a 50-msec interval between each element. The syllable sequences were spoken naturally to achieve the appropriate rates.

A.H. Ling worked with two groups of eighteen normal-hearing children, a five-year-old group and a nine-year-old group; and one group of eighteen hearing-impaired children whose ages ranged from six to fourteen years (mean age: 10.6 years) and who had residual hearing across the range of speech frequencies. In order to be selected as subjects, the children were required to

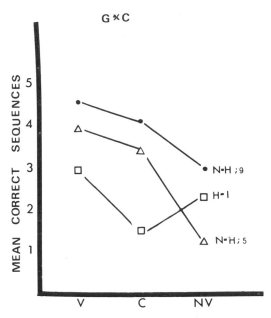

Fig. 2.5 Mean number of vowel, consonant and nonverbal sequences correctly recalled by the normal-hearing subjects aged 5 to 9 years and by the hearing-impaired subjects aged 6 to 14 years.

identify the elements when presented one at a time. In the case of syllables they had to repeat them distinctly, and for the nonverbal sounds, they had to point to the appropriate picture. In the experiment proper, they had to repeat the sequence of syllables or point in the correct order to the pictures representing the nonverbal sounds. The results are shown in Figure 2.5. For the syllable sequences, both those in which the consonants and in which the vowels were changed, the responses of hearing-impaired children were significantly less often correct than those of normal-hearing children. Also, the performance of older normal-hearing children, for consonant but not vowel sequences, was significantly superior to that of the younger normal-hearing children. Thus, the ability to process consonants in such sequences improved with age given normal hearing. For the sequences of environmental sounds, on the other hand, the performance of the hearing-impaired children was midway between that of the older and the younger normal-hearing children. In other words, for the environmental sound sequences, with which none of the children had any experience, the hearing-impaired children did about as well as the normal-hearing children on an identification task.

In Figures 2.6 and 2.7, the results for vowels, consonants, and environmental sounds are presented as a function of length of the sequence and of

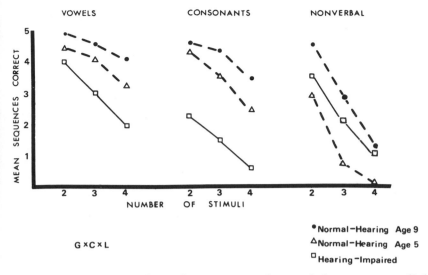

Fig. 2.6 Mean number of vowel, consonant and nonverbal sequences recalled by each group of subjects in relation to length of sequence.

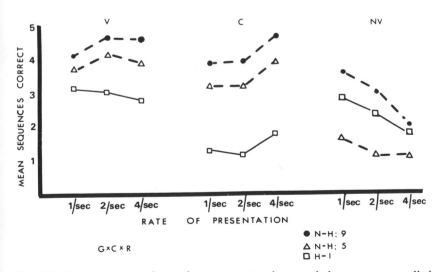

Fig. 2.7 Mean number of vowel, consonant and nonverbal sequences recalled by each group of subjects in relation to presentation rate.

rate of element presentation respectively. These figures show that the performance of the three groups of children manifests the same order from best to poorest for all sequence lengths and rates of presentation.

It can also be seen that recall of syllables in which the consonant is changing improves with increased rate of presentation. This is not true for syllables in which the vowel sounds are changing; these are recalled with essentially equal accuracy at all rates of presentation. Nor is it true of sequences of environmental sounds which are recalled less well at higher than at lower rates of presentation by all three groups of children. This effect is more pronounced for environmental sounds in the older normal and hearing-impaired subjects than in the younger normal subjects. The differences are all statistically reliable.

Strategies used in identifying nonspeech elements

Menyuk asked about the strategies the children used in responding to the environmental sound sequences. Ling said that, at the slow rates of presentation, subvocal naming activity was observed among both normal-hearing and hearing-impaired subjects. At the higher rates, this was not possible; different strategies had to be employed. The sequences gave rise to characteristic pitch patterns but it was very difficult to relate them to the pictures depicting sources of each element. Certainly the subjects could not give a verbal name and response at higher rates. It was noted that some hearing-impaired subjects made effective use of the spatial arrangement of the pictures as a cue to articulatory recall.

Types of confusion

Miller asked if the errors for the speech sequences of the hearing-impaired children were based upon visual confusions or auditory (articulatory) confusions. Ling replied that, since all of the stimuli were auditory, visual confusions were unlikely to occur. Also to reduce auditory confusions, each consonant selected was different by at least two features from the consonant it most closely resembled; and the vowels chosen were not adjacent to one another.

Recognition of phonetic and brief nonspeech elements

Liberman commented that it would be interesting to present sequences of phonetic elements included in a single syllable instead of polysyllabic sequences. The length of the sequence could then be varied from one as in 'a' to seven as in 'strengths.' In the latter case, the average element duration would be much lower than for the syllable sequences, say about 50 msec, and the rate of presentation much higher than four per second. If one were to compare recognition, ordering, or discrimination of such sequences with recognition, ordering, or discrimination of the sequences of nonspeech stimuli, the superiority of the normal-hearing subjects' performance with speech sequences would be even more impressive. Watson asked if the subjects were given feedback as to the correctness of their responses. Ling replied that the subjects were rewarded after each response with a set of poker chips. The number of chips in the set corresponded exactly to the number of elements that had been identified correctly but subjects were not told which of the elements of the sequence they had identified correctly, i.e., whether the first and the third were correct, or the second and the fourth. Watson felt that it would be interesting to provide more precise feedback to the subjects as to the correctness of their responses. He asked how long training on the task continued. He had found that even on difficult detection tasks, after thousands of trials in which tightly-linked feedback is provided, considerable improvements in performance may eventually be obtained (Watson et al., 1972). He believed that until such training is attempted one does not really know whether *capability* or *proclivity* has been demonstrated, and resolving this issue could mean a great difference to the appropriate treatment. Ling answered that the subjects had been given minimal training, that is, only sufficient to make sure they understood the task. It was the intention of his colleagues to continue to experiment with this kind of task and to provide intensive training, of the kind Watson had mentioned, to the subjects.

Role of training in identifying nonspeech elements

It was also noted that it became rather arbitrary as to when to end the experiment. Hirsh then commented that as far as processing of verbal vs. nonverbal stimuli was concerned, allegro music, which is often marked as 120 beats per minute or 2 per second, can be remembered and accurately reproduced. Melodies with sequences as long as a familiar theme from a Beethoven symphony, a sequence of considerably more than three or four notes, can easily be handled in this way. It would be interesting to push this kind of capability further and find out just how great the difference between processing of verbal and nonverbal materials really is. Ling felt that speech and music were likely to be processed somewhat differently but that both might be processed differently from all other kinds of auditory signals.

Recognition of elements of music

Discrimination of complex stimuli by hearing-impaired adults

Pickett saw some similarities between the responses of the subjects in Watson's experiments to temporal sequences of pure tones, and those he had obtained in a study of speech-cue discrimination. The latter study involved an oddity task, i.e., subjects were asked to say on which of three synthetically-produced vowels they detected a transition in the second formant, /F2/ (Danaher et al., in press; Pickett and Danaher, 1973). The listeners were all young college-age adults with moderate to severe bilateral sensorineural hearing losses. They fall into two groups according to contour of hearing loss vs. frequency. Their thresholds are shown in Figure 2.8, dB SPL.

Those in the first group (shown by a solid line) have thresholds which would yield a sloping curve in a conventional audiogram. The second group

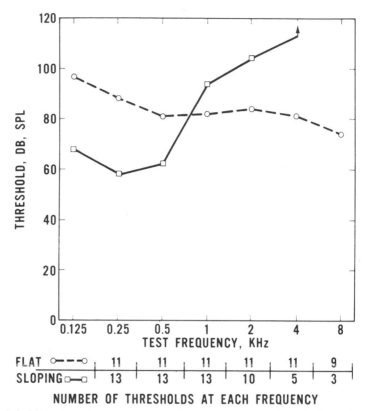

Fig. 2.8 Mean threshold hearing levels for pure tones of subjects, divided into the FLAT group (N = 11) and the SLOPING group (N = 13). Data of E.M. Danaher.

(shown by the dashed line) have a different profile which would show up as a flat curve in the conventional audiogram. The flat-loss subjects show consistently better discrimination of formant frequencies and formant transitions than the sloping loss subjects. All subjects listened at their most comfortable listening levels.

In Figure 2.9 the amount of F2 transition at threshold is plotted on the vertical axis. The higher this value, the greater was the extent of the transition that was necessary for detection and conversely the lower the value, the smaller the transition which could be detected. There were several conditions with respect to the first formant, /F1/, of the vowel. In the zero condition, the onset of F1 was simultaneous with the onset of F2. In the other conditions, F1 was cut back with respect to F2 by 50, 100, 150, and 200 msec; or in still another condition, F1 was completely absent. There was no

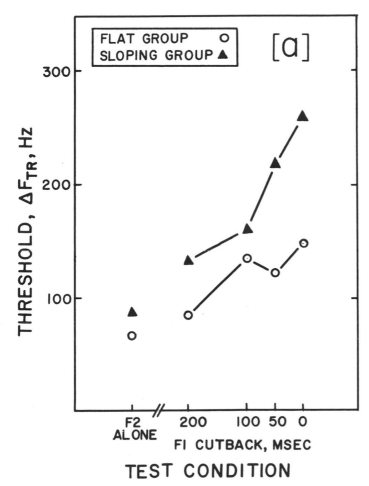

Fig. 2.9 Mean discrimination threshold for a transition in F2 depending on contour of hearing and amount of delay (F1 cutback) in the onset of F1 relative to that of F2. For more detail see legend of Fig. 2.10. Data of E.M. Danaher.

transition of F1 under any condition; the F2 transition was 70 msec in duration and the entire vowel sound was 250 msec in duration.

Figure 2.9 shows that discrimination of the F2 transition for the vowel /a/ was best in the absence of F1. Where F1 was present and had no transition, it affected the discrimination of the F2 transition adversely, and did so in proportion to the extent of its overlap in time with F2. Even where the first formant did not overlap with the period of the transition of the second formant, for example, in the 200-msec cut-back condition, detection of the F2 transition was adversely affected in the sloping group of listeners and also in one or two subjects in the flat group. The effect could be thought of as backward masking, similar to that observed by Watson in his subjects' responses to complex nonverbal sequences. Basic psychoacoustic experiments have shown that backward masking occurs in normal-hearing subjects when masking stimuli are presented at high sound levels (Pickett, 1959; Elliott, 1962). The sound levels at which many hearing-impaired subjects listen are sufficiently high to generate this type of temporal masking. If vowels do produce backward and forward masking, this might help to explain some of the speech discrimination problems that sensorineural subjects exhibit.

Pickett went on to describe an additional experiment in which the intensity of F1 relative to that of F2 was systematically varied, from equal intensity to minus 15 dB. In this experiment also, F2 was sometimes presented alone and sometimes in the presence of F1 as shown in Figure 2.10. Also, there was an F1 transition of 150 Hz in one set of conditions and no F1 transition in another. It should be noted, however, that the line representing the abscissa in Figure 2.10 is broken only for the sake of convenience and no change in the base line is being conveyed by means of this device. As in the experiment where F1 was cut back, the introduction of F1 made it more difficult for the listener to detect the presence of a second formant transition, even when it was 15 dB lower in intensity than F2 and had no formant transition. The disturbing effect of F1 increased with intensity and was greater when F1 had a 150 Hz transition than when it did not. The transition always began at the onset of the vowel and was complete in about 70 msec. The disruptive effect of the first formant transition might, however, be related to temporal masking. In its presence the stimulus tends to be heard as a stop-consonant combination, whereas in the condition where there is no F1 transition, the signal with the F2 transition sounds like a diphthong with a strange quality at its beginning and not like any consonant. As before, the sloping loss subjects were more affected by the presence of F1 at lower intensities than the flat loss subjects, especially when F1 had a transition.

Denes asked if any of these sensorineural subjects showed recruitment. He felt that this might be more important for the experimental task than *Effects of* threshold measurement. Gengel (observer) answered that when subjects lis- *recruitment on* tened at 110 or 120 dB SPL, as in this experiment, it was very difficult to *discrimination* establish the presence or absence of recruitment. The only indication the *of F2 transi-* experimenters had on this score was that after a comfortable listening level *tion* was established, subjects sometimes were asked to turn up the gain still further. Some subjects would turn it 10 or 15 dB higher before complaining of discomfort, others only 3 or 4 dB. The latter subjects might be suspected of having recruitment while the former would not.

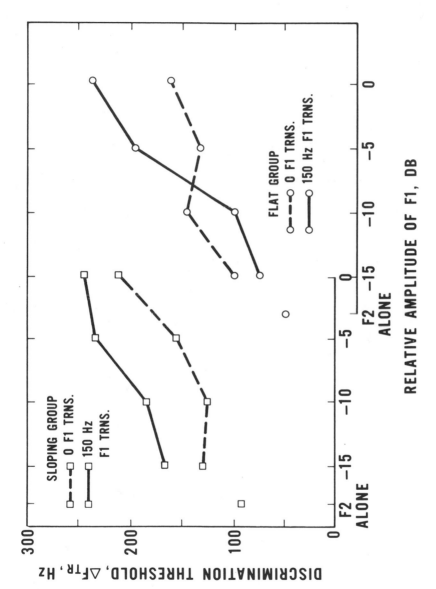

Fig. 2.10 Mean discrimination threshold, F_{TR}, for hearing an initial upward transition in the second formant frequency (F2) depending on type of hearing contour (SLOPING or FLAT) and various conditions of the first formant (F1). The threshold is the smallest frequency amount of transition necessary to discriminate that the transition was present. F2 ALONE = F1 not present; 0 F1 TRNS. = no transition on F1; the F1 transition rate is 150 Hz in 100 msec. Zero relative amplitude of F1 refers to its normal amplitude. Data of E.M. Danaher.

House wanted to know how closely the sounds with F1 transitions in them resembled CV syllables. Pickett replied that the presence of the F1 transitions caused the stimuli to be heard as stop-vowel syllables by some subjects at least. For them, the three speech sounds of the oddity task might sound like /da/, /da/, and /ba/, with the third one being the correct answer. Whether they heard the sounds as syllables or not, however, the hearing-impaired subjects showed a larger discrimination threshold in the presence of an F1 transition than in its absence. This was true for flat and for sloping sensorineural loss subjects.

A few comparison tests were run on normal-hearing subjects. The above effects seemed to occur for normals listening at high intensity levels, that is, at about 105 to 110 dB SPL. The normals listening at their own comfortable levels did not show such a large effect of the F1 transition; they could discriminate transitions of only 25 to 50 Hz and the masking effect of F1 was negligible on F2. Thus the reduced discrimination ability which was attributable to an upward spread of masking was present only when subjects listened at high intensity levels.

House felt that these experiments could not be compared directly with psychophysical experiments employing sequences of pure tones, however complex. If some subjects at least were responding to the combination of F1 and F2 as speech, they might be demonstrating their perceptual boundaries for phonemes rather than their ability to discriminate F2 transitions. Pickett replied that this was a question which had worried him too.

REFERENCES

Aaronson, D.: Temporal course of perception in an immediate recall task, J. Exp. Psychol. 76:129–140, 1968.

Bregman, A.S., and Campbell, J.: Primary auditory stream segregation and perception of order in rapid sequences of tones, J. Exp. Psychol. 89:244–249, 1971.

Conrad, R.: Short-term memory processes in the deaf, Brit. J. Psychol. 61:179–195, 1970.

Danaher, E.M.; Osberger, M.J., and Pickett, J.M.: Discrimination of formant frequency transitions in synthetic vowels, J. Speech Hearing Res. (In press).

Divenyi, P.L., and Hirsh, I.J.: Identification of the temporal order of three tones, J. Acoust. Soc. Amer. 54:315(A), 1973.

Elliott, L.L.: Backward masking: monotic and dichotic conditions, J. Acoust. Soc. Amer. 34:1108–1115, 1962.

Green, D.M., and Swets, J.A.: Signal Detection Theory and Psychophysics, New York: Wiley, 1966.

Liberman, A.M.; Cooper, F.S., Shankweiler, D.P., et al.: Perception of the speech code, Psychol. Rev. 74:431–461, 1967.

Ling, A.H.: Identification of auditory sequences by hearing-impaired and normal-hearing children, Doctoral dissertation, McGill University, 1973.

Patterson, J.H., and Green, D.M.: Discrimination of transient signals having identical energy spectra, J. Acoust. Soc. Amer. 48:894–905, 1970.

Peterson, G.E.: The significance of various portions of the wave length in the minimum duration necessary for the recognition of vowel sounds, Doctoral dissertation, Louisiana State University, 1939.

Pickett, J.M.: Backward masking, J. Acoust. Soc. Amer. 31:1613–1615, 1959.

Pickett, J.M., and Danaher, E.M.: On discrimination of formant transitions by persons with severe sensorineural hearing loss, Paper presented at Symposium on Auditory Analysis and Perception of Speech, Leningrad, 1973.

Pintner, R., and Paterson, D.G.: A comparison of deaf and hearing children in visual memory for digits, J. Exp. Psychol. 2:76–88, 1917.

Pollack, I.: Detection and relative discrimination of auditory "jitter", J. Acoust. Soc. Amer. 43:308–315, 1968.

Stevens, S.S.: The measurement of loudness, J. Acoust. Soc. Amer. 27:815–829, 1955.

Thomas, I.B.; Hill, P.B., Carroll, F.S., et al.: Temporal order in the perception of vowels, J. Acoust. Soc. Amer. 48:1010–1013, 1970.

Warren, R.M.; Obusek, C.J., Farmer, R.M., et al.: Auditory sequence—confusion of patterns other than speech or music, Science 164:586–587, 1969.

Watson, C.S.: Psychophysics, In: Wolman, B., ed.: Handbook of General Psychology, Englewood Cliffs: Prentice-Hall, 1973.

Watson, C.S.; Frank, J.R., and Hood, D.S.: Detection of tones in the absence of external masking noise. I. Effects of signal intensity and signal frequency, J. Acoust. Soc. Amer. 52:633–643, 1972.

6

Perceptual and Cognitive Strategies

DISCUSSION: AIDING SPEECH RECEPTION OF HEARING-IMPAIRED LISTENER

Hearing aid design

House asked how Pickett's data compared with results which would be obtained by pre-emphasizing the higher speech frequencies in a set of monosyllables and presenting these in an intelligibility task. It seemed to him that the concept of F1 masking was merely the concept of pre-emphasis of speech in another guise. In effect, he said, pre-emphasis raises the second and third formants to a greater relative amplitude. Then it becomes easier to discriminate /da/ and /ba/, for example, which was what Pickett's subjects appeared to be doing with the synthetic speech signal. Denes intervened to point out that the acoustics of speech production will necessarily make the intensity of F2 of vowels lower than that of F1; this intensity difference will increase as the frequencies of F1 and F2 move further apart (Fant, 1967). Pre-emphasis is merely a matter of equalizing intensity level across the frequency range, but is the speechlike character of the sounds affected?

Upward masking and pre-emphasis

Pickett pointed out that by means of pre-emphasis F1 would be suppressed much more when it is in a low-frequency range than when it is in a high-frequency range. In a synthesized signal, the intensity of F1 and of F2 may be controlled independently. House added that this depended on the roll-off characteristics of the filter involved. Pickett mentioned the classical data which showed that when low-frequency roll-off was used, listeners with sensorineural losses got higher discrimination scores on monosyllabic words (Davis et al., 1946). He believed, however, that these studies should be repeated with greater precision using new equipment and new methods.

In Pickett's laboratory, Gengel has been collecting data on word reception using rhyme test techniques. Both vowel and consonant discrimination were being tested in this way. The word stimuli were in the form of recorded natural speech. Scores for consonant and vowel discrimination for hearing-impaired adults with sensorineural losses were measured as a function of the gain level of the system. The group results are shown in Figure 2.11, which shows that at about 22 dB above their speech detection threshold, most of the subjects had reached their maximum vowel discrimination score and the curve was leveling off. For maximum consonant discrimination, the subjects

Reception of vowels and consonants as a function of gain of system

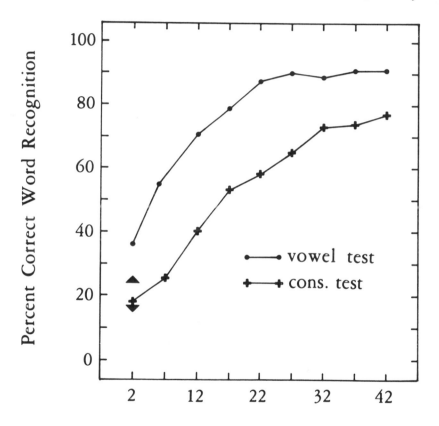

Fig. 2.11 Mean intelligibility functions of nine sensorineural hearing-impaired Ss for vowels and consonants. ▲ chance performance vowels; ▼ chance performance consonants. Unpublished data of R.W. Gengel.

had to be listening at about 33 dB above their speech detection threshold. Typically, however, subjects such as these set their hearing aids to receive speech at 20 to 25 dB or at most 30 dB above their detection thresholds. They probably set these levels with reference to the loudness of F1. It was possible for them to become accustomed to a higher gain setting; for good speech reception they should be doing just that, but for the most part they did not.

Pollack remarked that this seemed to reinforce House's suggestion with respect to pre-emphasis. House observed that the levels of 20 and 30 dB defined almost exactly the vowel-consonant ratio which Weiss (1968) reported in his master's thesis. Frequently the hearing-impaired subject sets a signal-to-noise level for listening to speech with respect to the vowels. Since the consonants are on the average 13 dB lower in intensity, pre-emphasis would improve their reception. *Vowel-consonant ratios*

Levitt asked if Pickett's curves for phoneme recognition represented a maximum score. If it was important to discover the level of maximum intelligibility, a sequential strategy could be used to seek this out very readily. Levitt had tried this with PB word lists. When there was in fact a maximum, the strategy worked very well and where there was no maximum it did not work at all, so that the situation could be clearly specified. Pickett said that only one or two of his subjects had shown a maximum with a subsequent decline in recognition score at still higher levels. *Levels of maximum intelligibility*

Blesser asked if amplitude compression and pre-emphasis had been used in combination in hearing aids to produce an optimal signal. Pickett answered that work along these lines was being done but was not yet definitive. Erber mentioned that peak clipping had been used experimentally at the Central Institute for the Deaf (CID), that is, the amplification system was over-driven so that the vowels were clipped and the consonants enhanced, but still received at a comfortable listening level (Witt, 1972). In some cases, severely hearing-impaired children understood words better than through an unclipped system. Denes noted that this was equivalent to the volume compression or pre-emphasis which House had been talking about. Boothroyd added that in the Harvard report on hearing aids (Davis et al., 1947), the articulation function in many cases continued to rise after peak-clipping levels had been reached. It was not necessary to look far for such evidence. *Peak clipping and articulation function*

Miller summarized the thinking of Niemoller, Miller, and Pascoe at CID with respect to vowel-consonant ratios and pre-processing, and how this relates to facts which have been known for a long time. He recalled Pollack's (1949) summary of field-to-eardrum and coupler-to-eardrum transfer functions (see Figure 2.12). These functions can be compared to the transfer functions from the 2cc coupler used in calibrating the hearing aid to the eardrum. The field-to-eardrum transfer function can be described as follows; *Hearing aid receiver-to-eardrum transfer functions*

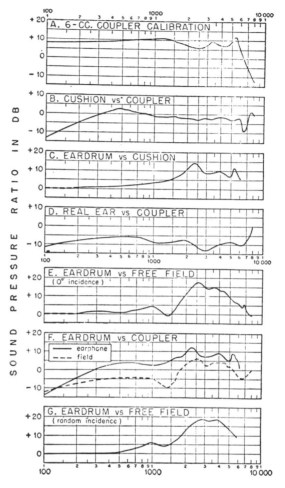

Fig. 2.12 Relations among different kinds of sound-pressure measurements. (A) Sound pressure developed in a 6cc coupler by a dynamic earphone. (B) Pressure measured with a probe tube under the earphone cushion relative to the coupler pressures in (A). (C) Sound pressures measured at the eardrum with a probe relative to the pressures under the cushion in (B). (D) Field pressures, measured relative to coupler pressures, that sound equal in loudness to the coupler pressures. (E) Eardrum pressures measured with a probe in an open ear canal (no earphone) relative to free-field pressures. (F) Eardrum pressures relative to coupler pressures in both covered and open ear canal. (G) Same measures as in (E), except that the free-field reference is for a sound whose angle of incidence relative to the sagittal plane of the head is random. The free-field reference for curve (E) is that of sounds directly in front. 0° angle of incidence. From Pollack, 1949.

there is a small peak at 500 Hz; the curve is flat to about 1 KHz and between 2 KHz and 4 KHz there is an increase in intensity of about 18 dB (see Figure 2.12, graphs E and G). This increase is due to the resonance of the ear canal and to head diffraction. The Harvard Report (Davis et al., 1947) stated that for an optimal output it was necessary to have a frequency response out to 3 KHz and to have a 6 to 7 dB per octave boost beginning from 300 KHz. This was defined as the voltage across a dynamic earphone which later was placed over the ear. In actual fact, when the investigators carried this out in practice, their subjects wore circumaural cushions. A characteristic of the earphone on the head is to add a 10 dB emphasis in the 2 KHz to 3 KHz region. Thus, the total high-frequency emphasis in this region was 18 to 20 dB. What these investigators were doing without recognizing it, or at least without stating it, was to reproduce almost exactly the natural listening condition provided by the acoustics of the external ear. In the laboratory at CID, Miller and his colleagues have taken as their design goal the reproduction for the hearing-impaired listener of the normal field-to-eardrum transfer function, plus a constant. They are testing this design extensively with a presbycusic patient whose average hearing levels are about 50 dB re normal hearing (ISO), and whose audiogram is nearly flat. They are finding that this patient can understand speech more easily in quiet and in noise when given the kind of pre-emphasis described. Miller added that when an insert receiver or hearing aid was calibrated, this is done in a 2cc coupler, but when the receiver is placed in the ear, there is a smaller volume between the tip of the insert and the eardrum than in the 2cc coupler. Thus, all frequencies receive a boost. There is still a slight high-frequency pre-emphasis, but these higher frequencies are in turn lowered relative to low frequencies because of the lack of external canal resonance and head diffraction. This together with the relatively greater loss in the high frequencies which is typical of many hearing-impaired subjects may result in the high frequencies being about 30 dB lower in amplitude for the patient than the low frequencies. This is very relevant to the problem, since as Pickett had pointed out, low frequency information in speech masks high frequency information. Miller and his co-workers were not yet certain at the time of the workshop whether it was necessary to have a sharp or a gradual increase in amplitude from 1 KHz to 2 KHz but felt that this was an important decision.

Miller and his colleagues had also observed that increases in vocal effort on the part of someone speaking to the presbycusic patient had an adverse effect on his speech reception. These increases in vocal effort affected amplitudes in a range where normal listeners' speech reception would not be affected; as the speaker changed from use of a confidential voice to a lecture room voice the patient's scores deteriorated markedly. Miller attributed this

Effects of increase in vocal effort

to changes in the vowel-consonant ratio of the kind documented by Fair-banks and Miron (1957); that is, as the speaker raised his vocal effort, the intensity of the vowels increased more than that of the consonants; thus, the vowel-consonant ratio became less favorable to the reception of consonants.

House thought that, within reasonable limits, just the opposite should have happened. As the vocal effort is raised in a more formal lecture presentation, the higher frequencies should become stronger relative to the lower frequencies and speech should become more, not less, intelligible, everything else being equal. Denes remarked that Noll (1969) had studied the intelligibility and acoustics of shouted speech relative to normal conversational speech and found shouted speech to be less intelligible than normal speech. One of the factors contributing to this effect was the compression of the pitch range in shouted speech.

Weiss (observer) stated that there were at least two factors affecting the intelligibility of formal lectured, not shouted, speech. One of these was the unfavorable change in vowel-consonant ratio documented by Fairbanks and Miron, that is, that the intensity of the vowel increases more than the intensity of the consonant. In addition, the higher frequencies in the vowels and thus, the second formant transitions, receive more emphasis as vocal effort increases. These two effects essentially operate in opposition to one another.

CROS hearing aid

Levitt asked if the difference in performance of the subjects using ventilated and unventilated earmolds could be explained on the basis of the change in acoustic characteristics introduced, that is, of greater pre-emphasis of high frequencies. Miller went further and argued that the success of the CROS Hearing Aid (Dodds and Harford, 1968), with its microphone on one side to eliminate feedback and a large hole in the earmold, is attributable to pre-emphasis. In fact, this configuration is exactly what is required to produce the field-to-eardrum transfer function described above (p. 110). He would regard such data as supporting his hypotheses until someone actually made the measurements required to show whether or not he was correct.

Conceptual strategies and speech recognition

Effect of redundancy on speech reception in noise

Blesser took issue with the previous discussants. It seemed to him that in the design of prostheses and in the choice of codes, two things were being confused, namely the ability to learn speech and the ability to perceive speech. As far as speech perception was concerned, it was clear to him that someone who has language competence can understand speech very well even when it is severely degraded. A review of the literature on perception and cognition in normal individuals showed that it is virtually impossible to destroy the intelligibility of speech for a normal-hearing person. For example, Kahn (1967) who reviewed the problem of designing speech scramblers to remove intelligibility, stated:

> Beginners in the study of privacy systems never fail to be amazed at the difficulty of scrambling speech sufficiently to destroy intelligence. The ear can tolerate or even ignore surprising amounts of noise, non-linearity, frequency distortion, misplaced components, superposition, and other forms of interference.
>
> The fact that the ear is such a good decoding tool makes the production of privacy systems very difficult. Scrambling systems which look effective on paper sometimes turn out on trial to degrade the intelligibility very little, although scrambled speech usually sounds unpleasant. (pps. 588, 599)

Comparable studies on visual capabilities also showed that in super high speed reading, most of the signals are essentially ignored. In this case also the reader uses context and the knowledge of what to expect and does not rely heavily on details of the signal. Blesser was reminded of an elderly airplane pilot who had a marked hearing loss and who could still understand badly garbled speech coming over his radio which normal-hearing nonfliers in the same cockpit would have much difficulty in understanding (Tonndorf, 1968). Blesser was convinced that cognitive processes are sufficiently flexible and powerful to dig meaning out of a speech signal provided that the whole framework is there. The signal itself has so much redundancy that if the listener has some knowledge of what to expect and if even a small part of it is intact, its meaning is very clear.

It seemed to Blesser that the problem with deaf and hard-of-hearing children is that the concept of the structure of language is not secure, and the confidence in redundancy is not very great. The choice of code should be based on these criteria, not simply on supplying features which are missing from the input. The absence of these features does not necessarily make speech unintelligible; if a child does not have a high confidence in his ability to use prosodic features to replace missing phonetic features or vice versa, then he will have a very difficult time. Because of this, the evaluation of various prostheses and codes becomes very difficult. This is because the question which is asked is not: Will this device make speech easier to understand? but: Will it make speech easier to acquire and to use under adverse conditions? There was also some lack of understanding of the implications of these two questions.

Lack of knowledge of structure of language in deaf subject

Why is it, then, that a hard-of-hearing or a deaf child has difficulty in understanding speech? Why can he not devote extra cognitive energy to make up for the missing detail of the signal? For Blesser the answer was, he does

Reception of overall pattern rather than phonetic detail

not have the confidence. He has a certain kind of rigidity which makes him hold onto small pieces of the pattern and not get a comfortable sense of the overall structure or patterning which would allow him then to supplement the degraded signal by supplying the missing pieces. Blesser would argue that our directions should be reversed. We should not tinker with the fine structure and try to restore missing phonetic features, taking for example high frequency frication and transposing it to a low frequency region. The child does not need to perceive feature distinctions like voiced/unvoiced to understand English. He needs to have confidence in the ability of global patterning to give him the context. That will enable him to learn language. The importance of mistakes in fine structure is a moot point. The concept of redundancy and comfortableness in dealing with the code, rather than completeness of the code, is the direction which will lead to greatest success.

Boothroyd pointed out the potential danger of such a global approach. He was reminded of an example of the deaf child's tendency to rely on small pieces of the signal. The supervising teacher of the lower school at Clarke School for the Deaf had asked him to examine two children who were very poor lip-readers, and to find out what their problem was. Boothroyd worked with these children for twenty minutes per day for a few days. He found that they had developed a one-word cue strategy. They had been trained from the beginning to work in lip-reading with very simple one-word messages which, taken in context, would convey meaning. They had never really broken away from this. If a teacher said to one of them, "Martha, will you close the door," the child would usually look for the last word, then scan the room to see what response could be demanded involving the door. Since she was smart and saw the door was open, she would reason that she was required to close it. This was considered to be a wonderful achievement at first. As the demands of communication increased, the one-word strategy ceased to work and the children who did not get beyond this stage came to be regarded as poor lip-readers. These children appear to use the same strategy in reading; they scan a written message, not with respect to its form, but randomly for one or two words which they think they recognize. They then attempt to relate those words in order to produce some independent meaning. Such strategies might be fostered by the global approach to language instruction suggested by Blesser.

Pollack then invited Blesser to describe an experiment (Blesser, 1969, 1972) which was an illustration of his point of view. In this experiment, Blesser said, he tried to simulate certain kinds of deafness in normal-hearing mature adults with language competence.

He developed some simple electronics which would invert the speech spectrum in real time, as in Figure 2.13. This shows the spectrum of the word "mayor" before and after introversion. The characteristic F2 transition can be seen in the upper part of the figure and the same transition turned

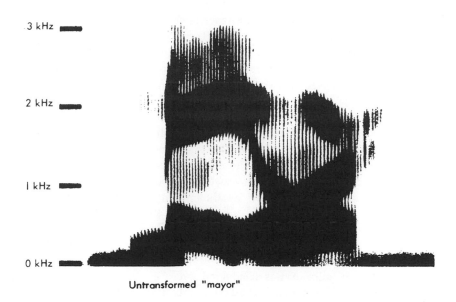

Untransformed "mayor"

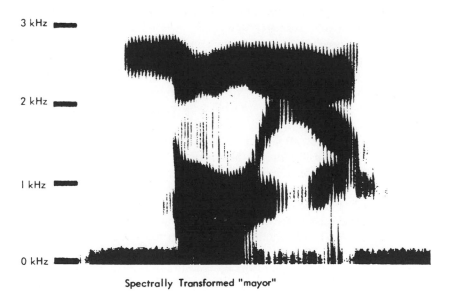

Spectrally Transformed "mayor"

Fig. 2.13 Spectrograph recordings of the word "mayor" before and after spectral transformation. From Blesser, 1972.

upside-down in the lower part of the figure. The subjects of the experiment worked in pairs and they already knew one another quite well. Thus, they were more willing to make mistakes in communicating with one another and were more familiar with their partner's personality, interests, and speech habits than if they had not been friends. Only male speakers were used since their lower fundamental frequency provided a richer harmonic content and a more pronounced envelope modulation than would have been obtained from female speakers.

The subjects were instructed simply to converse with one another using any strategy they found practical to establish communication, except that they were not to use a code which circumvented use of the transformed signal such as the Morse Code. The subjects were placed in a room with two acoustic chambers and were visually isolated. They were unable to hear the untransformed speech used by their partner. The transformed speech was conveyed to them by means of headphones embedded in ear-defenders of the kind used by jet plane mechanics. They were able to hear their own speech untransformed by bone conduction as well as transformed through the headphones.

The experiment was conducted over twenty sessions and each session lasted forty-five minutes. The first and the final sessions were test sessions. In the intervening sessions, during the first half hour, the subjects attempted to communicate with one another; during the final quarter hour, they were given pre-taped discrimination and identification tests similar to those used during the test session proper. The material presented in these tests was natural speech, obtained from a male speaker who was, in fact, Blesser himself. Blesser summarized the results of discrimination testing as follows:

(1) The source features voiced and unvoiced, and the features plosive, fricative, and nasal, were not affected by spectral transformation; thus, voiced plosives and unvoiced plosives, voiced fricatives and unvoiced fricatives, and nasals were easily perceived.

(2) Discrimination of consonant phonemes was generally very good except for those differing in place of articulation, for example /pa/, /ta/, and /ka/. The place feature was never learned.

(3) Discrimination of the tense/lax feature for vowels was quickly learned. For the tense vowels, perception of the front/back feature was initially reversed, for example, "boot" was heard as "beet" as one might expect. After only minimal exposure to the transformation, however, this feature was again perceived correctly.

(4) Discrimination of the lax vowels was never learned.

On identification tests, performance on monosyllabic words was abysmal. In the absence of context, identification of these words remained essentially zero throughout the experiment. Discussions held earlier in the workshop would lead one to predict on this basis that noncomprehension might have persisted throughout the entire experiment described. What happened, in fact, was quite different. The prosodic features of pitch, stress, and temporal ordering were not affected by the transformation. After a certain amount of learning of cues had taken place, that is, after the third or fourth session, sentence comprehension began to pick up and kept getting better and better. Furthermore, an examination of the sentences which subjects gave in their test responses revealed a very interesting fact. The first words to be recognized correctly in sentences were function words; for example, a contentless word like 'and' might be perceived correctly but nothing of the sentence on either side of it. As the subjects received more practice in conversation, they began to get phrase structure correct. For example, "under the stairs" was heard as "in the house." Notice here that the content words are wrongly perceived and also that the response to one of these content words doesn't even have the right number of syllables. The most dramatic example of this kind of thing was the response "Turn the page to the next lesson" for "Hoist the load to your left shoulder," a perfect grammatical match.

The conversations between the subjects were also studied. Some subjects learned to communicate very well, some moderately well, and some not at all. Their performance ratings varied from 0% to 100%. The best pair of subjects conversed as if there were no impediment to mutual comprehension and the worst pair essentially could not communicate with one another at all. Discrimination scores, phoneme identification scores, and single word identification scores were not correlated with one another or with the ability to converse. In other words, the subjects who showed marked ability to discriminate phonemes and who could even get place cues right occasionally, did not necessarily recognize words or sentences very well nor do well on conversation. The reverse was also true. The best pair of subjects in conversations were not necessarily particularly good in any of the other tasks. This is a somewhat uncomfortable result because it suggests a weak correlation between the sequences of operations that might go on in a process.

A further major finding was noted in analyzing the conversations. The subjects went through what might be called four stages of language acquisition. The first was a babbling stage or one of acoustic probing where the subject explored the medium, producing vowels for example like /a/, /o/, /e/, and listening to feedback from themselves and from each other. They were talking nonsense, just "playing around" as a baby might do in his crib.

The second stage which Blesser called ritualistic practice was communication using a very limited vocabulary, the items being repeated over and over in different contexts. "Do you understand?" "Yes, I understand." "Isn't understanding fun?" "Yes, we understand." The third stage, which was a little more advanced from a cognitive point of view, was called synthetic conversation. This was characterized by the establishment of a theme such as baseball or politics. Once that was done the subjects could converse on that theme, but it was extremely difficult for them to break away from it and establish another. For example, they might talk about baseball for ten minutes, then one of the subjects would become bored and try to switch to politics. It might take twenty minutes to establish the concept of politics but once that was done it was possible to talk about Nixon, Kennedy, or whatever happened to be relevant at that time. The last stage was the conversation where there were no inhibitions and no difficulty in changing the subject.

Blesser summarized the implications of these findings as he saw them. It seemed to him that speech abilities did not form any kind of sequence. In his experiment, a certain set of usually reliable spectral features were destroyed. At first Blesser looked for the subjects to learn spectral rotation, that is to rotate everything back perceptually in a manner analogous to the subject reinverting visual images which have been inverted by special lenses. The subjects of his experiment did not do this. Instead, they began to ignore certain features and to place a higher reliance upon others. In fact, they reversed their cognitive strategy. They abstracted the prosodic features first to gain some feeling for the context and then performed a phonetic match on the features that were intact, perhaps using their own articulation to assist them.

Blesser also found that personality factors were important to success or failure in learning to converse in this experiment. This had not been scientifically documented but observations suggested that certain personality factors were more highly predictive of success than performance on discrimination or identification tasks using isolated words. Blesser thought that the subject most likely to succeed was what he would call a synthetic generalist. This subject is not upset about not getting a perfect test score and is not upset by less than perfect communication. He will guess the sense of what is being said and try to find out if he is correct until he acquires some confidence in what he is doing upon which to build. In contrast, the subject least likely to succeed has an analytic approach. He will concentrate very hard upon the discrimination of sound elements. One pair of subjects approached this problem by trying to learn to speak with spectral rotation since the transformation performed by the system would turn the signal the right way about again. They spent a good deal of time trying to master this, but what they didn't appreciate was that they could not imitate their own rotated productions. They were able to hear themselves by bone conduction, speaking normally, as well as with rotation through the headphones. Their perceptions in this situation were plastic and unreliable. Even when they thought they were imitating their own rotated speech quite well, they were unsuccessful in doing so. Blesser saw certain parallels between this experiment and a deaf individual's situation. The deaf individuals who do well are not those, he thought, who try to recover lost information, but those who say, I shall do the best I can without. They use what is left to build up a sense of communication, rather than worrying about missing features. Blesser thought these findings were provocative for investigators concerned with the language problems of the deaf. Perhaps the present orientation led to emphasis on the wrong aspects of language.

Silverman commented that he had speculated about the relationship of personality variables such as those described by Blesser and lipreading. For example, he could recall an analytic type of subject, an eminent professor of physics trained to collect all the evidence before arriving at a conclusion, who was a very poor lipreader. The term "synthetic generalist," on the other hand described the good lip-reader very well; as an example, Silverman recalled a young man working on the river barges who had not gotten beyond the eighth grade. This man was one of the best lip-readers he had ever encountered.

Personality variables: lipreading

Boothroyd asked if the subjects were allowed to discuss the experiment with one another between sessions. Blesser said that this was specifically encouraged. It was clear that the subjects rehearsed certain kinds of strategies. One pair observed that they could converse freely once they had established a topic but that if they switched topics conversation was difficult. They brought in 3x5 cards with the numbers one to ten printed on them, each number signifying a different topic. They used these to facilitate switching of topics.

Strategies used with spectral rotation

Denes asked how long it took the subjects to go from one stage to another. Blesser answered that it was very variable. In a sense, the worst pair of subjects never did progress beyond stage 2, the ritualistic conversation, while the best pair of subjects went through the first three stages within three practice hours. Denes then asked what proportion of subjects were good at conversing and what proportion were poor. Blesser thought that if he rated them in this way, he would come up with a uniform distribution. The best pair of subjects were identical twins. This might be interpreted as indicating that these subjects did well because they might have similar bone structure and vocal tract configuration and greater familiarity with each other's voices.

Rating of subjects' progress

It was interesting that these subjects were also best at recognizing sentences in the test materials, that is, as produced by a third male speaker. It could be argued that this was not a well-controlled experiment on that score. It might very well be that the experimenter's voice more closely resembled that of one member of any pair who then should do better than the other.

Blesser added that he and his colleagues had visited Richey who worked on speech rotation at the Bell Telephone Laboratories in the 1930's (Richey,

*Perception
and produc-
tion of
rotated
speech*

1936). This man learned to speak in inverted speech in order to demonstrate its value as a privacy device for telephone conversations. Richey also made up a dictionary for the transformations which he found necessary to production of inverted speech. For example, for the word "one," something like "yun" was produced. It was Blesser's impression, however, that the subjects in his own experiment who began to be able to produce inverted speech were not those who were well able to perceive inverted speech.

Denes referred to a similar experiment which he had conducted (Denes, 1964). In this experiment, words subjected to the same kind of spectral rotation were presented to subjects over a period of several weeks. Blesser argued that this situation was profoundly different from the real-time inter-action which went on in conversation. Denes, as a matter of interest, mentioned that visible speech and the sound spectrograph had their origins in these early experiments with inverted speech.

*Systematic
training in
recognition
of words and
phrases*

Watson felt that it would be interesting to pursue the question of learning spectral rotation in two ways. Subjects could be given systematic training, with feedback from the experimenter as to the correctness of their responses, over a longer period of time. In the second type of experiment, they could participate in such an interaction situation as Blesser had studied. Blesser said that his subjects' performance on the tests conducted during each session had convinced him that they would do badly in the recognition of monosyllabic words, even with more intensive training. If all the information about place of articulation for consonants and the differentiating features of lax vowels were stripped from a monosyllable, then any word which would fit the remaining features set was a possible response. He could influence the results heavily, in such a case, by choice of a high-frequency or a low-frequency word as the stimulus; in other words, he could manipulate the probability of a correct response by choosing from low- and high-frequency word sets.

Watson said that his question was aimed at exactly this conviction of Blesser's, namely that subjects could not learn to use spectral rotation. In systemic training aimed at exploring this further, the materials need not be limited to monosyllabic words or even to single words, but should include phrases and sentences also. However, the subjects would be told what the word or sentence presented to them was, after each of their attempts to reproduce it. Boothroyd asked if any subject had learned to interpret spectral cues after rotation. Blesser replied that he had examined the confusion matrices very carefully. He had not found consistent patterns of response for place of information for any subject. In listening to second formant transitions and noise bursts for stops which were rotated and thus displaced, subjects could barely discriminate consonant-vowel pairs, let alone identify them. There was absolutely no learning of these cues.

Levitt and Watson both suggested that it would be of interest to deal with the confounding of spectral and prosodic cues in another way, namely, by presenting speech-modulated noise to the subjects in an interactive situation since this would have temporal prosodic features but no spectral features. Blesser objected that pitch features would then be absent and also any prosodic information in the spectrum. Pollack recalled a study in which one of the aims was to arrive at optimum masking of speech by means of speech-modulated noise. When this was devised, the technique was so effective that the masking speech-modulated noise itself became intelligible. Levitt said that it was precisely this that would be interesting to test, because the spectral cues would be stripped out and not confounded with the remaining prosodic cues.

Reception of prosodic and spectral cues

Liberman suggested that the experiment might be expanded in another way. Blesser had reported that his subjects responded very poorly to some kinds of cues in the test materials he had used, but it was difficult to interpret his results. It was not clear either how much redundancy there was in the test materials or, indeed, exactly what cues the subjects were able to hear. Liberman thought it would be interesting to control manner distinctions, voicing distinctions, and prosodic distinctions, for example, one at a time. Various conditions should be set up under which it would be clear what segmental cues of place, manner or voicing and which segments the subjects were in fact responding to. For example, how much poorer would performance be if the fundamental frequency were to be flattened or inverted or made to go in an opposite direction from normal?

Controlling spectral features separately

Blesser thought it might be best to use altered noninverted real speech or synthesized speech in order to examine such questions. His bias was to set up a context which was as close as possible to normal communication rather than to test performance in fine detail. He had wanted only to demonstrate that, left to their own devices, subjects could learn to master the altered code which he had used. Liberman assured him that he was not suggesting that this line of inquiry be abandoned but rather that it should be supplemented by studies of fine detail so that a better understanding would be gained of the precise means which the subjects in his type of experiment had at their disposal.

Prosodic and phonetic features in speech reception

Pickett thought Blesser's findings offered encouragement to some deaf people, that is, those who suddenly and drastically lose their hearing in adult life. His findings offered no encouragement to those born deaf who do not develop language competence. In Pickett's view, the subjects performed well in the experiment described above because they already had normal language competence. Blesser recalled that his point had been that hearing deficit does not prevent the understanding of speech but that it does prevent the acquisition of language. These two problems, he thought, could be separated fairly easily. Pickett reflected that in training adventitiously deafened adults, lipreading was useful for the recognition of certain specific phonetic events; Blesser's findings, however, indicated that the greatest progress would be made by helping the patient to take advantage of his knowledge of the language and his ability to predict speech events in context. Blesser argued that it was more important for the subject to have a concept of language than to worry about phonetic or articulatory details. Pickett said that the deaf person could not acquire language without having access to phonetic detail which was needed to resolve ambiguities.

Liberman stated the question in another way as follows. How could language be programmed without speech? If the deaf child could read, he would know all the syntactic and semantic constraints of the language and would be in exactly the same position as Blesser's subjects. The fact remained that deaf children did not seem to acquire language through reading very efficiently. If speech and its phonetic detail were merely ancillary to language, then why could syntactic and semantic constraints not be learned in their absence, that is, through printed matter instead? Blesser insisted that speech and syntactic and semantic constraints should be described separately.

Liberman went on to ask about the level of redundancy in the subjects' conversations and in the test materials presented to them. Obviously, the amount of phonetic information needed can vary from nearly zero for social greetings like "Good morning," to a great deal more when listening to a presentation such as Blesser's own, which was full of complicated constructions and unusual words. He wondered if Blesser's subjects could listen to the presently ongoing debate and understand any part of it. Blesser replied that his best subjects would have understood about 70% to 80% of the exchange provided that they knew it was the experiment in which they participated which was being discussed.

Liberman said that was hardly a fair test, since the subjects already knew a great deal about the experiment. What if the debate had been about a different experiment? Blesser thought that the point was well taken and that phonetic resolution might be important in such a case, but he claimed that most exchanges become redundant, except perhaps among intellectuals; even in their case, exchanges become redundant if the parties attend enough conferences. This made phonetic information unnecessary most of the time. Liberman answered while that might be true, the importance of the phonetic information which was occasionally required could not be assessed. It is not

Speech reception in congenitally and adventitiously deaf

Learning from spoken and written language

Phonetic information and comprehension of speech

Redundancy and phonetic information

possible to say that because 85% of normal conversation is highly redundant and can be understood if only 1% or so of the phonetic features are present, then phonetic detail is unimportant. In the remaining 15% of conversational speech, phonetic information may be quite critical. It may be just as important to the deaf subject to understand that nonredundant speech, as to understand highly redundant speech.

Ling added that in working with a young deaf child, it would be particularly foolhardy not to be concerned with phonetic information. Although information might be available about the level of auditory acuity in these children, there would often be no information at early stages of development about their ability to discriminate sounds or to process speech at supra-threshold levels. In the absence of such information, it was not possible to predict the child's responses to a natural language approach. If one put a hearing aid on the young deaf child and merely talked to him as if he were not deaf, the child might develop natural language, but he might not.

Phonetic information and the young deaf child

Hirsh thought that the issue was not one of the length of the unit to be used in teaching, that is, whether it was to be a phoneme or a sentence, but one of style of communication, that is, corrective teaching on the one hand versus the necessity for real communication on the other. Communication and its consequences for the child, for example, his ability to control others, seemed to be closely related to certain present day emphases in the education of young deaf children.

Style of communication

Eisenberg stated that she was fascinated by Blesser's experiment but troubled by his statement that with spectral rotation, one could simulate deafness. She did not think Blesser's subjects were comparable to deaf individuals but rather to people learning a second language. Blesser disagreed. Eisenberg said that at any rate, Blesser did not change his subjects' thresholds or the operation of their systems. He had taken the original code which they knew and replaced it with a distorted one which they did not know. What he had shown was that, given the knowledge and experience of certain rules of language, these rules could be applied to a distorted code, that is, to the features of the original code which remained.

Simulating deafness by spectral rotation

Blesser cited a more extreme example in which he felt subject performance could not be explained in this way. The example was a test of intelligibility for speech scramblers developed during World War II, which was not generally known (Schott, 1943). It was called the A-5 Scrambler and in it, the speech spectrum was broken up into five different frequency patterns. These patterns were randomly shifted and rotated in such a way that there were 3000 possible combinations. Of these, only eleven were considered to be secure against intelligibility. Highly trained subjects listened to sentences in which a new set of rotations was made ten or twenty times per second. Under these conditions, which amounted to complete destruction of spectral infor-

Effect of complete distortion of spectrum on intelligibility

mation, two highly trained subjects made a 50% to 70% score on recognition of sentence material.

Eisenberg pointed out that since under these listening conditions prosodic information was also not entirely removed, the subjects were reconstructing the original code from the totally scrambled one. They were able to have a conversation in the reconstructed code although it bore little resemblance spectrally to the original code, because they had the rules which Blesser could not get rid of.

Reconstruction of original code

Blesser thought that the reconstruction was performed in reverse order from that which is usually proposed. The subjects began with a framework, that is, the processing. From this, function words related to the framework emerged first and only later the content words. This was the reverse of the process usually proposed, that is, that of building up from phonetic features and phonemic features to syllables, words, phrases, and sentences. Menyuk commented that the subjects' ability to pick out function words in Blesser's experiment was clearly related to their knowledge of prosody, of pause and juncture, and those changes in fundamental frequency which are found in connection with phrasal pauses in English. The order of importance of different elements of language was quite different in so far as acquisition of language was concerned.

Prosody and function words

Blesser conceded that this was true, but, he added, prosodic features are available to the hearing-impaired child. If language instruction were to begin with these features where he is already on good ground, that is, with fundamental frequency, juncture, and so on, then he could be taught to have some confidence, first in communication of his feelings and later in formulating questions and statements. His progress would be much better than if instruction began with the more difficult learning of phonetic features and later attempted to put these back into the prosodic framework. It was better to do what was natural to the child than to force him to learn according to some theory of language acquisition.

Menyuk suggested that it would not be appropriate, however, to start with function words. Blesser agreed, but said that he might start with pitch. That, said Menyuk, was an open and empirical question; but function words were acquired by his normal adult subjects because of their knowledge of the language and, in particular, of the relation of function words to the prosodic values in the sentence. This was far from the state of affairs in a little child acquiring language.

Function words in language acquisition

Blesser replied that he had initially built a portable device which he carried around with him in everyday situations. He tried to communicate with others while listening through its headphones, with little success. What he lacked was a "mother." He found that people talked to him in what he perceived as too clipped and quick a manner. They were not used to talking with high redundancy. It was like being thrown into a foreign country. No one would take the time to babble or go through ritual phrases with him. Thus, he was not able to acquire a limited vocabulary to start with or to expand it by introducing new words. He could not persuade any symbolic mother to translate complicated thoughts which had been expressed into simple language. Thus he found it very difficult to acquire any skill in communicating with rotated speech. It was for this reason that he had adopted the paradigm of the experiment where subjects learned in pairs.

Mother's role in language acquisition

Miller said that the discussion had raised once again an issue which had been identified as important in a previous conference (Miller, 1972). If, in designing an aid for a hearing-impaired adult who has language competence, it is possible to present only a limited number of cues, which cues is it important to select? Is this same set of cues or a different set important in the case of the child who is still in the process of acquiring language?

This, said Menyuk, brought the participants back to the question of the infant's responsiveness to different aspects of sensory input with which the conference began.

REFERENCES

Blesser, B.: Perception of spectrally rotated speech, Doctoral dissertation, Massachusetts Institute of Technology, 1969.

Blesser, B.: Speech perception under conditions of spectral transformation: I. Phonetic characteristics, J. Speech Hearing Res. 15(1):5–41, 1972.

Davis, H.; Hudgins, C.V., Marquis, R.J., et al.: The selection of hearing aids, Laryngoscope 56:85–115, 135–163, 1946.

Davis, H.; Stevens, S.S., Nichols, R.H., et al.: Hearing Aids: An Experimental Study of Design Objectives, Cambridge: Harvard University Press, 1947.

Denes, P.: On the motor theory of speech perception, Paper presented at Proceedings of the 5th International Congress on Phonetic Sciences, Munster, Germany, August, 1964.

Dodds, E., and Harford, E.: Modified earpieces and CROS for high frequency hearing losses, J. Speech Hearing Res. 11:204–218, 1968.

Fairbanks, G., and Miron, M.S.: Effects of vocal effort upon the consonant-vowel ratio within the syllable, J. Acoust. Soc. Amer. 29:621–626, 1957.

Fant, C.G.M.: On the predictability of formant levels and spectrum envelopes from formant frequencies, In: To Honor Roman Jakobson, The Hague: Mouton, 1967.

Kahn, D.: The Codebreakers: The Story of Secret Writing, London: Weidenfeld and Nicolson, 1967.

Miller, J.D., ed.: Directions for research to improve hearing aids and services for the hearing-impaired: A report of working group 65, NAS-NRC Committee on Hearing, Biomechanics and Bioacoustics, Washington, D.C.: National Academy of Sciences, 1972.

Noll, A.M.: The intelligibility of shouted speech, Advisory Report No. 19,

AGARD Publication, Clearinghouse for Federal Scientific and Technical Information, Springfield: December, 1969.

Pollack, I.: Specification of sound pressure levels, Amer. J. Psychol. 62:412–417, 1949.

Richey, J.L.: Instruction sheet used to demonstrate Record #4599, Bell Telephone Laboratories, 1936.

Schott, L.: Frequency-time division speech, Privacy system: Final Report. Project C-66, National Defense Research Committee, Office of Scientific Research and Development, Western Electric Company, Inc., 1943.

Tonndorf, J.: Why do we hear what we hear? Decibel 2:21, 1968.

Weiss, M.S.: A study of the relation between consonant-vowel amplitude ratio and talker intelligibility, Master's thesis, Purdue University, 1968.

Witt, L.H.: Reception of acoustic speech signals as a function of sensation level by hearing-impaired children, Student Project, Central Institute for the Deaf, 1972.

Language Processing

7

Language Processing:
State-of-the-Art Report

A. M. Liberman
Haskins Laboratories

To provide a framework for our discussion, I will set down in outline form the questions that arise in my mind when I wonder how we might get language into the hearing-impaired child. Some of these questions were raised by Hirsh in his keynote speech the other evening, which reinforces my belief that they will help to organize our discussion this morning.

I should confess at the outset that I know very little about deaf children, even less than I know about language processing. It is more appropriate, therefore, that I should try to make the outline neutral. But I do have views (even biases) that may, in one way or another, influence what I say, so before proceeding with the outline, I should get them on the record. The most relevant of these concern the function or purpose of grammar. My colleagues and I have written about those views in other places, and at length (Liberman, 1973; Liberman, Mattingly, and Turvey, 1972; Mattingly, 1972b); if only for that reason, I should be as brief as possible.

I believe that grammar—or, more exactly, grammatical recoding—serves to reshape information so as to enable the speaker-listener to move it efficiently between a nonlinguistic intellect, which has facilities for the processing and long-term storage of ideas, and a transmission system, where sounds are produced and perceived. Without the grammatical reshaping that comes so naturally to all normal human beings, we should have to communicate our ideas by means of sounds that were uniquely and holistically different from each other—one sound pattern, however simple or complex, for each idea. In that case, the number of ideas we could transmit would be limited to the number of sounds we can produce and identify. (Precisely that limitation applies to the normal communication of nonhuman animals if it is true that those creatures lack the capacity for grammatical coding.) We do not know exactly how many messages could be transmitted by that kind of "language." But given the richness of the intellect and the comparative poverty of the transmission system, the scope of such a nongrammatical "language" is orders of magnitude less than that which is afforded by the grammars that are so readily available to human beings and that, in my view, set language apart from other perceptual and cognitive processes (Liberman, 1973; Liberman, Mattingly, and Turvey, 1972). All this is to imply what some of my colleagues and I believe about the biology of grammar, which is that the capacity for grammatical processing evolved as a kind of interface, matching the output of the intellect to the vocal tract and the ear. If that is so, the biological development of those grammatical processes should have been influenced by the possibilities and limitations of the mismatched structures they connect. Natural grammatical processes should, then, reflect those influences. Unfortunately, we do not know how far "up" and "down" the grammatical interface the effects of intellect and transmission system go. I have some guesses, based on the formal resemblances between speech and the rest of grammar (Mattingly and Liberman, 1969), but I see no point in inflicting them on you. I will, however, suggest that the point of view I have expressed here is relevant to our concerns. When congenital deafness prevents the use of the normal transmission system, what are the consequences for grammar? If the deaf child bypasses speech entirely, as in the case of natural sign, must he then use a grammar different from the grammar of spoken languages? If so, what are the differences and, more to the point, how far "up" the system do they extend? If the grammar of spoken languages is not appropriate for the transmission system used in sign, how adequately can the signer adapt it? Or must he contrive a more suitable grammar? If so, how well does this more suitable grammar work, and at what cost in effort?

My views about grammatical recoding take a more specific form the more closely we approach to speech at the transmission end of the system. They also become more directly relevant to our concern, since we must surely try to understand speech if we want to know how the deaf child might cope with it. Thus, I think we should want to understand the function of the phonetic representation so that we can better appreciate the consequences, if any, of the failure to develop it in a proper way. We should also want to understand the relation between the phonetic representation and the sound, for we cannot otherwise see how the deaf child might use prosthetic devices that drastically alter the acoustic signal or, in the extreme case, transform it for delivery to the eye or the skin. (See: Liberman et al., 1968.)

Let us consider first the function of the phonetic representation in the interconversion between ideas and sounds. We do not know the shape of ideas in the intellect, but we should doubt that they are strung out in time as they are after they have been transformed into sound. If that doubt is well founded, we should suppose that the meaning of the longer segments of language (for example, sentences) must transcend the meaning of the shorter segments (for example, words) that they comprise. There is, then, a need for a buffer in which the shorter segments can be held until the meaning of the longer segments has been extracted. I suspect that the universal phonetic features became specialized in the evolution of language as appropriate physiological units for storage and processing in that short-term buffer. (See: Liberman, Mattingly, and Turvey, 1972.) Since the substitution of sign for speech does not remove the need to spread ideas in time, we must wonder how or how well the need for short-term storage is met. We should also wonder what happens when, instead of bypassing the normal transmission system entirely, as in natural sign, one rather enters directly (if only approximately) at the level of the phonetic representation by finger spelling or by writing (and reading) the letters of the alphabet. For if those substitute signals do not engage the phonetic features, then the deaf child may have to make do with other representations—for example, visual or kinesthetic images. How efficient are these nonphonetic representations for the storage and processing in short-term memory that the perception of language may be presumed to require? (See, for example, Conrad, 1972.)

But suppose that instead of avoiding the sound by representing the phonetic message directly, as in finger spelling or alphabetic writing, we try to present the acoustic signal to the deaf child in a form (for example, spectrographic) suitable for presentation to an organ other than the ear. One of the problems we will then encounter arises from the nature of the relation between the sound and the phonetic message. There is a great deal of evidence for the conclusion that speech is not an alphabet or simple substitution cipher on the phonetic representation, but rather a complex and grammatical code (Liberman et al., 1967, 1968). Indeed, if speech were not a complex code it could not work efficiently, for just as the transmission system is not well matched most broadly to the intellect, so also is it unable, more narrowly, to deal directly with the phonetic representation. Thus, the rate at which the phonetic message is (or can be) communicated—up to twenty or thirty phonetic segments per second—would far exceed the temporal resolving power of the ear if, as in a simple cipher, each phonetic segment were represented by a unit sound. But there is another, equally important problem we should expect to have if the phonetic representation were transmitted alphabetically: the listener would have great difficulty identifying the order of the segments. Though little is known about the ability of the ear to identify the order of discrete (nonspeech) sound segments, recent work suggests that it fails to meet the normal requirements of speech by a factor of five or more (Warren et al., 1969). That is, when segments of distinctive nonspeech sounds are arranged in strings of three or four, their order can be correctly identified only when the duration of each segment is five or more times longer than speech sounds normally are.

The complex speech code is a grammatical conversion that nicely evades both those limitations of auditory perception: several segments of the phonetic message are commonly folded into a single segment of sound, which takes care of the problem posed by the temporal resolving power of the ear; and there are context-conditioned variations in the shape of the acoustic cues that provide nontemporal information about the order of segments in the phonetic message, thus getting around the ear's relatively poor ability to deal with order on a temporal basis. (See Liberman et al., 1967; Liberman, Mattingly, and Turvey, 1972.) But for our purposes the important point is that these gains are achieved at the cost of a very complex relation between phonetic message and acoustic signal. We are not normally aware of how complex this relation is because the decoding is ordinarily done by an appropriately complex decoder that speech has easy access to. Unfortunately for the needs of the deaf child, however, that decoder is connected to the auditory system. What happens then when we try to present the raw (that is, undecoded) speech signal to some other sense organ, such as the eye? On the basis of what we know about speech we can understand some of the difficulties that are encountered; we can also see opportunities that might be exploited.

I should like to turn now from a more specific concern with grammatical processes near the transmission end of the system to consider some hypotheses about language that deal with grammatical processes more generally. In speaking of the function of these processes, I have suggested that by appropriately interfacing mismatched structures of intellect and transmission, grammar makes possible the efficient communication of ideas from one person to another. But I believe that an equally important function of a grammar is to enlarge the possibilities for communicating ideas to oneself. By getting ideas out of the inarticulate intellect and down at least part way into the language system, we conceivably achieve a kind of control that we could not otherwise have managed. If so, having a grammar confers on us much the same kind of advantage that a mathematics does. A significant part of normal human cognitive work may then depend in one way or another on grammatical processes. In that case we have reason to be concerned about the consequences that may follow when these processes are tampered with.

I have also spoken of the human intellect as though it were in no sense linguistic—that is, as if all the accommodating to the transmission system had been done by the development of the grammatical interface. That leaves out of account the possibility that in the evolution of language the intellect and the transmission system themselves underwent alterations that tended to reduce the mismatch. In the case of the vocal tract, indeed, there is evidence that such an accommodation did occur. The vocal tract of human beings is different from that of other primates (Lieberman, 1968; Lieberman, Klatt, and Wilson, 1969; Lieberman, Crelin, and Klatt, 1972), and the difference appears to have produced for us a greater ability to transmit the phonetic message, thus easing somewhat the job that the speech grammar has to do. But what of the other end of the system? Was the originally nonlinguistic intellect also altered in the direction of a better fit to the other structures in the linguistic system? We do not know but, if it was, then we should have to suppose that the human intellect is to some extent specifically adapted to normal grammatical processes. Given that possibility, we have another reason for wondering whether alteration of normal grammatical processes might have consequences for intellectual ability.

Throughout this introduction I have spoken of "natural" grammatical recodings, which implies a bias that I particularly want to get on the record—namely, that such recodings are not arbitrary inventions or cultural artifacts, but rather the reflections of processes that are deeply biological. I believe, as do many other people who concern themselves with language, that human beings come equipped with the capacity to develop grammars, including, as I have already emphasized, the grammar of speech that connects the phonetic message to the acoustic signal. To the extent that we force these processes into unnatural channels we can expect to encounter difficulties. Unnatural grammars will very likely be hard to learn, especially if they are as complex as they may need to be. Indeed, the fact that people do not learn to read spectrograms suggests that we cannot, by learning, acquire a grammar of speech or make the natural grammar work with an organ other than the ear (Liberman et al., 1968).

Now let us turn to the outline I spoke of at the beginning, the one that might help us organize our discussion. Though the shape of the outline conforms rather well to the views I have just talked about, the outline itself does not prejudge any of the issues it raises, or so I hope. The larger division in the outline is between those methods that would aim at delivering to the hearing-impaired child as close an approximation to the spoken language as possible, and those that would use a different transmission system, such as the gestures of sign. The first method is further divided between those that present speech in unencoded form (that is, as a signal from which the phonetic message has not been extracted) and those that present it in decoded form (that is, as a phonemic or phonetic transcription, for example). With undecoded speech there is an additional, subordinate choice among modalities: do we present the signal to the ear, the eye, or the skin?

I. COMMUNICATION OF A STANDARD, SPOKEN LANGUAGE

It seems reasonably obvious that we should want, if possible, to develop in the deaf child a reasonable approximation to standard, spoken language. Because the greatest number of natural grammatical processes is then used, the fullest possible development of language becomes a relatively easy matter, and there is the least risk of crippling the kinds of cognitive processes that normal grammatical processes ordinarily serve. Those advantages are, of course, in addition to giving the child access to standard literature of all kinds as well as the ability to communicate more readily with normal-hearing people. I do not mean to propose that we eschew all other possibilities, since the advantages of trying to give the child an approximation to a standard language can be outweighed by many considerations. Indeed, I do not mean to propose anything here, but only to frame the possibilities.

A. Transmission of the undecoded speech signal

I said in my introductory remarks that there is a complexly encoded relation between the phonetic message and the acoustic signal. The salient characteristic of the speech code is that information about successive segments of the phonetic message is often transmitted simultaneously on the same parameter of the sound. As a consequence, there is, in general, no acoustic criterion by which one can identify segments of sound that correspond in size or number to the segments of the phonetic message, and the acoustic shape of the cues for a phonetic segment will often vary greatly as a function of context. The perception of speech requires, then, a complex decoding operation. In this section we will consider those ways of presenting speech, including even rather elaborately processed speech, in which, no matter how well the speech signal is gotten through (or around) the person's deafness, the decoding job has yet to be done. But first, by way of introduction, I should say more about the speech code and the speech signal. Thus, I should emphasize that the relation between phonetic message and sound is not always that of a complex grammatical code; there are, intermittently, quite transparent or unencoded stretches. In those parts of the speech signal that carry the phonetic message in encoded form, there is, as I have pointed out, the complication that information about more than one phonetic segment is carried simultaneously on the same acoustic parameter. In the transparent or unencoded stretches, however, there is no such complication: a segment of sound carries information about only one phonetic segment. In slow articulation the vowels and fricatives, for example, are reasonably transparent, as are some aspects of the distinctions among phonetic manner classes. The fact that the phonetic message is sometimes encoded in the speech signal and sometimes not becomes important later in this section of the outline when we consider how to present the speech signal to an organ other than the ear.

I should also emphasize here that there is an aspect of the speech signal that has, in principle, nothing to do with encodedness, but that nevertheless can make speech hard to deal with, especially for the deaf. I refer to the well-known fact that speech is, from an engineering standpoint, a very poor signal. The acoustic energy is not highly concentrated in the first two or three formants, which carry most of the important linguistic information, but is rather smeared broadly through the spectrum. Moreover, some of the most important acoustic cues are rapid frequency changes of the formants, the so-called formant transitions; such rapid frequency swings are, by their nature, physically indeterminate. In the processing that we normally do in speech perception, therefore, there is not only the need to decode the signal so as to recover the phonetic segments which are so complexly encoded in it, but also, apparently, a need to clean up the signal—to track the formants, as it were—and deliver to the decoder a clearer parametric description of a signal that is still undecoded. I know of no evidence that human beings have devices (shall we call them property filters?) to do that job. It is nonetheless relevant to our concerns, however, to know that the linguistically important acoustic cues *are* poorly represented, and to wonder, then, whether we might help the deaf by altering speech so as to make it a better signal.

1. Getting the undecoded speech signal by ear. If we are to deal with the undecoded speech signal, then we should want, if possible, to get it in by ear in order to take advantage of all the physiological equipment, including especially the speech decoder, that is naturally connected to the auditory system. But we must then alter the speech signal in some way that is calculated to evade the condition of deafness. The simplest and most common alteration is amplification. I will not discuss that remedy further, except to remark the obvious and say that it does not always solve the problem.

I would rather consider other, more complicated alterations in the speech signal. Here I have in mind that, as I said in the introduction to this section, the speech signal may be hard to deal with, not only because of its peculiarly complex relation to the phonetic message, but also because the important cues are not among the most prominent features of the acoustic landscape. By using what we now know about those cues, and by taking advantage of the techniques that enable us to manipulate them in convenient and flexible ways, I should think that we might be able to make speech significantly more intelligible to the deaf. We should want first, for this and for other more general purposes, to extend our knowledge about the acoustic cues by discovering exactly which ones deaf people can and cannot hear. Then we should explore the possibility that by putting the acoustic energy where it counts, and by specifically reinforcing certain cues, we could produce a more effective signal. Many of the alterations that might, on a common sense basis, be expected to help could only be managed with totally synthetic speech, since it is beyond our present technological capabilities to process "real" speech in such a way as to produce those patterns that are likely to prove most effective. But it is nonetheless worthwhile, I think, to see how much better we can do with even the most extreme, synthetic departures from normal speech. We all know that what is technologically not feasible today is child's play tomorrow, so if we find that certain kinds of synthetic speech can be got through to the deaf better than natural speech, we can look forward realistically to the possibility of some day being able to produce such signals from "real" speech. But there might also be an immediate application. I have in mind the problems of the congenitally deaf child and the possibility that the development of his linguistic system might be promoted—or, more exactly, not held up—if speech could more effectively be got through to him. Of course, if we could only provide him with exposure to appropriately tailored synthetic speech, he could not interact with it in the normal way. Still, he might, like the chaffinch, gain something important if his normal language mechanisms had proper data to work on.

There are other possibilities for alterations in the speech signal that might also increase intelligibility for the deaf. In that connection I should like to take particular note of some work done recently by Timothy Rand (1973). That work is the more relevant because a member of our conference, Pickett, has results that are related to those of Rand, and Pickett will, I believe, describe those results for us at this session. What Rand has found is that when the formants are split between the ears the two higher formants are, to a significant extent, released from the masking effects of the lowest one. More specifically, the procedure and the findings are as follows. Using synthetic speech so as to have the stimulus control he needs, Rand presents binaurally the syllables /ba/, /da/, and /ga/, which are distinguished only by the transitions of the second and third formants. He then determines by what amount he must reduce the intensities of the second and third formants to bring the subjects' accuracy of identification down from nearly 100%, where it is before the intensity reduction, to a level just slightly above chance. In another condition, he carries out exactly the same procedure, but this time with dichotic rather than binaural presentation. In the dichotic condition the first formant is presented to one ear, the second and third formants to the other. The first thing to be said about the results is that, as had been known before, the listener fuses the two inputs quite readily and hears an intelligible utterance. But, for our purposes, the more important result is that, in order to produce a reduction in intelligibility equal to that of the binaural condition, Rand must, in the dichotic condition, reduce the intensities of the second and third formants by an additional 15 dB. That is, in the dichotic condition the transition cues for the stop consonants can, other things equal, be heard (and used) by the subjects at a level 15 dB lower than that required in the normal binaural condition. Thus, it is as if the dichotic presentation produced a 15 dB release from masking. I should emphasize that Rand's work has been done with normal-hearing subjects, and the degradation in the speech has so far been only in the form of intensity reduction. Still, we might want to consider the implications that Rand's work could have for improving speech intelligibility with the deaf. Perhaps Pickett will do that.

2. Getting the undecoded signal in through a nonauditory modality. Over the years, and especially in the recent past, attempts have been made to help the deaf by presenting the speech signal to the eye or the skin. Those attempts were very adequately reviewed by Pickett at the 1970 meeting in Easton, Maryland. As our contribution to a previous meeting at Gallaudet, Cooper, Studdert-Kennedy, and I undertook to describe the difficulties that face anyone who tries to decode the acoustic stream of speech without the aid of the physiological decoder that normally does it for him (Liberman, Cooper, and Studdert-Kennedy, 1968). The source of those difficulties should be apparent on the basis of what I have said here today about the complexly encoded nature of the relation between the acoustic signal and the phonetic message. If the sounds of speech were an alphabet on the phones— that is, if there were a discrete acoustic segment for each phonetic segment, or if the segments were merely linked as in cursive writing—then it should be no more difficult to read spectrograms than to read print. (Of course we should still have to contend with the fact that signal-to-noise ratio of speech would be poorer by far than that of print; that would, however, pose no very serious problem, or so I think.) But as I have said already, the relation of the speech signal to the message it carries is not that simple. Though the speech code matches the requirements of the phonetic representation to the particular limitations of the transmission system, thus permitting these two structures to work well together, it does so at a price; to extract the phonetic message from the acoustic signal requires a special and complex decoder. Such a decoding mechanism is apparently quite readily available to all human beings, but, unfortunately for our present purposes, it is connected to the auditory system, and experience in trying to learn to read spectrograms suggests that it cannot be transferred to the eye (or the skin).

Given what we know about the speech code and the way it is normally perceived, we have reason to be pessimistic about the possibility that the eye or the skin can ever be a wholly adequate substitute for the ear as a pathway for speech sounds or even as an alternative entry to the speech decoder. It does not follow, however, that no useful information about the speech signal can be transmitted through nonauditory channels. There are, as I have pointed out, relatively transparent or unencoded stretches of speech in which the relation between acoustic signal and phonetic message is quite straightforward. Since these stretches are not in need of complex decoding, they might be more readily "understood" when transmitted through the eye or the skin.

At all events, I would suggest that in the design of prosthetic aids for the deaf we take into account what we now know (or could by further research learn) about the speech code. We should then more clearly see both the difficult problems and the promising possibilities.

B. Transmission of the decoded speech signal

In an alphabetically written language there is a fairly straightforward relation—a rather simple substitution cipher, indeed—between the segmented optical shapes and the phonetic or phonemic segments they represent. We might suppose, therefore, that in presenting language to the eye of the deaf child it would be the better part of wisdom not to offer the raw speech signal which requires decoding, but rather an alphabetic representation which does not. Indeed, this seems the more reasonable because we know that, while normal-hearing people have not learned to read spectrograms, some have learned to read language in an alphabetically written form.

But the matter is not that simple. There is abundant evidence that reading is a secondary linguistic activity in the sense that it is grafted onto a spoken-language base (Mattingly, 1972a). Thus, reading came late in the history of our race. Moreover, an alphabet, which represents the decoded phonetic segments, is the most recently invented orthography, and it is significant that it has been invented only once. Most relevant of all, of course, is the fact that among normal-hearing children there are many who speak and perceive speech perfectly well who nevertheless cannot learn to read.

We should not be surprised, then, to discover that congenitally deaf children, having had little or no chance to master the primary spoken language, find it exceptionally difficult to acquire a secondary, written form of it. Indeed, the fact that such children have more than the normal amount of trouble learning to read, and that they do not normally attain so high a final level of achievement, is itself strong evidence for the essentially secondary nature of reading. It seems intuitively reasonable to me that a child (or anyone else) should have difficulty mastering the grammatical (as opposed to the lexical) elements of language if his initial and only exposure is to the written forms, but I don't know how to talk about that in any intelligent way. I will only say, therefore, that it is surely important to us that reading *is* significantly harder for those who do not speak—that it is, in effect, difficult to acquire the language by eye. How much do we know about this and what else should we try to learn? Is the deaf child's success in reading related to his ability to deal, by whatever means, with the spoken language? If so, what is the nature of the relation? Is there some kind of threshold effect—that is, is some certain amount of competence with the spoken language enough to enable the child to break through and acquire the rest of the language by reading? Can we discover whether experience with particular aspects of the spoken language is more important than experience with some others? And what does it mean, precisely, to say that a congenitally deaf child reads poorly? What kinds of errors does he make, for example, and how do those compare with the errors made by normal-hearing children? Are the deaf child's errors spread evenly (or randomly) over all aspects of language, or do the difficulties pattern in ways that make sense in terms of anything we know about language? Is there any factual support for my intuition that the deaf child might have more trouble with the grammatical items than with the lexical ones? Is that what is reflected in the comment I have heard from one of the participants at this conference, which was that teachers sometimes refer to the performance of deaf children in reading as "noun calling"? If, as I suggested earlier, the phonetic representation normally provides an efficient vehicle for storage and processing in short-term memory, what kinds of alternative representations are available to the deaf child, and how well do they work for the same purpose?

Our outline would be incomplete if we omitted another method of communicating decoded speech to the deaf child, though in this case the decoding is not complete and only some aspects of speech are communicated at all. I refer to "lipreading." The gestures of articulation occur at a stage just prior to the one where much of the most severe encoding occurs. Though the gestures do not thereby escape as many complications as my colleagues and I had once supposed, still they are, by contrast with the acoustic signal, more simply related to the phonetic message. To the extent that the deaf child can see at least some of the articulatory gestures, he has access to a reasonably straightforward representation of the phonetic message. Conceivably, we will want to consider today what we now know or ought to try to learn about lipreading. We may also want to wonder whether there are greater possibilities with that method than have yet been realized.

II. COMMUNICATION BY AN OTHER-THAN-SPOKEN LANGUAGE

Given the problems that the deaf child has with speech, we must consider alternative means of communication. Surely the most obvious and important of these is sign language. Unfortunately for our purposes, and for me, I know almost nothing about sign, so I will not presume to talk about it. All that I can do is to include it in our outline as a subject that you may want to discuss, and, more presumptuously, raise a few questions that my own biases lead me to ask.

Seeing grammar as a kind of interface, I assume in my introductory remarks that it might bear the marks of the several structures, intellect and transmission system, that it connects. On that basis I raised questions about the consequences of using a different transmission system. In sign the transmission system is very different, involving neither the vocal tract nor the ear. I should ask, then, as I did earlier, whether the grammar of sign is different from that of any spoken language, and if so, exactly how different? (Apart from its relevance to our understanding of the deaf, an answer to that question should be of interest to students of language, because it tells us something about how far up the grammatical interface the effects of the transmission system extend.) If the grammar of sign is very different, is there a price to be paid, either in effort or in efficiency, for not being able to use, as the normal speaking person does, those grammatical processes that presumably evolved with language and are now a part of our physiology? You probably know more than I do about research on sign, including, for example, the work of Stokoe (1965) or that of Bellugi and Fischer (1971). If so, I hope you will include sign in our discussion. In any case, it is time for me to stop talking and, instead, to invite the comments from you that are the principal purpose of this meeting.

ACKNOWLEDGMENTS

The preparation of this talk, and much of the research on which it is based, has been supported by a grant to Haskins Laboratories from the National Institute of Child Health and Human Development.

REFERENCES

Bellugi, U., and Fischer, S.: A comparison of sign language and spoken language, Cognition 1:173–200, 1971.

Conrad, R.: Speech and reading, In: Kavanagh, J.F., and Mattingly, I.G., eds.: Language by Ear and by Eye: The Relationship between Speech and Reading, Cambridge: M.I.T. Press, 1972.

Liberman, A.M.: The specialization of the language hemisphere, In: Schmitt, F.O., and Worden, F.G.: The Neurosciences: Third Study Program, Cambridge: M.I.T. Press, 1973.

Liberman, A.M.; Cooper, F.S., Shankweiler, D.P., et al.: Perception of the speech code, Psychol. Rev. 74:431–461, 1967.

Liberman, A.M.; Cooper, F.S., Shankweiler, D.P., et al.: Why are spectrograms hard to read? Amer. Ann. Deaf 113:127–133, 1968.

Liberman, A.M.; Mattingly, I.G., and Turvey, M.T.: Language codes and memory codes, In: Melton, A.W., and Martin, E., eds.: Coding Processes in Human Memory, Washington, D.C.: Halsted Press, 1972.

Lieberman, P.: Primate vocalizations and human linguistic ability, J. Acoust. Soc. Amer. 44:1574–1584, 1968.

Lieberman, P.; Crelin, E.S., and Klatt, D.H.: Phonetic ability and related anatomy of the newborn and adult human, Neanderthal man, and chimpanzee, Amer. Anthrop. 74(3):287–307, 1972.

Lieberman, P.; Klatt, D.H., and Wilson, W.A.: Vocal tract limitations of the vowel repertoires of rhesus monkey and other nonhuman primates, Science 164:1185–1187, 1969.

Mattingly, I.G.: Reading, the linguistic process, and linguistic awareness, In: Kavanagh, J.F., and Mattingly, I.G., eds.: Language by Ear and by Eye: The Relationship between Speech and Reading, Cambridge: M.I.T. Press, 1972a.

Mattingly, I.G.: Speech cues and sign stimuli, Amer. Sci. 60:327–337, 1972b.

Mattingly, I.G., and Liberman, A.M.: The speech code and the physiology of language, In: Leibovic, K.N., ed.: Information Processing in the Nervous System, New York: Springer Verlag, 1969.

Pickett, J.: Speech teaching aids, In: Levitt, H., and Nye, P.W., eds.: Sensory Training Aids for the Hearing Impaired: Proceedings of a Conference, Washington, D.C.: National Academy of Engineering, 1971.

Rand, T.: Dichotic release from masking for speech, In: Status Report on Speech Research, SR-33, Haskins Laboratories, 1973.

Stokoe, W.C.; Casterline, D.C., and Croneberg, C.G.: Dictionary of American Sign Language on Linguistic Principles, Washington, D.C.: Gallaudet College Press, 1965.

Warren, R.M.; Obusek, C.J., Farmer, R.M., et al.: Auditory sequence: Confusion of patterns other than speech or music, Science 164:586–587, 1969.

8

Language Processing and the Hearing-Impaired Child

DISCUSSION: LANGUAGE PROCESSING AND LANGUAGE ACQUISITION IN NORMAL AND HEARING-IMPAIRED CHILDREN

In opening the discussion, Liberman summarized briefly the model of language processing, i.e., of the grammatical interface between the nonlinguistic intellect and the transmission characteristics of vocal tract and ear, implicit in his state-of-the-art report.* Furth then presented a model which dealt with the symbolic behavior of the deaf child coming into an educational program at the age of four years. This is shown in Figure 3.1. He proceeded to discuss this model in relation to Liberman's model of the language behavior of the normal-hearing adult. The first thing that commanded one's attention, Furth said, was that the deaf child is normal at certain of the levels discussed by Liberman. Intellect and long-term memory are intact (Vernon, 1968). Secondly, at the age of about one year, he begins, like hearing children, to develop a capacity for symbol formation (Furth, 1973). In the hearing child, this takes the form of spoken language. In the deaf child, the symbols derive from kinesthetic and visual input. Why then does the deaf child when he comes to school at the age of four years have difficulty in learning language? Furth thought that the answer was obvious. The deaf child has quite happily advanced in the development of his intellect and of his personality without the acoustic input which the hearing child has had. Language has no place in his development and biologically the deaf child now has no need of it. The main reason for his failure to make use of the acoustic or visual cues available to acquire language is that he has no motivation to do so. This is a point of particular interest and it should be considered by those who believe that acoustic input and the spoken language input which follows from it is vital

Model of symbolic behavior of 4-year-old deaf child

*See also Liberman (1970), p. 305.

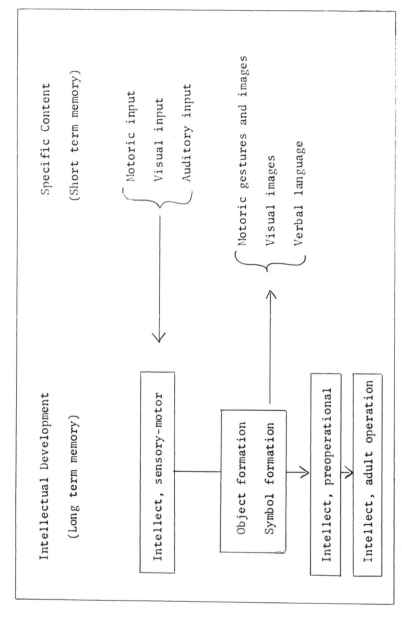

Fig. 3.1 Schematic model of intellectual development in relation to the specific sensory input. Lack of auditory input does not substantially affect the child's basic development.

for the development of certain intellectual and personality variables. Furth proposed that the profoundly deaf child does have all the adequate and necessary mechanisms for cognitive and personality development. He has nonverbal symbols, he has grammar, he does not need verbal language.

It requires a great deal of motivation, Furth indicated, to learn a language in a formal manner. Few Americans learn French or German or any other language in high school well enough to use it. In the same way, it is very difficult to motivate a four-year-old deaf child to learn language. It is hardly sufficient to tell him that ten years from now language will help him in school. It is necessary to realize that this child has a symbol system. He has whatever underlies linguistic competence or he would not be a human being. He organizes his world, he memorizes the world, he stores his experiences, he can recall them. If we continue to think that verbal language is necessary to all of these operations, we shall be on the wrong track. Furth did not wish to convey the idea that language is unimportant to these operations once it is acquired, but what is really important is the underlying capacity which allows us to make use of language. Whatever that is, the deaf child has it and he has it whether or not he has acquired verbal language. It is important to realize this. Otherwise, we may continue to place a burden upon verbal language which it simply does not carry.

Motivation for language learning

Furth believed that Conrad's findings (Conrad, 1970), that profoundly deaf children make visual rather than auditory confusions in reading, provided very weak evidence for a short-term memory problem in deaf children. Conrad tested only memory for phonemes. Obviously, the deaf child will behave differently from the normal-hearing child in memory for phonemes. He is not so familiar with verbal language and with acoustic information. Why would he not have difficulty in remembering its features? In any case, what is the importance of short-term memory for phonemes in real life? When did anyone intentionally try to recall phonemes? Furth felt that it was important to keep in mind that many things remain to be discovered about the deaf child. One thing known about him, however, is that he is a human being, with all the capacities that human beings have. This is a very important point and the one from which we should start. To summarize, he said, the deaf child has long-term memory, short-term memory, general development of intelligence; his difficulties are related only to his lack of motivation for learning linguistic cues which are quite meaningless to him.

Short-term memory

Eisenberg objected that the deaf child did not organize his world in the same way as the hearing child. Furth was looking at the four-year-old child as an end product but she thought it was more meaningful to begin at the beginning, that is, to trace the development of the child who is deprived of auditory input from birth up to four years of age. From a physiological or a psychological standpoint, a child who has input from five sources is not going

Deaf child's organization of his world

to be the same organism as the child who has input from only four sources. She thought it to be a matter of debate as to whether long-term memory is the same in such children. This question is equally applicable to children with other sensory deficits. If one sensory modality is not usable, there is a real question as to whether the affected organism organizes his world in the same way as the intact organism. She would agree with Furth wholeheartedly that the deaf child has a natural way of dealing with his world, but that way is different from normal. Also, she would argue that verbal language is not the only naturally occurring language. What is natural language depends on the nature of the organism; if he does not have auditory input, then certainly his language cannot be a verbal language. At the same time, she did not think Furth could say that the deaf child was like a hearing child, in that the same rules or concepts could be applied in thinking about him.

Intelligence and personality of deaf child as independent of sensory input

Furth replied that no two human beings were the same, and individual differences depended on personal experience. But he would maintain that characteristically, human intelligence is not bound to any particular sensory input. If you make a bird blind, it cannot function as a bird because visual input is an essential part of its life in a way in which no form of sensory input is characteristic of human intelligence. What really counts in human life, on the other hand, is human intelligence and human personality. Eisenberg protested that blind children were different from deaf children.

Bringing deaf child into natural language community

Hirsh felt that it would not be profitable to spend time defining language in the broadest sense and its different manifestations. With some caution he would summarize one of Furth's arguments in the following way: All human beings have the capacity for language. On this point there was no contest. Therefore, it might be more profitable to talk about how the deaf child could be brought into a language community which extends to the majority of human beings, than to indulge in metaphysical debate. We should ask how best to help the deaf child acquire the natural language in which newspapers and books are written, and in which people talk.

Grammatical coding and mental operations

Liberman wished first to reply to Furth. What a person does with his biologically given intellect, he said, might depend in certain interesting and important ways on the extent to which he can gain access to the grammatical system. Grammatical recoding was necessary for efficient communication with others in terms of semantic representation. More than that, the consequences of acquiring the grammatical system might be immense, even for communicating with oneself. Conceivably, much of the information in a prelinguistic or nonlinguistic system could be moved around in different ways and perhaps even more efficiently, once the conversion from one level to another (for example, from the semantic to the syntactic level) is available to the individual. If we assume for the moment, he said, that the levels which the transformational grammarians have talked about are real, then we might think of these mental operations in terms of deep structure. In deep structure, we have strings like [the + man + present tense + play + the + piano], [the + man + present tense + be + young], [the + man + present tense + love + the + girl], [the + girl + present tense + be + blond]. But we do not talk in deep structure strings. Rather, we apply the rules of syntax and come out with a surface structure which says "the young man who plays the piano loves the blond girl." If we ask why we do that, intuitively it seems to be because it is easier to talk in surface structure than in deep structure. We might turn the question around and say, if that is so, why do we have deep structure at all? The answer has to be because the deep structure is closer to the semantic representation.

Liberman wished to suggest that in talking to ourselves, and by this he did not refer to subvocal articulatory activity but to an inner system of communication, it might be a lot easier for certain kinds of tasks at least, to operate closer to the surface structure, that is, at a level in his model somewhere below the intellect and long-term memory. Liberman also thought that it was an open question as to what kinds of nonlinguistic processing could be managed at the level of the intellect without the need for grammatical conversion and what kinds of processing did require the ability to make grammatical conversions. If grammatical processes contributed to the ability to move ideas around in our own heads, then the consequences for the effectiveness of the intellect could be great.

Menyuk thought it worthwhile returning to Conrad's work since it had been mentioned by both Liberman and Furth in presenting their models. One of Conrad's most interesting findings, she thought, was that within the same population of deaf youngsters, aged twelve to fourteen years, one group made articulatory confusions and another visual confusions in their recall of verbal materials. She assumed that this difference was not related to degree of hearing loss nor to educational experience since the children apparently all came from the same school. Both assumptions had been verified by Conrad in print (1972). She felt it was important to clarify this point. If the different types of confusions were related to individual differences in the utilization of information, rather than educational experience, this meant that all deaf children did not respond in the same way to the same training methods. If so, it was important to find out why.

Diverse responses of deaf children to training methods

Miller stated that on the occasion of a recent visit by Conrad to the Central Institute for the Deaf, Miller had taken him to the classrooms of children at grade levels one to eight. The children in these classes were six to fourteen years of age and were using text books appropriate for their respective grade levels. Miller and Conrad had conducted some informal experiments of the kind that Conrad described in his reports. They found that none of the children who had been in oral training programs for more

Short-term memory of children from oral training program

than one or two years responded with visual confusions on a short-term memory task. On items designed to elicit articulatory or so-called auditory confusions, only one child responded atypically, i.e., in a way which Conrad himself would classify as typical of the nonarticulatory error pattern.

Ling stated that Conrad's work was done at Burwood Park, a secondary school for the deaf which derives its population from all over England. It is one of two major secondary schools which deaf students are selected to attend. The other is Mary Hare Grammar School, where deaf students with high verbal abilities are admitted. The students attending Burwood Park have high nonverbal I.Q. scores but have poorer verbal language. Some of them fall just short of the verbal requirements of the grammar school while others fall very far short of these requirements. It is not surprising, therefore, that in a population of this kind drawn from a wide variety of elementary schools for the deaf, there should be some children who encode on an articulatory basis and others who encode visually. Ling suggested that students who used finger spelling would encode digitally and possibly show confusions based on similarity of hand configurations.

Short-term memory of children from nonoral training program

In discussing the deaf child's language acquisition, Boothroyd pointed out the danger of assuming that the child is the only changing element in an unchanging environment. Verbal communication is an active, evolving entity, and the deaf child causes changes in his linguistic environment just as this environment causes changes in him. The development of communication follows a natural law; what does not work will be dropped and what does work will be accepted and survive. The motivation of the child to adapt to the language of a larger community is reduced as the community adapts to his language. This process could be seen even in a purely oral school for the deaf. The language environment in that school and the oral language used between teacher and child are not necessarily the same language as that dealt with in Liberman's model.

Menyuk thought it would be useful to relate what was known about normal language acquisition in the deaf child to both Liberman's model and Furth's model. She believed that the period before words were first acquired was extremely important for language acquisition (Menyuk, 1971), but wished for the present to discuss the one-word stage of development in two of its aspects. One of these aspects was the context in which the word was uttered. The other was the word itself, i.e., what was said in that context (Greenfield et al., in press). When the young child produces holophrastic utterances, these relate to the situational context in which they are produced and also have a certain acoustic shape (Menyuk, 1971). The child produces the morpheme /ba/ and the mother responds to his production in very interesting ways. The utterance has certain phonological and certain prosodic features. It might be produced with a falling intonation or a flat or rising

Holophrastic utterances of normal child

intonation and with different kinds of stress. The mother responds both to the phonological shape of the utterance and to its prosodic features within the context obtaining at the time it is produced. What does that context consist of? It consists of what is present in the environment plus the behavioral repertoire of the mother and of the child, that is, pointing, gesture, and facial expression. All of this is part of communication. The interesting thing about it is that in terms of verbalization the child seems to be selecting both particular phonetic features to use in talking and particular semantic relationships to talk about. Let us take an example, Menyuk said. In the presence of a car, the child may produce the word "daddy." He is not confusing the words "car" and "daddy," he is expressing a relationship between car and daddy, in this case one of possession. He cannot yet express this relationship in a complete utterance ("That's Daddy's car"). The mother understands him and responds appropriately by saying, "Yes, that's Daddy's car." Both in terms of the form and the meaning of the utterance, there are certain very interesting regularities about this stage of development. These have to do with form, which was at the bottom of Liberman's model, and with meaning, which was up at the top. What Menyuk wished to suggest was that unlike the fully competent speaker-listener of the language who has the whole grammatical model available to him, the child is selecting from two categories which are widely separated. It may be that the features of these categories are the most salient ones for the normally developing child.

It is also of importance to consider how mothers talk to their children. They do not talk to their one-year-old infants in the same way as they talk to their ten-year-olds. There is now a body of research which indicates two things; first, mothers of normal-hearing children direct their verbalization toward the infant by means of position, body contact, and eye contact; secondly, the structure of their utterances changes over time (Phillips, 1973). Also, the mothers use reiteration and segmentation in a fascinating way (Snow, 1972). For example, if the mother wishes to direct the child to give her the red truck, she says, "Give me the red truck. The red truck. Red truck." In other words the mother segments this fairly complex sentence for the child. This applies to mothers communicating with normal-hearing children, not to mothers who are trying to devise a special learning situation for the deaf child.

Mother's speech to young children

It is important to think of the implications of selection of form features and meaning features for the training of the deaf child. This question is closely linked with that of motivation, which Furth had identified in presenting his model. All young children are motivated to communicate; in fact, they have a need to communicate whether they are deaf or hearing, and whether their parents are deaf or hearing. It is true that the deaf child with multiple handicaps has to be considered separately. As Eisenberg pointed out, very

Language training of deaf child

little is known about their abilities or needs. However, it was impossible to put too much emphasis on Furth's statement that the deaf child without additional handicaps has the capacity for language learning. The problem is one of finding a channel of communication for him.

Menyuk was uncomfortable with this problem because she did not think deaf children could be divided up into two groups for the purposes of training, those with true residual hearing and those with vibrotactile sensation only. Whatever sensory input was used, the form and meaning features which would have special significance in the development of the young normal child *Exemplars* should be presented with particular salience to the young deaf child. These *from nor-* might be the features which Liberman had referred to as transparent, present *mally devel-* on the surface and not coded in complicated ways, i.e., those semantic, *oping child* phonological, and syntactic features of the language which universally appear at the earliest stages of development (Menyuk, 1972). The normal-hearing child's behavior was giving us exemplars of these features. The best way to learn to recognize them and to understand their use was by studying mother-child interaction in normal-hearing children and in deaf children of deaf and hearing parents.

Stark suggested two additions to Menyuk's model of the one-word stage of language acquisition. One of these was the exaggeration of prosodic features on the part of the mother with respect to stress, fundamental frequency and word duration (Phillips, 1970). The other was the tendency of mothers, at least with infants up to the age of one year, to ask a question and then provide the answer to it (van Uden, 1972).

Menyuk agreed that mothers do exaggerate prosodic features, even to the point where contrastive stress is introduced in sentences which would not be *Chaining in* natural in speech addressed to adults. She added that mothers not only ask *communication* questions of their infants and answer them, but they also ask questions and *of mother* wait for an answer (Bateson, 1971); thus, one can see training in communica-*and child* tion between mother and infant. When infants produce a cooing sound the mother replies, "Yes, is that so?" and waits for the infant to come back with another sound. Chains of up to six exchanges of this sort may be set up, even in the earliest months of life.

Miller commented that the work on language development had now graduated to a new stage. Previously when such statements were made, he knew that they referred to only one or two subjects. Now that more data were available, he thought it was important that the statements should be qualified by details as to number of subjects, social class, and so on. Menyuk said that part of the difficulty in accumulating data had been that of developing techniques for measurement. It was now the case, however, that *Universals of* many young children, perhaps a total of two hundred, had been studied. *language de-* Differences due to both sex and socioeconomic status had been identified.
velopment

However, these factors were not important for the aspects of communication which she had been describing. These appeared to be universal aspects of mother-child exchanges, occurring across five ranges of socioeconomic status (Lewis and Freedle, 1972).

Furth reverted to a point made by Menyuk, namely, that the child abstracts features from the context of a situation and also from the language spoken in his environment. As a result, the normal-hearing child eventually learns the intelligent use of language. Furth pointed out that the deaf child, on the other hand, abstracts features from situational contexts but not from verbal language. The deaf child has no difficulty in understanding a variety of different concepts, such as concepts of possession, for example, that daddy has a car. He has understood this without receiving the impact of any verbal system. Furth found it strange that scientists should presume that the deaf child is likely to be deficient in abstraction of such relevant contextual features, in the absence of any meaningful evidence for this. It seemed to Furth more scientifically valid to assume that the deaf child is not deficient in this way. This assumption does not lead to the conclusion that language is unimportant. But as long as the deaf child is treated as deficient in concept formation, and as long as the teaching of language is considered a means of overcoming this deficiency, his motivation for language learning will be poor. We must accept the deaf child as he is and not explicitly or implicitly convey to him the message that he is deficit or failing.

Boothroyd commented that Menyuk's description of the one-word stage of development would fit the language behavior of school-age deaf children extremely well. Where the context was clear, these children would frequently use one word to convey a whole sentence. He wondered if Menyuk would be prepared to follow her description by accounting for the normal child's progression from the word "daddy" in the context of "car" to the sentence, "That's Daddy's car."

Menyuk replied that first the child acquires the understanding of a relationship, for example, possession. He then expresses that relationship with the aid of contextual features. He has also abstracted some phonologic and prosodic features and uses these. Subsequently, he begins to observe the formal rules of syntax. Order begins to play a role in his utterances so that he may produce "Daddy—car," to convey possession or "There Daddy" to convey location. As to how he moves from one stage to the next, it is possible at present to offer only a speculative answer. At the stage described above, he certainly is selecting two aspects of relationship: a topic or focus and a modifier. He adds to this until eventually he is producing full grammatical sentences. Why does he do this? Perhaps this question gets closer to the nature of the human organism and what is important in that organism. Perhaps the child needs to communicate in a progressively clearer way in an

Development of syntax

expanding environment (Cazden and Brown, in press). New people are introduced into that environment so that the mother and father are no longer the only listeners. All of these aspects play a role. One can describe what happens stage by stage, but the progression is influenced by many variables.

Menyuk then asked if this progression was found in the language development of deaf children. Did deaf children go through a one-word stage "daddy" and then a two-word stage like "daddy—car"?

Use of syntax by deaf children

Boothroyd said that after the one-word stage, the deaf child produces a series of single words, for example, "You. Car. White." On some occasions, Boothroyd had taken the role of the mother and expanded the utterance to "Yes. I have a white car."; but this didn't seem to make any difference to the child's speech patterns or to teach him to produce a proper sentence. Is it too late for these children? he asked. Are their communicative needs so great that their ability to modify language patterns is overwhelmed? Menyuk pointed out that "You. Car. White," was a beautiful example of a sentence in which all the necessary content relationships were expressed without syntax. When this kind of an example of the spoken language of deaf children was mentioned to her, she said, her first question was always, How do you sign it? Very frequently, the utterance appeared to be a translation from a native to a second language.

House said he was struck by the fact that mothers speak in such nonadult ways to their normal-hearing children. As a result, these children learn their native language. He wondered if young children in oral schools for the deaf did not learn to speak unnaturally because they were spoken to in unnatural ways in the classroom.

Interaction of mothers with normal-hearing and hearing-impaired infants

Ling said that he had some data on the ways in which mothers communicated with normal-hearing and with hearing-impaired infants, which he and his wife had collected (Ling and Ling, in press (a), in press (b)). These data were from a study aimed at documenting different aspects of communication between mother and child, i.e., the verbal aspects and the nonverbal aspects of communication that Menyuk had referred to; for example, body contact, facial expression, eye contact, and gesture. The nonverbal aspects are used by the child to arrive at the speaker's meaning (Macnamara, 1972) which he then maps onto the verbal symbols used by the speaker.

Within the one- to thirty-six-month age range, the Lings had examined infants on a cross-sectional basis, aged 1, 3, 5, 7, 9, 11, 14, 18, 24, and 28, 32, and 36 months. There were four infants in each age group and all were from middle class English-speaking families. The data were collected by two

observers who recorded independently what was taking place between the
mother and the child over one-second sample periods. The one-second sample
was recorded every thirty seconds until 100 observations had been obtained.
This kind of approach was very useful, Ling noted, for detecting patterns of
behavior characteristic of children with different communication disorders,
for example, the deaf child and the autistic child.

The types of interaction used by the mothers in communicating with a
normal infant are shown in Figure 3.2. Initially, body posture and action

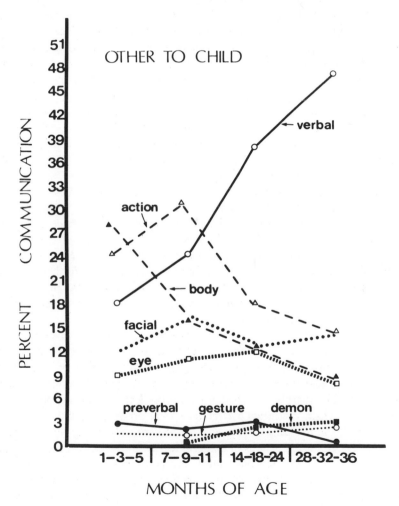

Fig. 3.2 Modes by which mothers communicated with their children at
various age levels.

directed toward the infant had the highest rate of usage. Verbal communication was next in order for the very young infant. It increased sharply for older infants as compared with younger infants throughout the age range studied, while action and bodily posture declined. Pre-verbal sound making, gesture, and demonstration had a low but stable rate of occurrence from three to thirty-six months. Facial expression and eye contact, on the other hand, were major modes of communication throughout this age range. Verbal communication was almost always related to the situation obtaining at the time of its use. In this way, verbal expressions addressed to the child were made meaningful to him. It was also Ling's impression that there was a strong semantic component in the language learning that was taking place. However, Ling did not observe changes in the style of verbal communication addressed to the child over the age range studied. Furthermore, he did not observe the use of expansions of the child's utterances on the part of the mother with anything like the frequency (30%) reported by Brown and Bellugi (1964), nor did he observe many imitations on the part of the child. He felt that this was extremely important in view of the fact that, in the effort to model training of the deaf child upon normal mother-infant interaction, teachers were utilizing expansions of the kind reported by Brown and Bellugi. If expansions were not typical of mothers of normal-hearing children, then this practice might be a bad one to follow with hearing-impaired children. Teachers were also attempting to elicit imitations of expansions. If these procedures were not based on normal development, they were not likely to be successful. This was all the more unfortunate, since it was difficult to check up on what the deaf child was actually receiving. Eventually he might produce an abnormal pattern of language of the kind House had referred to. It would then be very difficult to say whether the pattern was abnormal because the input based upon imitation models or expansion models of language acquisition was abnormal, or from some other cause.

The types of interaction initiated by the infant are shown in Figure 3.3. In the earliest months, eye contact and facial expression were used most often in communication. These types dropped off in frequency of usage. The sound making increased in importance until about eighteen months of age and then declined sharply. Ling had also observed a chaining in mother-infant interaction in which the infant's utterances were pre-verbal and the mother's replies verbal. Action directed toward the mother and bodily posture were relatively less important modes of communication in the earliest months, but their frequency of usage remained fairly constant across the period of study. Verbal communication, gestures, and demonstration did not appear until about nine months of age. Thereafter, verbal communication increased very sharply in frequency of usage, while other modes of communication became relatively less frequent. Gesture and demonstration appeared at the same time

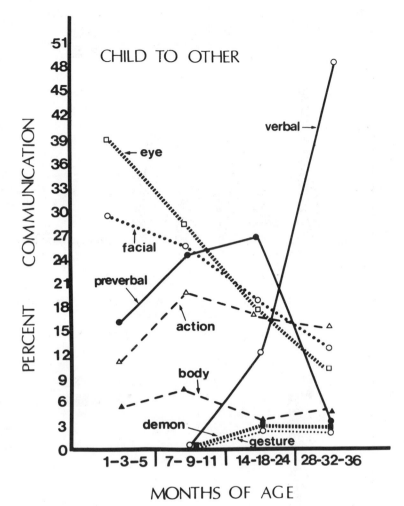

Fig. 3.3 Modes by which children of various ages communicated with their mothers.

as verbal communication, but did not increase in importance in the same way. The latter finding had cast some doubt upon the references in literature to verbal behavior developing out of gesture (McCarthy, 1954).

The Lings had also studied a number of deaf infants on a longitudinal basis. One of these, an infant whose hearing level was between 85 and 90 dB (ISO) across the frequency range 125 Hz to 4 KHz, was first studied at fifteen months of age. At this time, he had not been given amplification or training of any kind. In Figure 3.4, the percentage usage of different modes of com-

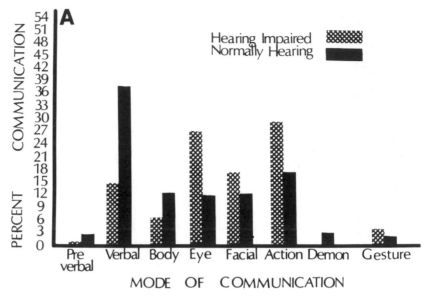

Fig. 3.4(a) Communication of mother with B.J. at 15 months of age with no training. Data shown in relation to norms for same age.

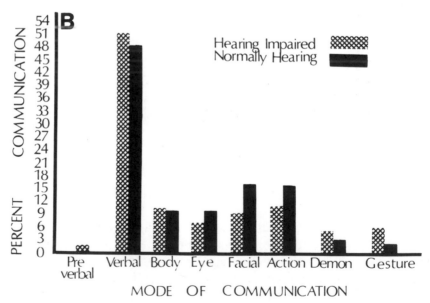

Fig. 3.4(b) Communication of mother with B.J. at 32 months of age after 17 months of training. Data shown in relation to parents of normal children of same age.

munication of the mother with this infant, B.J., is shown (a) pre-training at fifteen months of age and (b) post-training at thirty-two months of age. The data are shown in the form of a histogram. The percent usage of different modes of communication is compared with the usage of those same modes in mothers of normal-hearing infants at fourteen and thirty-two months of age.

The mother of B.J. at fifteen months is using less pre-verbal sound making, verbal interaction, body contact, and demonstration, than the mothers of normal-hearing fourteen-month-old infants. At this time, the mother of B.J. was aware that he was deaf, but she had not fully accepted this fact and would not admit it to anyone else. However, the use she was making of action, facial expression, and gesture might provide a substrate for the development of sign language and finger spelling. This follows from the notion that action and gesture have a nonsymbolic and a symbolic level of function in communication, in the same way as sound making. Similarly, the use of eye contact and facial expression at a nonsymbolic level can lead to communication by means of lipreading. In fact, after a period of seventeen months of training, the mother of B.J. resembles the mothers of normal infants of the same age much more closely than in the pre-training period when B.J. was only fifteen months old.

The modes of communication used by B.J. (a) interacting with his mother pre-training at fifteen months and (b) post-training at thirty-two months, are shown in Figure 3.5. The percent usage of different modes of communication is compared with the usage of those same modes in four normal-hearing infants at fourteen and thirty-two months of age. At fifteen months, B J. is using pre-verbal behavior, that is, babbling, but he is using it less than the normal fourteen-month-olds. Also, he has no verbal behavior at all and uses no demonstration. Action and body posture are used to the same extent as in the case of the normal-hearing infants; and eye contact, gesture, and facial expression, somewhat more.

After seventeen months of training, B.J. was using more pre-verbal communication than before; also some verbal communication had begun to appear. This was in the form of single word utterances such as Boothroyd had described for older deaf children. All other forms of communication were close to normal in percent usage. It is of interest that this child at age three years, six months went to a nursery school for normal-hearing children and subsequently to a grade school for normal-hearing children. He learned to communicate normally by means of spoken language. This illustrates the importance of early interaction for the deaf child's language development and ability to communicate with others.

Gengel (observer) asked for further audiological data on infant B.J. Ling replied that the hearing loss was thought to be related to a sporadic genetic defect although there was no history of hearing loss in the immediate family.

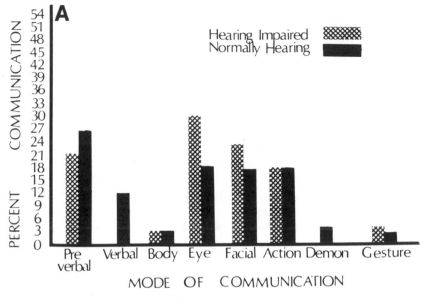

Fig. 3.5(a) Communication of B.J. with mother at 15 months of age with no training. Data shown in relation to normal children of same age.

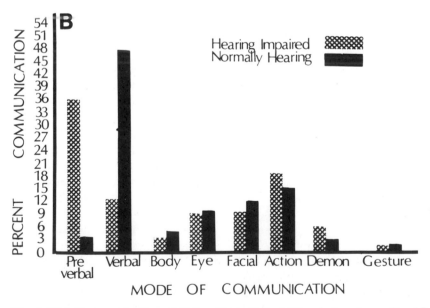

Fig. 3.5(b) Communication of B.J. with mother at 32 months of age after 17 months of training. Data shown in relation to normal children of same age.

The child's loss was bilateral and severe, but it was also a flat loss at about 85 dB (ISO) for all frequencies.

Menyuk said that Ling's report was consistent with the work of other investigators. Expansions were found at somewhat later stages of development in mothers' verbal interactions with their infants, for example, the infants Adam, Eve, and Sarah. Imitations of expansion on the part of the infant were a very infrequent occurrence (Menyuk, 1971).

Ling said that he had been interested in the mother's use of expansions. In his study the mothers of the normal children rarely used them. As for the mothers of the deaf children, when they were asked to use expansion as a teaching technique, they found it extremely difficult to do so.

Menyuk replied that much depended on one's definition of expansion. It is not the case that the mother takes the two-word utterance and expands it to a three-word utterance in an artificial or deliberate manner. She is actually communicating with her child. If expansions are used artificially in any teaching situation, for example, with children in a head-start program, they do not effect improvement (Cazden, 1965). Moreover, it is not the case that a normal child imitates his mother's expansions. What would be even more damaging would be to correct the child and say to him, "No, don't say 'boy running,' that is wrong. Say, 'boy is running.' " This kind of thing is not what happens in the natural situation. Indeed, until the child is ready to produce a structure because it is within his competence, he will frequently repeat the structure in the manner which he originally produced it rather than imitate the mother's form (Klima and Bellugi, 1967).

Verbal expansions and imitations in mother-child interactions

Ling agreed that he had not observed mothers requesting imitations or expansions from their normal children. He regretted to say that this approach, however, might sometimes be used in the teaching of deaf children.

Pollack felt that the quality and amount of mother-infant interaction was as important as its verbal and nonverbal forms. He commented that investigators in Israel (Kahneman, personal communication) had tried to account for the difference in verbal skills between children of European or of African or Asiatic origin. Child psychologists examining these families had reported that the greatest difference between them was in these aspects of mother-infant interaction at an early age. Investigators in the United States had also reported on such differences among cultural groups.

REFERENCES

Bateson, M.C.: The interpersonal context of infant vocalization, Quarterly Progress Report, No. 100, Research Laboratory of Electronics, M.I.T., 1971.

Brown, R., and Bellugi, U.: Three processes in the child's acquisition of syntax, In: Lenneberg, E.H., ed.: New Directions in the Study of Language, Cambridge: M.I.T. Press, 1964.

Cazden, C.B.: Environmental assistance to the child's acquisition of grammar, Doctoral dissertation, Harvard University, 1965.

Cazden, C.B., and Brown, R.: The early development of the mother tongue, In: Lenneberg, E.H., and Lenneberg, E., eds.: Foundations of Language Development: A Multidisciplinary Approach, UNESCO (In press).

Conrad, R.: Short-term memory processes in the deaf, Brit. J. Psychol. 61:179–195, 1970.

Conrad, R.: Speech and reading, In: Kavanagh, J.F., and Mattingly, I.G., eds.: Language by Ear and by Eye: The Relationship between Speech and Reading, Cambridge: M.I.T. Press, 1972.

Furth, H.G.: Deafness and Learning: A Psychosocial Approach, Belmont: Wadsworth, 1973.

Greenfield, P.M.; Smith, J.H., and Laufer, B.: Communication and the Beginnings of Language, New York: Academic Press (In press).

Klima, E.S., and Bellugi, U.: Syntactic regularities in the speech of children, In: Lyons, J., and Wales, R.J., eds.: Psycholinguistic Papers, Chicago: Aldine, 1967.

Lewis, M., and Freedle, R.: Mother-Infant Dyad: The Cradle of Meaning, Princeton: The Educational Testing Service, 1972.

Liberman, A.M.: The grammars of speech and language, Cognitive Psychol. 1:301–323, 1970.

Ling, A.H., and Ling, D.: Communication development of normal and hearing-impaired infants and their mothers, In: Proceedings of the Conference of Effects of Blindness and Other Impairments on Early Development, Ann Arbor: American Foundation for the Blind (In press, a).

Ling, D., and Ling, A.H.: Communication development in the first three years of life, J. Speech Hearing Res. (In press, b).

Macnamara, J.: Cognitive basis of language learning in infants, Psychol. Rev. 79:1–13, 1972.

McCarthy, D.: Language development in children, In: Carmichael, L., ed.: Manual of Child Psychology, 2d. edition, New York: Wiley, 1954.

Menyuk, P.: The Acquisition and Development of Language, Englewood Cliffs: Prentice-Hall, 1971.

Menyuk, P.: Aspects of language acquisition and implications for later language development, Eng. Austrl. 19:3–23, Feb., 1972.

Phillips, J.R.: Formal characteristics of speech which mothers address to their young children, Doctoral dissertation, The Johns Hopkins University, 1970.

Phillips, J.R.: Syntax and vocabulary of mother's speech to young children: Age and sex comparisons, Child Develop. 44(1):182–185, 1973.

Snow, C.E.: Mother's speech to children learning language, Child Develop. 43:549–565, 1973.

van Uden, A.M.J.: The reflection method of language acquisition, Paper presented to The Alexander Graham Bell Association for the Deaf, Washington, D.C., May 15, 1972.

Vernon, M.: Fifty years of research on the intelligence of deaf and hard-of-hearing children: A review of literature and discussion of implications, J. Rehab. Deaf 1(4):1–12, 1968.

9

Language Processing

DISCUSSION: COMMUNICATION AND THE HEARING-IMPAIRED CHILD

In discussion, the participants concentrated upon communication of a standard, spoken language. This was chiefly because they knew more about spoken language than other forms of language, and were thus able to contribute most to questions concerning its acquisition by deaf children. At one point Gengel (observer) remarked that no one had as yet discussed Liberman's suggestion that some other system than natural language should be used in training profoundly deaf children. Lipreading had received much attention, but the issue of sign language to which Liberman had referred had not been discussed. Gengel thought it was important that someone should talk about that visual mode of transmission which, at least according to its advocates, was unambiguous. *Sign language*

None of the participants felt himself to be sufficiently well-informed about sign language to accept Gengel's suggestion. Ling mentioned the fact that until recently, the lexicon of sign language amounted to only 2500 words and that it must lack the range in subtlety of a natural language such as English on that account (Hoemann, 1972). This restriction did not apply to use of the visual-kinesthetic system of finger spelling. Finger spelling combined with other forms of language training had been advocated by a number of authorities (British Department of Education and Science Report, 1968). One of the programs of this kind used the so-called Rochester Method. *Finger spelling*

Ling had conducted an experiment designed to test this approach specifically. He wished to find out if lipreading plus residual hearing and finger spelling would supplement one another in speech reception. It was his belief that they would not do so unless finger-spelled information could be perceived in terms of larger units or chunks such as syllables or words, as well as in terms of individual letters, just as speech may be perceived in terms of syllables and words as well as phonemes.

The subjects of this experiment were nine children, aged thirteen to eighteen years, whose average hearing loss was in excess of 70 dB (ISO). Most had no measurable hearing for frequencies above 1 KHz. The subjects were rated by their teachers as being equally well able to lip-read and finger spell. They were of at least normal intelligence and had no handicaps other than hearing loss. Verbal materials at three levels of complexity, namely syllables, words, and phrases, were presented to these children (1) by means of finger spelling alone, (2) by means of lipreading alone, and (3) by means of finger spelling and lipreading. All children wore their hearing aids under each condition. It was found that as the speaker accompanied the production of all materials with finger spelling, the rhythm of his speech tended to be abnormal. All stimuli were spoken at three different rates: fast, normal, and slow. The speaker was video-taped and a diagonal mask was placed over the image of his hand on the T.V. monitor in the lipreading only condition, and over his face in the finger spelling only condition. No mask was used in the lipreading plus finger spelling condition.

The lipreading scores of the "Rochester" group were poorer than expected. The materials were therefore presented under condition 2 to a more

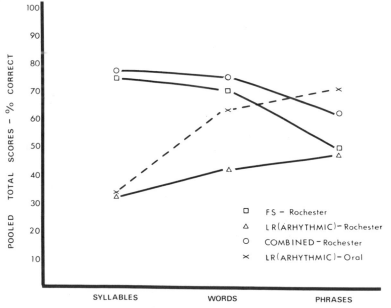

Fig. 3.6 Percent correct responses to words, syllables and phrases by hearing-impaired children trained with the Rochester method and tested with finger spelling (FS) alone, lipreading (LR) alone, and with the two modes combined. Data obtained for lipreading from a group of children trained exclusively by oral means are also presented.

severely hearing-impaired group of children matched in age and intelligence, but who had been trained exclusively by the oral method. The results are shown in Figure 3.6. The data are pooled over the three rates of presentation. It is clear that syllables are perceived best when finger spelling is used, that is, in the finger spelling only and in the combined conditions. Performance under the finger spelling only condition is poorer for words than for syllables and better for phrases than for words. Also, lipreading, even of the arhythmically spoken phrases, was more successfully achieved by those whose communication training had been exclusively oral.

Although not shown in Figure 3.6, the lipreading of words and phrases was better at faster than at slower rates of presentation, while with finger spelling the reverse was the case.

Transmission of the undecoded speech signal

Discussion of conventional amplification is reported on page 107. The presentation of synthetic speech to deaf subjects has not been tried out except in pilot work (Pickett, personal communication). However, other types of processing of the undecoded signal have been used.

Presenting processed acoustic signals to the ear

Pickett stated that his colleague, Ellen Danaher (Danaher, Osberger, and Pickett, in press), had been investigating the effects of dichotic presentation of the first and of the second formant of vowels to hearing-impaired listeners. The aim of the study was to find out (1) if dichotic presentation of speech would reduce the amount of upward spread of masking from F1 to F2, and (2) if this improved discrimination. The subjects of this experiment were eighteen college-age adults who had bilateral moderate to severe sensorineural losses of long standing. Their losses are described in Figure 3.7.

As in previous experiments, the subjects were asked to perform an oddity task, that is, they were to select the one synthetic vowel out of three which has an F2 transition at its beginning. Their thresholds for this discrimination were defined as the amount of transition in hertz, which had to be present at the beginning of F2 before the transition could be detected.

Subjects of the experiment listened under three conditions. One was a monotic condition, where the subject listened with F1 and F2 both in the preferred ear. The second condition was a dichotic one, in which F2 was presented to the preferred ear and F1 to the opposite ear. In the third condition, the subjects listened to F2 alone in the preferred ear. The subjects

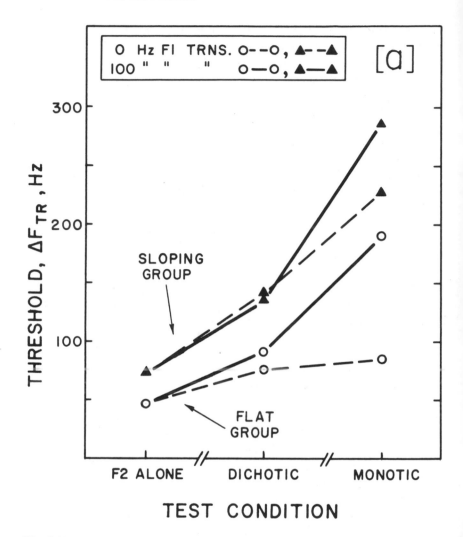

Fig. 3.7 Mean discrimination threshold for a transition in F2 depending on whether F1 and F2 are presented in the same ear (MONOTIC) or in opposite ears (DICHOTIC), the absence of F1 (F2 ALONE), contour of hearing, and the presence or absence of a transition in F1. For more detail, see legend of Figure 2.9. Data of E.M. Danaher.

set their listening levels at their most comfortable level for the monotic condition, that is, where F1 and F2 were presented in the preferred ear, at the beginning of the experiment. The levels were not subsequently changed.

In some of these conditions, F1 had a transition while in others it had none. The order of the test conditions was randomized. The data are summarized in Figure 3.7. As in the studies Pickett had reported earlier (pps. 99–102), when F2 was presented in isolation, the discrimination threshold for the F2 transition was normal (see left side of Figure 3.7). The introduction of F1 produced a marked masking effect in the monotic condition, especially when an F1 transition was present (see right side of Figure 3.7). Subjects with flat losses again did better than subjects with sloping losses under all conditions. In the dichotic condition, both groups of subjects showed a better performance than under the monotic condition. There was no evidence of an F1 transition masking effect under the dichotic condition; the presence or absence of an F1 transition had little effect on F2 discrimination. However, the dichotic discrimination was poorer than that for the F2-alone condition. This suggests that F1 can produce a type of central masking.

Pickett felt that this study might have implications for the habilitation of the hearing-impaired individual. The data suggest that high- and low-pass hearing aids, placed on opposite ears, might be of benefit to some of these individuals. However, in some cases, a mismatch due to unequal amounts of distortion in the two ears or to long-term hearing aid usage in one ear only, might give rise to poor integration of dichotically presented high- and low-frequency components.

Levitt mentioned that he had followed a suggestion from Pollack (1959) and used a comb filter to extract narrow (third octave) bands from the speech signal. One set of frequency bands was presented to the right ear and the set of intervening bands to the left ear. This was intended to reduce the peripheral masking between adjacent frequency bands. An alternate approach would be to use only two bands, a low-frequency band in one ear and a high-frequency band in the other, so as to reduce masking of high frequencies by low frequencies. The higher frequency bands might also be pre-emphasized. The device, he said, is a feasible one to build and to wear. He had tried it out in a preliminary way with six deaf children. A small but fairly significant improvement in speech reception was found when the children wore the comb filter type hearing aid as compared with their reception scores when wearing a conventional aid. Although he had not followed up on this idea, two of his graduates (Barbara Franklin and Ruth Rosenthal) were pursuing this line of research and had found improvements with the two-band system (Franklin, 1969; Rosenthal et al., 1972).

Liberman thought that in such a device the width of the filter bands would be important. Because it was not certain what kinds of masking effects were produced in the unfiltered signal, it was difficult to decide upon filter width, but a very narrow comb might not reduce the maskings significantly. The setting of the filters would be important from another point of view. It is quite possible that with a given setting, second formants might be flipping

Selection of filter widths

back and forth between ears and although he knew of no research in the area, he thought that the constant switching might be confusing to the listener. Perhaps the only course would be to set the filter so that the first formant was always in one ear and the rest of the signal in the other.

Ling added further observations with respect to dichotic listening in hearing-impaired children. He described a study carried out by his wife (A.H. Ling, 1971) in which digits were presented both monotically and dichotically to nineteen hearing-impaired and nineteen normal-hearing children. The mean age for both groups was about ten years, one month. The hearing losses of the impaired group were moderate to profound; the difference in average hearing level between ears did not exceed 5 dB.

When sequences of the digits were presented monotically, the normal-hearing children obtained higher scores for recalling them than the hearing-impaired children. However, neither group had a higher score for the right than for the left ear under this condition. When the digits were presented dichotically, the normal-hearing children again had a higher recall score than the hearing-impaired children. They also showed a small but reliable superiority for right ear scores as would be expected (Kimura, 1963). The hearing-impaired children, on the other hand, showed a nonsignificant trend toward right ear superiority. As shown in Figure 3.8, there was greater variability of response among the hearing-impaired children and in some cases, individuals showed large right or left ear advantages. In addition, they frequently reported the digits heard in one ear only. Some subjects responded to the left or the right ear only while others responded to either ear on an apparently random basis. Their poor performance appeared to be due to their inability to process the simultaneously presented members of a dichotic pair. Ling had concluded that hearing-impaired children may have a dominant ear and may suppress sounds arriving at the other ear rather than integrate them as normal listeners do. The suppression effect may have to be taken into account in prescribing hearing aids, particularly aids utilizing comb filters described above.

Stark commented that similar findings with respect to dichotic listening had been reported for normal-hearing children of less than five years (Yeni-Komshian, personal communication). Thus, the suppression effect reported by Ling might reflect some kind of immaturity with respect to language skills.

Presenting processed acoustic signals to a nonauditory modality

Because of lack of information about sensory systems and sensory deficits, we do not at present know whether it is better to present speech information to the visual or to the tactile sense in nonauditory prostheses.

In addition, we do not know what analysis systems and forms of display are likely to be most efficacious. Those at present available are (1) the vocoder, a device which performs a spectral analysis by means of a set of filters and presents the output of the filters to the skin or the eye (Pickett, 1971; Stark, Cullen, and Chase, 1968), (2) a feature extractor, a device which makes decisions about the presence or absence of features such as nasality, plosion, and frication, and presents this to the tactile or the visual sense (Risberg, 1968), or (3) a traveling wave display which presents the traveling wave like that von Bekesy proposed in his model for the basilar membrane of the cochlea (Keidel, 1968). The traveling wave display and the vocoder are capable of presenting a great deal of information, but it is not known whether the deaf child can extract important features from this information when it is presented to the eye or to the skin.

Analysis systems in sensory aids

Sherrick felt that there were certain merits to tactile devices in the form of cochlear analogs such as those developed by Keidel in Germany. Such devices have become more sophisticated as knowledge of the mechanisms of hearing have advanced. Also, the tradition of research in tactile speech-mediating devices is much older in Germany than in the United States. Lindner (1937), for example, who worked in Leipzig early in the 20th century, produced a tactile device which he named Ferntaster, i.e., Teletactor, the name chosen by Gault for his device. Keidel's device, deriving from von Bekesy's model of the basilar membrane, though the most recent and the most complexly organized, is not necessarily the most sophisticated device of its kind. The problems that Keidel has encountered with frequency transposition in real time are not insurmountable. His device, moreover, has the

Tactile aids

Right-Minus-Left-Ear Scores	Number of Subjects	
	Normal-Hearing	Hearing-Impaired
30 to 39	0	4
20 to 29	0	1
10 to 19	5	5
1 to 9	6	4
0	4	1
−1 to −9	4	1
−10 to −19	0	0
−20 to −29	0	1
−30 to −39	0	2

Fig. 3.8 Frequency distribution of dichotic difference scores for normal-hearing and for hearing-impaired subjects. From Ling, 1971.

advantage that the traveling wave yields a delay in microtime in the development of patterns of the skin. The delay may allow for elaboration within the time occupied by the speech signal, an elaboration which is not present in a traveling wave that has infinite velocity. The latter is a property of vocoder-like devices, where patterns develop simultaneously on all parts of the skin.

Traveling wave display

Pickett expressed an interest in Keidel's approach and asked if the time delay cues available in his model generate themselves automatically, that is, if they are due to the travel time through the model which would be different for different frequencies. Sherrick replied that the delay times were of the order of 1 or 2 msec. A spatiotemporal display of frequencies at various amplitudes was developed rapidly on the skin. This display would be consistent for a given speech sound each time it was repeated. The patterns are related to lateralization time, which gives rise to peaking at one point, that is, stress or emphasis at a certain frequency on the membrane and a depression or inhibition at another.

Lateralization of mechanical signals on skin

Pickett asked him if by referring to lateralization he meant that the input to the skin was in some sense binaural; Sherrick explained that a single portion of skin will act like a binaural ear. Von Bekesy (1967) showed that the phenomenon of lateralization can take place over a five centimeter stretch of skin; that is, if you present transient stimuli separately to two points of the skin separated by five centimeters and balance them for perceived amplitude or loudness, then simultaneous presentation of these stimuli will give rise to perception of a phantom stimulus, localized between these two points. Also, as you offset time or intensity, a slow movement between the two points will be perceived. This is a relatively delicate experiment to perform, but then, so is lateralization for hearing.

Sherrick went on to explain that this phenomenon is of a much lesser degree of magnitude than the phi phenomenon (Sherrick and Rogers, 1966) which takes longer to evolve and complete itself. What is really interesting about lateralization of the skin is that no matter how far apart the two points on the skin to be stimulated may be, the lateralization phenomenon occupies only 1 msec, a time span which is comparable with that found for the ear. On the other hand, the frequency transitions of speech which signal the succession of one phoneme upon another, occur in macrotime. Any frequency shift will be perceived as patterns developing simultaneously on all parts of the skin.

Visual vs. tactile displays

Denes said he was not clear what basic principle of data or information processing was inherent in the von Bekesy model which would facilitate speech learning. There were, after all, any number of electronic devices which analyze the speech wave and display variation of formant structure or of pitch as a function of time. None of these had aided speech learning. It seemed as if the speech waveform was translatable as language only if it came through the ear. There is great similarity in information content between, on the one hand, an acoustic signal as processed by a vocoder and presented to the ear (which is perfectly understandable) and, on the other hand, a visible speech record (which is difficult to read). We do not know how to read or to learn to read visible speech so why should we experiment with the von Bekesy model? What does it offer that the plethora of devices available today that give visual or tactile transforms of the acoustic speech signal do not already offer? Pickett replied that it seemed to offer a way of making things salient to the skin which are salient to the ear. Denes asked why it should be easier to learn speech through the skin than through the eye. Pickett said perhaps it was because the skin behaves more like the ear than the eye; however, he would like to know how much more like the ear it is. A lot depended on the answer to that question. Denes still felt that the eye was a better substitute for the ear than the skin. For example, we can learn to read the written word in a manageable period of time.

Hirsh pointed out that in a spectrogram, time is converted to a spatial display. It is not at all clear that a spatial display presented to the eye is the equivalent of temporal transitions as they are presented to the ear. The skin when it handles complicated vibratory patterns responds in a time-associated sensory modality. In this sense, it is more like the ear. The detection of the transition in speech and movements across the skin occurs as Sherrick had pointed out, in macrotime. For example, transition rates must be perceived as different for plosives and for glides; but such events occupy 10 to 50 or 60 msec. The installation of a time delay in the order of one millisecond in a traveling wave model is not going to aid that kind of perception. Plosives and glides can be equally well discriminated from a vocoder array of spectrum channel outputs on the skin even although all arrive simultaneously. The time differences Sherrick had discussed played no significant role in the times that are involved in perception of transitions in speech.

Rates of speech transitions

In reply to Denes' comments on the difficulty of reading visual patterns of speech, Liberman said that there were at least two reasons for the difficulty in reading spectrograms. The first had to do with the fact that the spectrographic signal is a very poor one. The acoustic energy is not concentrated where the important linguistic information is, but is smeared over the spectrum. Some of the most important linguistic information is to be found in the rapidly changing formant transitions which often have an excursion of as much as 500 or 600 Hz in 40 msec and those are physically indeterminate in the spectrogram. So, the acoustic signal has to be cleaned up before it can be perceived. From this point of view, the skin might produce a more efficient input channel than the eye.

Visual processing of acoustic speech signal

But the second source of difficulty should apply equally to the skin and eye. That difficulty has to do with the fact that many important aspects of the phonetic message are complexly encoded in the acoustic signal. Normally the decoding is done by a processor that accepts an auditory input. When the acoustic signal does not go through the normal auditory channel, it cannot be dealt with by the appropriate processor. In that case we do the best we can by using a deliberate, iterative guessing operation. It might take fifteen minutes to decode a phrase in that fashion; it might take fifteen years.

Decoding acoustic speech signal

Pickett suggested as an example of this kind of problem the entirely different appearance of the second formant transition for /ga/ and for /gu/ in the spectrogram. In spite of this, the acoustic signal elicits the perception of the same initial consonant /g/ for both signals. Liberman said that this was perfectly true. If the second formant transitions are abstracted from the speech context in the case of /ga/ and of /gu/, and presented to the ear, they do, indeed, sound quite different just as they look different in a spectrogram. But in the appropriate speech pattern, they produce, in perception, the same phonetic segment. This is presumably a result of the operation of the speech decoding apparatus all of us have in our heads. We have no idea of how this decoder works, but from the point of view of designing sensory aids for the deaf the practical question is whether or not it can in fact be hooked up to any sensory modality other than hearing. After twenty-five years of trying to read spectrograms, Liberman thought that it could not. The difficulty encountered in this task did not have to do primarily with cleaning up the signal and obtaining the important information. It had to do with decoding the signal so as to recover the phonetic information.

Visual decoding of acoustic speech input vs. lipreading

Hirsh agreed that speech was difficult to process visually if that statement were restricted to the acoustics of speech, the sounds already transmitted. The visual display of pre-phonetic categories, that is, of the articulatory gestures about which Liberman himself had written so elegantly, might be much easier to process. Speech reading was an excellent example of this kind of processing. Some individuals find speech highly intelligible and achieve high rates of transmission simply from looking at the talker, that is, so long as they are not required to process speech on a phoneme by phoneme basis. Comprehension in this case must be achieved by entirely different processes. Ling expressed the opinion that sensory aids should supplement lipreading. For this purpose, they should operate in real time. In addition, he felt that visual display devices detract from lipreading rather than supplementing it since the deaf individual cannot pay attention to both at once. For this reason, Ling had turned his attention to developing a tactile aid. Theoretically, such an aid should be capable of supplementing both hearing and lipreading.

Sensory aids as supplementing lipreading

Perception of frication in speech with aid of a tactile device

Ling felt that the most promising approach with tactile aids was one of feature extraction. He described an experiment carried out by one of his students (Sofin, 1972) in which this approach was tried.

The tactile aid she used presented information to the skin about the presence or absence of frication. She presented sets of four French words to deaf students from a French language background. These subjects, aged nine to thirteen years, had an average hearing loss of 81 dB for the frequencies 125 Hz to 1 KHz. None had measurable hearing over 2 KHz. In each set of words, two words contained frication and two did not. The results are shown in Figure 3.9. The responses of the children were analyzed in terms of the number of errors in recognition. The mean number of errors is shown before and after a period of training, (1) when the children were wearing the tactile aid (unbroken line), and (2) when they were not (dashed line). The number of errors made within the class of fricatives did not decline as a result of training. Moreover, it did not differ for the condition where the child wore the aid and the condition where he did not. The number of errors in discriminating fricatives vs. nonfricatives, on the other hand, declined significantly with training; in addition, these errors were fewer, both before and after training, when the child was wearing the aid than when he was not.

Miller felt that it was important to deal with the optimism/pessimism issue with respect to nonauditory aids which previous speakers had raised. In order to put this in perspective, he asked a very simple question, namely, Does a profoundly deaf child who has essentially no usable hearing have the sensory capability to learn language? He felt that the answer was, some deaf children do. There is considerable evidence that this is possible in the achievement record of alumni of oral education programs (Quigley et al., 1968). Denes had said that the visual system could not be used in acquiring speech, but clearly, he had not meant to extend this statement to lipreading. Some deaf children learn to lip-read with astonishing accuracy. Their skill is such that everyone wishes to check that they do not have some residual hearing after all, and they do not. They receive only time-intensity patterns from the ear. They may not learn language as fast nor as well as one would like, but they have the sensory capability for doing so ultimately.

Optimism vs. pessimism re: sensory aids

The experimental evidence thus far, Miller said, shows that nonauditory aids improve the speech recognition of deaf children, perhaps not by very much, but consistently and reliably (Erber, 1972; Kringleboten, 1965, 1968; Pickett, 1963; Pickett and Pickett, 1963). Ling had offered evidence for this as had Erber; thus, we do have to temper the super-optimism of the engineer

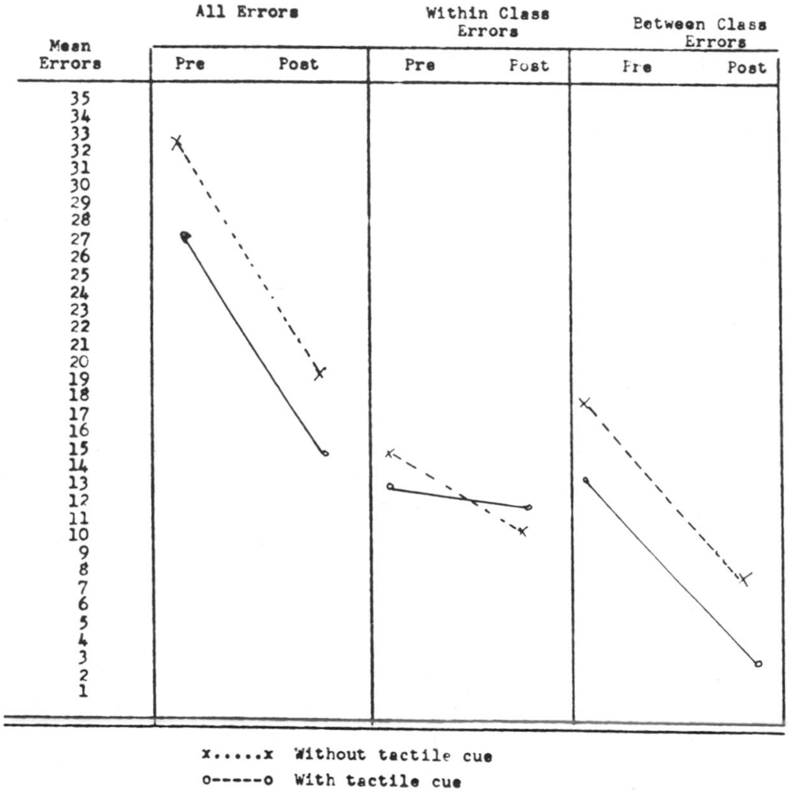

Fig. 3.9 Mean errors for the pre- and post-tests with and without tactile cue.

who has just discovered the speech spectrogram and wants to know why the deaf are being deprived of this aid to speech acquisition. The spectrogram is hard to use and Denes and Liberman provide a valuable service in making this clear. But, there is room for modest optimism. We should remember President Lincoln's experience with his generals: McLellan, the cultured and elegant orator who left every battlefield saying "We lost," and Grant, who upon similar outcome, said "We won." Miller recommended Grant's attitude to the participants as encouragement for further work on the problem.

Transmission of the decoded signal

Hirsh reverted attention to the feasibility of displaying speech information to the deaf child at a level somewhere above the raw acoustic signal in Liberman's model. He asked whether paraphrase was involved in going from the raw acoustic signal to phonemic categories.

Liberman replied that in principle the process was similar, but that essentially all of what we normally think of as paraphrasing occurs in moving from the phonetic level upward. Hirsh explained that he was really interested in the statement that some of the levels in the model were suitable for transmission and others for memory and processing. That implied, if taken literally, that forms which were suitable for memory and processing but not for transmission were not the best candidates for display to the deaf child. How then, would phonemic categories fare if they were used to convey speech information to the deaf child instead of the raw acoustic signal? Liberman replied that it was not entirely clear where transmission left off and storage began. The extremes could be identified but the function of way stations might be less clear. For example, a feature analysis at the level of semantic representation might involve thousands or even millions of features, but at the phonetic level, there are only about eighteen features and only twice that many phonemic categories. Thus, the phonetic message is much more nearly appropriate than the semantic level for transmission through the vocal tract and the ear. But the phonetic message is not itself transmitted. It is a vehicle for storage, if only of the short-term variety. How successful we will be when we present these phonemic categories directly to the deaf child cannot be predicted a priori. Experience in teaching deaf children to read a phonemic transcription suggests that we won't do very well.

Transmission vs. storage

Hirsh then asked why articulatory information in the form of lipreading should be easier to use than the acoustic signal. In the case of lipreading, the signal is also in a raw state. Liberman thought that the information in lipreading might, in fact, be partially decoded and thus closer to the phonetic level than the acoustic signals were, although this was arguable. Also, the success of displaying articulatory information might depend on just what information was selected for display. For example, display of cross-sectional vocal tract shapes might yield different results from lipreading with respect to the use of the phonetic level.

Display of articulatory information

Stark mentioned a tentative observation which still remained to be tested. She had given speech training to a group of profoundly deaf children aged eight to eleven years from oral training programs. Visual displays of the raw acoustic signal were used as an adjunct in this training. Prior to training, the children had marked difficulty with speech intelligibility. In the course of training the children learned to produce sounds and combinations of sounds which could be recognized as words by the people with whom they were most familiar. It had been reported by the parents and teachers that these same children showed a small but quite noticeable and unexpected improvement in reading skills at this time.

Facilitation of reading skills by means of speech acquisition

House stated that he had always felt that the best output for an automatic speech recognition system would be a typescript in English. Was it, then, worthwhile thinking about moving in the opposite direction? In other words, was there any evidence at hand that learning how to read would facilitate speech acquisition or make it easier for the child to communicate? What was the evidence that deaf children can actually be taught to read even when they cannot speak? Stark replied that according to Stuckless and Birch (1966) and Vernon and Koh (1971) deaf children who have acquired manual communication skills from their deaf parents learn to read rather better than deaf children who have no manual communication skills, and who, in addition, have not succeeded in acquiring speech or lipreading skills. However, the deaf children of deaf parents are still below normal in their reading achievement. House asked if this did not suggest that it would be worthwhile to develop prostheses which skipped the acoustic-articulatory level and instead, displayed information at the phonetic level in the form of a typescript.

Facilitation of speech by acquisition of reading

Stark objected that in speech training, it would be difficult to use a typescript display as feedback. Either the subject would give a correct response and see a typed version of what he had said; or an incorrect response in which case he would see nothing or some incoherent pattern. What he needed was a visual display which showed how far off target his production was. This could not be done with graphemes.

House asked, leaving the speech production aside for the moment, what would be the effect of an ideal system in which the hearing person spoke and/or typed and the typescript was registered on a display at the other end; and the deaf person who could not speak typed a reply which was then produced as speech? Would such a device aid language development or speech training in a school for the deaf? Stark said she thought this might be valuable if the deaf child received an auditory signal simultaneously with the typescript display.

Menyuk felt that the discussion was dealing in gross oversimplification. At this time, no one could answer the questions such as House had raised, i.e., whether one has to learn to speak before learning to read or whether learning to read would aid the acquisition of speech. Children, she said, use very different strategies and styles in learning to read (Clay and Imlach, 1971). The role of subvocal verbalization in reading, for example, was an important one, as the work of Conrad (1972) had shown. Measurements of eye scan and of how much chunking is being used in reading would have to be considered.

Availability of technology

Denes said that if there was real evidence that use of a visual display device would aid language acquisition, it would not be difficult to implement the system. The teacher would not have to speak into the device, but would merely type a message. The deaf child would receive it visually and could type his answer. If it was important for him to hear the exchange, it could be presented to him in the form of synthetic speech; also the acoustic representation of the synthetic speech could be presented to him visually.

Erber pointed out that a typewriter wasn't necessary for written communication, but Denes answered that the system he had described offered an experimental approach to the question raised about speech and reading which was within our present technology. Also, it would be much speedier than paper and pencil.

Levitt thought it was of value to consider all those systems where rates of transfer of speech information were close to that of normal speech. The data on spectrum analysers and vocoders of various types as communication aids showed that their output displays effect small improvements in recognition of syllables or of monosyllabic words, say as much as from 50% to 70%; but none of these systems had yet shown substantial improvements when used with continuous running speech. Similarly, methods of coding relying on other modalities (e.g., Morse Code or typed messages) are too slow to be a practical substitute for continuous speech. There are, however, a few exceptions where the rate of information transmission is comparable to that of typical, conversational speech. These include:

Systems whose transmission rates are close to those of normal speech

1. Touch Shorthand, where speech information is transmitted by means of a small keyboard and the design of which has taken into consideration some important characteristics of speech (Levitt, 1973);

2. Speech Reading, where a very good lip-reader can read most of a message without auditory input; and

3. Reading by means of tactual coding, such as braille or with the aid of the Optacon (Taenzer, 1971). These techniques should be studied to determine the essential considerations that will allow for the development of rapid, practical communication systems for the deaf.

It occurred to House that the comparison between the nonspeech systems such as braille or touch shorthand and speech itself were not very good ones. In trying to read braille faster or to write shorthand faster, one devises short forms. Short form derivation and shorthand braille are ad hoc operations. A different process takes place in rapid reading. A teacher diverts the student from one way of coding to another. However, this change of coding is not really understood. Also, recoding in the processing of speech appears to be a natural procedure, but we cannot describe it or identify it. It does not really have a recognizable analog in other sensory modalities.

Use of short forms

Sherrick spoke further of the use of braille as paired-associate learning where the individual is taught to identify a tactile pattern as a letter of the alphabet, or a word. This is one level of compatibility which can be achieved by arbitrary symbols. There are many different versions of embossed print besides braille, for example, Early Dalton, Moon type, New York Point, and Boston Line (Zahl, 1950). All of these tactile signal systems are perfectly

Perception of larger units in nonspeech systems

readable. The next question is, can the reader now fuse or chunk letters into larger units, that is, into syllables or words? Is this always due to the use of shorthand symbols or does the reader develop the ability to do this for himself? If so, is there a period in the life of the organism beyond which it is difficult for him to learn this chunking?

House returned to the speech versus reading issue. This, he said, could be settled without the inclusion of a talking machine. That is, reading could be separated from the other communication skills and studied by means of a laboratory experiment in which all communication was effected by a type-writer. The effect, if any, upon speech, could be documented separately.

Miller said that since all that was really necessary for this experiment was paper and pencil, he felt sure that it had been run by someone in history of the education of the deaf. He would like to know what results were obtained. Silverman commented that this form of communication predominated in the teaching in many schools for the deaf. That is, the teacher wrote on the blackboard, the child read silently, and answered questions in writing about the material. Whether the program was an oral one or not, this happened regularly. The transmission rate was slow, however, and the teaching nonconsistent when mediated in this way. Levitt again suggested that since the main problem with handwritten messages is the time taken in getting them across, it might be worthwhile learning to communicate in phonetic symbols or touch shorthand, as the stenotypist does. Then, both sender and receiver could operate in real time, communicating with the speed of the spoken message. Alternatively, the typed message could be used only by the teacher, the deaf student replying with a spoken message. Or the typed message could also be presented to the deaf student auditorially in the form of a synthetic acoustic speech signal. Questions could then be asked about the value of teaching language by means of any or all of these modalities. Silverman answered that in utilizing teaching techniques such as this, it would be important to deal with exceptional deviation from the accepted symbol system. Already, teletype systems were used in communication with the child and experience had accumulated in dealing with such deviations. Levitt said that the teletype was slow compared with what he had in mind.

Absence of contextual features in written language

Ling felt that a problem inherent in such an approach to the teaching of language, first used by Alexander Graham Bell (1939), was the matter of content. The language has to be about something, he said. How is it possible to give the child cues as to the meaning of an utterance when he is attending to shorthand or to visual displays? How is the child to acquire semantic features, or grammatical relations in the absence of context? Ling remarked that the speech addressed by mothers to young children was often quite complex as he had stated earlier (p. 152–157), but almost everything the mother said was related to events, actions, or objects that were present as she spoke. It was very difficult to organize this kind of experience around a blackboard or a teletype. In Ling's view, children needed to form concepts and to be given the language symbols for these concepts. They needed to be able to express relations by putting words together in some form before they could proceed to learn to read. Only when they had learned to define words in terms of other words were they ready to take off and read entirely on their own.

Rosenstein thought these matters could be related to Furth's observation about motivation in language learning and also to the finding that deaf children of deaf parents show some superiority in reading skills over deaf children of hearing parents. He warned, however, that deaf children of deaf parents make up less than 8% of the entire population of deaf children. Theoretically, these are the children Bellugi (1972) has studied; she has shown that they acquire language naturally and in a manner which is analagous to that of the hearing child with hearing parents. Thus, they have concepts and symbols, and are able to express relations with these symbols. In addition, the deaf parents of these children know when their child has succeeded in making an association and when they have to present a stimulus or a language pattern again and again because the child has not yet made that basic association. This happens quite naturally as they communicate with their child between one and four years of age. It is not as easy for the hearing parents of a deaf child to know when an association is made. Those parents who *are* most successful are highly sensitive to their child's abilities and to his successes and failures in this direction; they give appropriate reinforcement and/or additional input. Rosenstein further noted that deaf students, even profoundly deaf students, who have been given amplification early and sensitive handling in the early preschool years, tend to make phonetically based errors rather than visual errors in reading (Gibson et al., 1970).

Natural language acquisition

Blesser felt that speech and written language were not interchangeable for rather different reasons than Ling's. Both involved cognitive activity it was true, but written language as the child experienced it was socially passive, introspective, without emotional responsiveness or motivation for contact. These differences, he thought, were fairly clear and related directly to questions of motivation for learning. He would postulate that if there were written forms of the language which had instead the characteristics of speech, namely social and emotional responsiveness, extroversion, and contact, then the linguistic contrast between them might disappear. Perhaps, a signed version of written language would produce this effect, or a written language conveyed by a hand-held teletype whose output was received by other miniteletypes or in the form of subtitles written across a pair of spectacles. The grammatical structure of the language model might be different if the visual system were to be employed, but use of this system might actually be

Social differences between spoken and written language

more efficient than speech. The short-term memory requirements for a skillful reader might actually be less than for speech, since one can take in much larger amounts of information by reading in the same period of time, than when listening to speech. Speech requires more memory partly because it is necessary to wait until the end of a spoken sentence before realizing its meaning. A person who can read at high speeds can take in a whole line or a whole paragraph at one scan.

Liberman asked Blesser to clarify, pointing out that there was a physiological constraint on the rate of scanning print. Blesser replied that it was not the number of scans per second that increased in speed reading, but the amount of information incorporated in a given fixation or scan. At these speeds phonetic recoding could not be taking place; what is used is visual imagery. In other words, if the reader is asked to recall material read some ten pages previously, he does so not on the basis of an acoustic signal, but of a visual image of the events represented. Thus, highly developed speech and highly developed reading might be different in their grammatical structure, but might be equally efficient. Their inability to replace one another was due to the social and emotional factors he had discussed earlier. Liberman answered that there was nothing incompatible in his view between so-called speed reading and phonetic recoding in reading, nor was there anything about phonetic recoding which would slow the reader down. Articulation was not involved, but merely a transfer in the way in which items were represented in the central nervous system.

Watson requested a few moments to develop some speculation about the possible role of extracurricular reading for deaf children. He suggested that engineering of circumstances could be used to encourage the deaf child who has reached a third or fourth grade level in reading skill, to read for pleasure. In developing this idea, he expressed the opinion that most investigators start from a number of tacit assumptions, namely:

1. that intellect and language abilities are intimately related;
2. that language abilities are primarily receptive and transmissive; and
3. that language abilities are acquired in the developmental era of greatest and most plastic intellectual and physical growth, the era of birth to puberty emphasized by Freud, Piaget, and many others. Watson first questioned that cognition and receptive and transmissive language abilities were really intimately related; he gave the example of cases of extremely intellectual and able deaf individuals whose speech is unintelligible, and of a child mentioned to him by Shaplin (personal communication) who had an IQ of 50; this child's verbal output was syntactically well-ordered and seemed to demonstrate a good vocabulary, yet was completely lacking in content. He also pointed out that the intellect and personality in civilized man continued to develop and to change after puberty (Loevinger and Wessler, 1970). Watson

also questioned a further assumption, namely, that education is what goes on in the classroom.

Since most deaf children succeed in reading at least at a third or fourth grade level, it would not appear that sensory or major cognitive barriers exist to limit their progress beyond this level. Normal-hearing children do so partly because they begin to read for pleasure. Why shouldn't deaf children become ardent consumers of the printed page also, since for them this input channel is even more important than for normal-hearing youngsters? Fader and McNeil (1968) had succeeded in getting black children from disadvantaged homes to do so. It might be necessary to begin with comic books or pornography or whatever the youngsters really like to read. Adults should restrain themselves from making judgements of these materials as "trashy." Teenagers like to read "trash." Watson recommended that when a deaf child engages in self-motivated, self-paced, self-selected reading, he should be treated as though he were doing something that is very important. This might be the most effective kind of reinforcement for him. Private reading consumption, for normal children who later show major academic success, far exceeds their reading in formal academic settings. It must lead to significant increase in volume of vocabulary and concepts. This may or may not interact with other language skills. Watson believed that it would, even if only by increasing the volume of material in long-term memory.

House replied that Watson had understood the drift of his question about reading very well. There were two channels of research that ought to be exploited more fully than at present: The use of reading per se and the use of a typescript prosthesis. In other words, should education be putting more emphasis on reading as a way of teaching language skills? Is reading a more practical and profoundly important way of getting language in a deaf population than present approaches? In his own experience, learning to read had introduced him and also his children to a completely different world. It was also one way to acquire language. He felt that efforts to try out a prosthesis with typescript output might be profitable.

Reading as a means of teaching language skills

Miller replied that there were counter-arguments to this point of view which should be considered. There was a very real fear among teachers of the deaf which essentially had been expressed earlier by Boothroyd. These fears were that without a strong base in spoken language, that is, in receptive and productive spoken language, the child might learn reading strategies which are extremely destructive. These strategies are of the kind where the child looks for a sequence of noun words and guesses the meaning from looking at them, and possibly at pictures accompanying the text. These strategies might interfere with the later learning of more constructive reading habits. He anticipated that Watson would say the youngsters should go ahead and get some basic reading skills first, but Miller felt that this issue was a real one

Destructive reading strategies in deaf children

which should be kept in mind. Ling again took the view that spoken language should come first. It was important before engineering conditions conducive to acquisition of reading to engineer conditions conducive to spoken language acquisition. He recalled that he had begun this work as a teacher of the deaf in a school in which such conditions did not obtain. Later, he saw to it that as many deaf children as possible were integrated into schools for the normal-hearing. The teachers did not see their jobs as lecturing in a classroom but as one of mediating between the child and his total linguistic environment. Ling was not surprised at the low standard of verbal achievement and of reading achievement on the part of deaf children in huge state schools for the deaf. The conditions were such that they mitigated against intellectual and language growth, speaking and reading. However, he thought Miller's caution about destructive reading habits was a timely one. Some deaf children, he thought, did learn from reading in a counterproductive way which was reflected in their spoken language. He had recently tested a number of deaf children who had been integrated into schools for normally-hearing children under less than ideal conditions. These children were reading at a seventh grade level and they read for their own pleasure. Yet their responses on a test requiring them to supply missing morphemes (Berry and Talbott, 1966), showed that they did not have a grasp of morphological rules, for pluralizing nonsense words, for example, or for marking tense or the possessive relation. Ling thought these children might in fact be using a noun search to get a vague impression of the content of what they read. They might be satisfied with that and thus miss much of the subtlety of written language.

Knowledge of morphemic system and reading

Watson responded that he was not proposing self-motivated reading as a substitute for performance in a formal curriculum, but as a supplement to that curriculum. The logic of the argument that too much reading for pleasure could have negative results seemed weak to him. Normal children too begin by looking for key words, using the pictures as crutches, and so on. But the reinforcement associated with accurate information eventually corrects faulty strategies for the normal child; why do we assume a like process will not occur for the deaf child, *if he reads a lot?* Liberman thought that it would be instructive to examine the reading proficiency of congenitally deaf children in China or Japan. The information displayed in print, for example, in Kanji in these countries was morphemic rather than phonologic.

Rosenstein thought that cued speech would also be taken into consideration as a phonetically-based system which should facilitate reading (Cornett, 1970). In this system, hand gestures are used to disambiguate all gestures which look alike on the lips. The hand gestures have the important property that they cannot be read in the absence of speech gestures at the mouth; they only supplement the information of speech gestures. The system has not been widely practiced in the United States, and initial evaluation reports from an Australian school that adopted the system were not detailed or quantitative but general and descriptive (Cornett, 1972). The system, however, could be used in natural learning situations and Rosenstein thought it should facilitate reading also.

Miller suggested that if conditions were to be engineered, it might be well to consider how best to do just that. One way, possibly, was to use reinforcement to modify behavior. He wished to present some recent thinking in animal learning in which Seligman (1970) suggested that it is useful to classify learning situations in three categories:

Behavior modification

1. those for which the animal is prepared;
2. those for which he is unprepared; and
3. those for which he is contra-prepared.

Since animals differ with respect to these categories, we cannot think of laws of learning as universal. Auditory behavior, for example, is linked in different species to different kinds of nonauditory behavior. These might be classed as food getting, social, and defensive. If we list species as in Figure 3.10 and then examine auditory learning in these species, and how this relates to the main types of auditory behavior, we find some interesting differences. A barn owl, for example, uses auditory behavior in food getting. It has been shown by Konishi (1971) that it is very simple to teach a barn owl to discriminate sounds if food is used in reinforcing correct judgments. A Rhesus monkey, on the other hand, who is much more intelligent and has a greater long-term memory, has a very difficult time learning to discriminate sounds if food is used in reinforcing correct judgments (Wegener, 1964). The Rhesus monkey is totally unprepared for this kind of task. His auditory system, like that of most species of laboratory animals, is linked with defensive action in response to a pure tone or other auditory signal. Even

	Defense	Foodgetting	Social
Barn Owl		+	
Rhesus	+	-	+
Chinchilla	-		
Human	+		+

Fig. 3.10 Auditory behavior in different species.

when defensive behavior is used as the operant, however, problems may arise, as for example in the case of the guinea pig whose defense is to freeze (Miller and Murray, 1966). This is awkward if the purpose is to train avoidance behavior, i.e., flight to another part of the cage. In Rhesus monkeys, auditory signals are also strongly linked with social behavior. Thus, tasks involving social behavior may be useful in training them to discriminate auditory signals.

This has implications for the training of human subjects. Sounds are certainly involved in an important way in human defensive behavior. They are also involved in an extremely important way in social behavior. Miller was willing to say that the human is prepared to learn auditory tasks in a social situation. He may, however, be totally unprepared to learn tactile tasks in this way. This is not to say that he cannot learn such tasks, but that he would have great difficulty in doing so. Humans have evolved in such a way that they are likely not only to behave in certain ways, but also to learn specific behaviors in response to certain kinds of signals.

REFERENCES

Bekesy, G. von: Sensory Inhibition, Princeton: Princeton University Press, 1967.

Bell, A.G.: Teaching language to a young deaf child, Volta Rev. 41:437–441, 1939.

Bellugi, U.: Studies in sign language, In: O'Rourke, T.J., ed.: Psycholinguistics and Total Communication: State-of-the-Art, Washington, D.C.: American Annals of the Deaf, 1972.

Berry, M.F., and Talbott, R.: Exploratory test of grammar, 4332 Pine Crest Rd., Rockford, Ill., 61107, 1966.

Clay, M.M., and Imlach, R.H.: Juncture, pitch and stress as reading behavior variables, J. Verb. Learn. 10:133–139, 1971.

Conrad, R.: Speech and reading, In: Kavanagh, J.F., and Mattingly, I.G., eds.: Language by Ear and by Eye: The Relationship between Speech and Reading, Cambridge: M.I.T. Press, 1972.

Cornett, R.O.: Effects of cued speech upon speech and language patterns of the aurally-handicapped child, In: Proceedings of the International Congress on Education of the Deaf, vol. I, Stockholm, 1970. (Proceedings available from A.G. Bell Assoc., Volta Place N.W., Washington, D.C. 20008)

Cornett, R.O.: Cued speech, parent training and follow-up program, Final Report OEC-8-009137-4348(019) and (615), U.S. Dept. of Health, Education, and Welfare, Office of Education, Bureau of Education of the Handicapped, August, 1972.

Danaher, E.M.; Osberger, M.J., and Pickett, J.M.: Discrimination of formant frequency transitions in synthetic vowels, J. Speech Hearing Res. (In press).

Department of Education and Science: The education of deaf children: The possible place of fingerspelling and signing, London: Her Majesty's Stationery Office, 1968.

Erber, N.P.: Speech-envelope cues as an acoustic aid to lipreading for profoundly deaf children, J. Acoust. Soc. Amer. 51:1224–1227, 1972.

Fader, D.N., and McNeil, E.B.: Hooked on Books: Program and Proof, New York: Berkeley Publishing Corp., 1968.

Franklin, B.: The effect on consonant discrimination of combining a low-frequency passband in one ear and a high-frequency passband in the other ear, J. Aud. Res. 9(4):365–378, 1969.

Gibson, E.J.; Shurcliff, A., and Yonas, A.: Utilization of spelling patterns, In: Levin, H., and Williams, J.P., eds.: Basic Studies in Reading, New York: Basic Books, 1970.

Hoemann, H.W.: Communication skills in deaf and hearing children, Res. Relat. Child. 29:61–62, Sep., 1971-Feb., 1972.

Keidel, W.D.: Electrophysiology of vibratory perception, In: Neff, W.D., ed.: Contributions to Sensory Physiology, vol. III, New York: Academic Press, 1968.

Kimura, D.: Speech lateralization in young children as determined by an auditory test, J. Comp. Physiol. Psychol. 56:899–902, 1963.

Konishi, M.: Sound localization in the barn owl, J. Acoust. Soc. Amer. 50(148A), 1971.

Kringlebotn, M.: En Ny Vibrotaktil Vokoder-Hjelper Dove A Hore Med Fingerene Fysik, Institutt Norges Tekniska Hogskole, Trondheim, 1965.

Kringlebotn, M.: Experiments with some visual and vibrotactile aids for the deaf, Amer. Ann. Deaf 113:311–317, 1968.

Levitt, H.: Speech processing aids for the deaf: An overview, IEEE Trans. Audio Electroacoust. AU-21(3):269–273, 1973.

Lindner, R.: Physiologische Grundlagen zum elektrischen Sprachetasten und ihre Anwendung auf den Taubstummenunterricht, Ztschr. f. Sinnephysiol. 67:114–144, 1937.

Ling, A.H.: Dichotic listening in hearing-impaired children, J. Speech Hearing Res. 14:793–803, 1971.

Loevinger, J., and Wessler, R.: Measuring Ego Development, vol. I, San Francisco: Jossey-Bass, 1970.

Miller, J.D., and Murray, F.S.: Guinea pig's immobility response to sound: Threshold and habituation, J. Comp. Physiol. Psychol. 61:227–233, 1966.

Pickett, J.M.: Tactual communication of speech sounds to the deaf: Comparison with lipreading, J. Speech Hearing Dis. 28:315–330, 1963.

Pickett, J.M., and Pickett, B.H.: Communication of speech sounds by a tactual vocoder, J. Speech Hearing Res. 6:207–222, 1963.

Pollack, I.: Binaural communication systems: Preliminary examination, J. Acoust. Soc. Amer. 31:81–82, 1959.

Quigley, S.P.; Jenne, W.C., and Phillips, S.B.: Deaf Students in Colleges and Universities, Washington, D.C.: A.G. Bell Association, 1968.

Risberg, A.: Visual aids for speech correction, Amer. Ann. Deaf 113:178–194, 1968.

Rosenthal, R.D.; Lang, J.K., and Levitt, H.: Effects of low-frequency speech bands on intelligibility, Communication Sciences Laboratory Report No. 3, August, 1972.

Seligman, M.E.P.: On the generality of the laws of learning, Psychol. Rev. 77:406–418, 1970.

Sherrick, C.E., and Rogers, R.: Apparent haptic movement, Percept. Psychophys. 1:175–180, 1966.

Sofin, B.: Vibrotactile cues in the discrimination of speech by deaf children, Master's thesis, McGill University, 1972.

Stark, R.E.; Cullen, J.K., and Chase, R.A.: Preliminary work with the new Bell Telephone Visible Speech Translator, Amer. Ann. Deaf 113:205–214, 1968.

Stuckless, E.R., and Birch, J.W.: The influence of early manual communication on the linguistic development of deaf children, Amer. Ann. Deaf 111(3): 452–460, 499–504, 1966.

Taenzer, J.O.: Some psychophysical limitations on reading performance, Doctoral dissertation, Stanford University, 1971.

Vernon, M., and Koh, S.D.: Effects of oral preschool compared to early manual communication on education and communication in deaf children, Amer. Ann. Deaf 116:569–574, 1971.

Wegener, J.G.: Auditory discrimination behavior of normal monkeys, J. Aud. Res. 4(2):81–106, 1964.

Zahl, P.A., ed.: Blindness: Modern Approaches to the Unseen Environment, Princeton: Princeton University Press, 1950.

Summary and Overview

10

Summary

S. Richard Silverman, Ph.D.
Central Institute for the Deaf

This summary is based primarily on the edited transcript of the Conference supplemented by my own notes. I have resorted in the main to excerpting significant items from the transcript, interspersed by my own condensations and interpolations. I felt it would add to the value of the summary to identify participants with the thoughts which they expressed. For the pressed-for-time reader I have included enough detail to communicate significant substance along with the "flavor" of the Conference. On the other hand, I hope that the summary will tantalize the reader to read the entire text. Any inaccuracies of summarizing are my sole responsibility.

The keynote address for the Conference on the processing of information by hearing-impaired children was delivered by Hirsh. Then the Conference considered in sequence, sensory capabilities, perceptual and cognitive strategies, and finally, language processing, as they relate to hearing impairment.

Keynote Address

Hirsh emphasized the contribution to the education of deaf children of contemporary research in speech perception, psycholinguistics, the psychology of memory, the development of motor skills and language acquisition. Investigations of perception raise important questions, namely, (1) to what extent can we predict how well a listener will process, discriminate and recognize acoustical patterns from his performance on a detection task and (2) does the deaf child process supra-threshold signals in a normal manner? We need to understand the coding that must take place when the signal enters the peripheral sensory system and the requirement put on short-term memory and storage of long sequences of stimuli. Are verbal and nonverbal stimuli coded in the same way? Furthermore, are short-term memory images to be thought of as acoustic or transformed auditory images? Is there a motor component to a perceived and stored image? Language communication may involve perceiving and producing in a way somewhat different from that suggested by nonlanguage experimentation.

Hirsh cited the emergence of the model of language acquisition that imputes to the young child the capacity to induce grammatical rules of language and to reveal them in his own utterances. How applicable is this model to the child deprived of normal language input? And how does it mesh with the requirements of reinforcement theory in the education of the child? For example, how do we program acoustic input to provide an optimum catalogue of acoustic cues for a very young child?

This leads to a consideration of prosthetic coding that encompasses a continuum from genuine acoustic representation of spectral and temporal features of language to online transformations for the skin or the eye, graphic illustrations, signs or finger spelling, and to the printed word. Our major task is to provide reasonably specific instructions for the prosthetic engineer as to the use of sensory and stimulus modalities.

As for concept formation, is the deaf child's ability to think, at least at high abstract levels, impaired seriously by his lack or deficiency of comprehension and use of his language system? The subtle interweaving of the learning of language and the forming of concepts still needs clarification.

State-of-the-art report

SECTION I: SENSORY CAPABILITIES

Sherrick first defined sensory capabilities as "the capacity of the organism to exhibit relatively simple behavioral or physiological responses to sets of simple and well controlled stimulus conditions." He focused attention on infants and on the relation between diagnosis and the compensatory use of deficient sensory channels.

Research in sensory testing, he said, can be categorized as follows:

A. Methods involving unlearned responses to stimuli.
  1. Bioelectric potential changes.
  2. Automatic behavioral responses.
B. Methods requiring learned responses.
  1. Classical conditioning.
  2. Operant conditioning.

A major problem has been the lack of standardization and normalization of tests from laboratory to laboratory. Three sources of variance of current interest are: (a) the effect of the state of alertness of the infant on his responsiveness; (b) the problem of habituation; and (c) the problem of the detection of "true" responses in "noisy" response patterns. Related to the problem of state is the question of the effect of the stimulus on state. Responsiveness is not necessarily correlated with increasing activity. Repetitive stimuli, particularly noxious ones, may arouse defensive activity but others may lull a child to sleep. Response decrement may also be due to adaptation and habituation. The interaction of adaptation and habituation with the state of alertness is particularly noticeable in neonates. In general, much of the earlier work on states needs to be reexamined.

The understanding of the problem of response detection has been greatly influenced by the Theory of Signal Detection which created an awareness in psychologists of the need to monitor a subject's behavior in psychophysical studies. The investigator or clinician also needs to have signal detection methods applied to his own behavior in testing.

The development of sensory aids for the deaf has been dealt with extensively elsewhere (Pickett, 1968; Levitt and Nye, 1971; Smith, 1972). Illustrative investigations cited by Sherrick include the evolution from the Gault teletactor to the tactual vocoder developed by Pickett aimed at auditory analogues for tactile communication by speech. The limited sensitivity of the skin stimulated modifications of the Helmholtz place model featuring filter bands. Higher frequencies were transposed to more easily discriminated lower frequency regions. The problem with transposition was the sluggish transmission rate. Real time display devices would be pedagogically more desirable. One of the major problems in spatiotemporal displays is the difficulty subjects experience in fusing letters into chunks. Is there a display that permits fusion; does the skin lack the capacity, or is fusion the product of either massive overlearning or very early experience?

Problems of research in sensory aids

DISCUSSION—SENSORY CAPABILITIES

Sherrick suggested that diagnosis should be based on a battery of relatively independent tests. Such tests were of vital importance not only for diagnosis but also for the design of prosthetic devices. Evaluation of devices presents tough problems of experimental design, but the tying together of questions of sensory testing, including definition of the deficit to be aided, and sensory aids in a kind of "bootstrap" operation had some appeal.

Sensory testing

Eisenberg expressed concern that the use of the non-specific word "deficit" lies at the crux of our problem with the pediatric-aged, both from a diagnostic and a treatment standpoint. The word has not been defined, for example, in terms of the difference in coding of speech and nonspeech sounds or of the influence of development on these different types of coding. Eisenberg felt that one sensory system could not be substituted for another

Defining the deficit

until (1) the ways in which each system functions normally are understood and (2) there is some reasonable body of information on how the auditory system is affected in the hearing-impaired child who is to receive the substitute. Sherrick took issue with this point of view, stating that such a stand would not advance progress.

Sherrick reminded us that the study of habituation can be useful in itself. Its disappearance upon introduction of a novel stimulus can demonstrate differentiation of the familiar and novel system. Habituation may provide an index as to the level of maturity of the central nervous system. Pickett felt that there must be significant functional reasons for differences in adaptation, which should be studied.

Eisenberg stated it was quite impossible to keep an infant organism in the same state throughout testing. She felt that tests of young infants especially (a) should require no cooperation on the part of the subject, (b) should not depend on the maintenance of a proven state, but should be so designed that they separate out the effects of different states from his ability to respond, and (c) should not be age dependent. Such tests should enable us to look at functions on a developmental scale. Pollack suggested that continuous naturalistic observations of infants might have an advantage over episodic testing for early detection of impairment.

Electrophysiological measures for assessment of auditory function

Eisenberg described her experience in assessing sensory functions in infants. She was interested in determining (1) how the young organism operates when the test signals are at levels of average conversation and (2) the predictive value of measures obtained in her work with neonates. Over the past ten years she has employed three indices of stimulus-bound auditory behavior: overt behavior, which is defined by a standardized coding system, heart rate measured by cardiotachometry, and EEG. In summarizing her present judgement of these indices Eisenberg felt (1) that behavioral measures had value in terms of their correlation with electrophysiologic measures; (2) that heart-rate measures now in the "refining" stage at her laboratory have potential as foolproof measures of hearing loss; and (3) that EEG, though past the stage of preliminary exploration, would require considerably more basic research before it could serve as a widely useful clinical tool. However, heart rate as a correlate of auditory function still presents problems. Among these are lability of response, temporal conditioning, choice of stimulus, detection of response, response-time boundaries, mode of response, diagnostic significance of responses and also the validity of the cumulative treatment of the data which she herself had utilized.

In the discussion that followed Eisenberg's exposition, Hirsh commented that Hallowell Davis' group was reasonably comfortable with the evoked response as basis for estimate of auditory threshold. Agreement with behavioral thresholds has been close. Eisenberg agreed, but felt that EEG audiometry was more apt to be misused than heart-rate measures. She emphasized the greater convenience and economy of heart-rate measures but encouraged the continued use of EEG in proper hands, particularly to learn more about the functioning of the auditory system.

Watson described work at CID to develop systematic procedures for conducting and interpreting evoked response audiometry (ERA) on anesthetized patients. Tests on anesthetized infants have sufficient reliability and validity to reduce our concerns about the requirement that subjects be quiescent. Watson described a CID study that suggested caution in drawing inferences about perception from cortical evoked responses. In an adult subject whose individual responses were so large that it was not necessary to sum responses over a number of trials to average out random waveform components, the only significant correlation, among a number that were determined, was between stimulus magnitude and subjective rating (.8). The correlations implied that, for a narrow range of stimuli, differences in evoked responses may be essentially meaningless when compared to an observer's subjective judgment even though those judgments are closely tied to the levels of stimulation.

There was unquestionable agreement that the auditory function of the child with significant hearing impairment should be studied in detail and the nature of his deficit more fully understood. There was disagreement, however, about the usefulness of the audiogram as a predictor of the child's ability to learn, or to understand and produce speech.

Boothroyd emphasized the value of residual hearing and warned against the distraction caused by the search for tactile or visual sensory aids. In studies at Clarke School he found a clear and interesting relation between hearing level and speech intelligibility. The relation was fairly good up to about 90 dB, and then there was a marked drop-off in intelligibility. This step function raised the question of the value of auditory approaches to training of children with losses exceeding 90 dB. Boothroyd described a pitch-matching experiment which led him to conclude it would be wrong to ignore hearing channels just because the loss exceeds 90 dB.

Relation of hearing level to speech production and speech perception skills

Levitt described an experiment carried out by Smith at the Lexington School for the Deaf, relating hearing loss to speech perception and intelligibility of read speech. He and Smith felt that an L-shaped curve with a sharp transition in the 90 dB region would fit their speech intelligibility data very well. Levitt also found some children (8 out of 40) with hearing levels better than 90 dB who had poor intelligibility scores. These children came predominantly from homes in which parents were also deaf. The effect of language environment upon speech intelligibility needs to be examined further. Menyuk felt that the "magic" number of 90 dB hearing level might not show the same relation to intelligibility of spontaneous speech as to that of reading an isolated sentence. Pickett recalled some Swedish work which showed high correlations between degree of hearing, speech intelligibility and auditory reception but no correlation between hearing loss and other linguistic skills such as reading, lipreading and use of grammar.

Erber reported studies which led him to conclude that the audiogram is *Effect of to-* an inadequate predictor of speech recognition in the case of some profoundly *tal loss of* deaf children, probably because their responses to pure-tone signals were *hearing: vi-* vibrotactile. Erber used word-recognition scores to classify children as se- *brotactile re-* verely or profoundly hearing-impaired. Through hearing alone, the severe *sponses to* group could make consonant discriminations involving low-frequency voicing *sound* and nasality cues, but not place cues, while the profound group could perceive only time and intensity cues in speech. The analysis of error categories in both groups suggested that the profoundly impaired group need to have voicing and nasality information as well as place of articulation made clearly available to them through some other sensory modality.

Ling reported an experiment in which training improved the ability of profoundly deaf children to discriminate manner and nasality cues but not place cues, and suggested that Erber might have found similar increments after a period of training. Erber maintained that the children he designated as profoundly deaf perceived only vibrotactile clues which carried information about the waveform envelope of speech. Erber had also found that information from lipreading was being supplemented by the information presented to the ear; but that the supplementary cues, whether from real speech or speech-modulated noise, were those present in the time-intensity envelope of the speech signal in every case. His results suggest the nature of the speech signal which the profoundly deaf child must deal with in communicating receptively. Ling felt that real speech was more effective as a supplementary signal than speech-modulated noise. He cautioned about using a 95 dB pure-tone average threshold as a means of classifying deaf children. He pointed out that slope of the audiogram was important since the speech reception of hard-of-hearing and profoundly deaf children was frequency dependent. Hirsh felt that the evidence was particularly strong in favor of a dichotomy among the hearing-impaired population. This was based upon an average threshold for lower frequencies and upon a predominance of vibro-tactile responders among the more profoundly deaf, those children who are difficult to teach.

Lipreading Lip-reading scores need also to be considered as predictors of a child's *skills* ability to acquire language skills. Erber quoted his own work and Berger's, pointing out that, while consonants were perceived categorically as far as place of articulation was concerned, vowels were more difficult to discrimi-nate and were perceived on a continuum, confusions with "neighboring" vowels predominating. Silverman thought that deaf children tended to produce vowels, particularly front vowels, that were slightly off target with respect to tongue position. Levitt noted that in Berger's study of lipreading, the findings had indicated some clustering in the confusion matrix on the tense/lax vowel dimension. Erber thought the deaf child could be helped to resolve this confusion by training in the use of information in the time-intensity envelope. Silverman said that there was a reasonably good relation between lipreading and speech production skills but that this might be influenced by the child's language capabilities and the frequency with which lipreading was used in his school. Levitt observed that the speech production errors documented in Smith's thesis showed confusions very similar to those which Erber and Berger had shown in lipreading.

If lipreading contributes not only to the reception of speech but also to speech production, it is important to help the child make maximum use of it. Erber described his investigation of the effects of word length and stress and concluded that the child should start with multi-syllabic input in lipreading. House was skeptical of the high lip-reading scores obtained by Erber's subjects, which might have been due to exaggerated articulation and unusual lighting at the mouth. Erber thought there might have been some exaggeration, which is quite typical of many teachers of the deaf, and Miller suggested that special illumination could be as important as hearing aids. Sherrick also called attention to the Tadoma Method used with the deaf-blind in which the hand of the subject is presented articulatory gestures by feeling the throat, lips, nose and cheeks of the speaker.

Sherrick further commented that there did not seem to be agreement with respect to questions of some kind of fixed sensory task or system of evaluation to use with hearing-impaired children of more than three or four years. Bordley expressed concern about the need for consideration of the child's total mental capacity, i.e., his nonauditory sensory and perceptual capabilities which he must use in responding to the tests that had been described. Elliott (observer) said that such data were available on children admitted to CID. She related the children's IQ's to educational outcome and felt that such data could be assembled for the children who had been in the speech reception studies at CID. Levitt cited one of his studies in which the intelligibility of speech was correlated only moderately with IQ score. Bordley illustrated the real point of his question by citing the child with high IQ whose nonauditory perceptual deficit would hinder his acquisition of language.

Nonauditory sensory and perceptual capabilities

Sherrick suggested that it would be important to study somesthesis, especially oral stereognosis, in deaf children, using the approaches of Bosma. House cited a study by Bishop in which predominantly manually taught deaf children had higher error rates than a normal group on an oral stereognosis task. This might imply that deaf speech was defective because of an oral sensory deficit or that the deficit resulted from the deaf child talking less than the normal child. House said that Bishop's study was extended to compare orally educated deaf children, manual deaf, and normal-hearing high school students. The discrimination scores separated the manual from the other two groups. These results led to the view that while a failure in oroperceptual functioning may lead to disorders of articulation, a failure to use the oral mechanisms for speech activities, even in persons with normal orosensory capabilities, may result in poor performance on oroperceptual tasks.

State-of-the-art
report

SECTION II: PERCEPTUAL AND COGNITIVE STRATEGIES

Pollack gave it as his personal view that it was useful to preserve the distinction between perceptual and cognitive processes "as a useful heuristic for sharpening our theories." Nevertheless, the distinction had been blurred by a steady stream of brilliant theorists and empiricists.

First, there is the impact of the Theory of Signal Detection which attempts to achieve a pure measure of sensory discriminability apart from bias and other response factors, usually labelled cognitive. Although the theory handles well the case of the attentive subject with a consistent response bias in one direction it has trouble with inconsistent biases. It has difficulty, as does any theory of discriminability, in discriminating sensory factors from motivational or attentive factors. Then, there are an increasing number of ingenious experiments on attention, many stimulated by Broadbent, where parallels between perception and cognition in terms of attentional demands have been studied. Pollack noted that most cognitive tasks suffer under competing activities and Neisser's ingenious notion of "focal cognitive stream" and a cognitive background stream preserves the flavor of a perceptual focus and a perceptual background.

Studies in pattern perception have also generated the hypothesis that we recognize patterns by constructing a model against which we test the to-be-recognized pattern. The unknown pattern may be recognized because the list of features which enter the construction are known to the observer. A special problem of speech recognition, namely, that it depends heavily on context, suggests that speech theorists need to take a broader view of speech recognition. Neisser's concept of cognition which refers to all the processes by which the sensory input is processed has contributed to the unitary view of perception and cognition. (We regret that Neisser was unable to accept our invitation to attend the Conference.) Also Garner shows that performance in tasks typically considered to be perceptual depends strongly upon the structural properties of sets of stimuli, not just properties which are immediately relevant to the discrimination. The measure is of the properties of the set from which that stimulus could have been chosen. There is a unity of perception and cognition or as Garner put it "to perceive is to know." However, in "finessing" the distinction between perceptual and cognitive processes, Pollack pointed to evidence that rates of presentation influence the kind of behaviors elicited. Cognitive behavior is elicited in response to slow presentation and perceptual behavior in response to fast presentation, given the same set of tasks. He also pointed to evidence from his own work that task requirements differ in the presentation of visual displays for perceptual processing and for cognitive processing. In general, Pollack favored the idea of essential continuity between cognition and perception.

In discussing the study of psychological processes in children, Pollack found it difficult to distinguish failures in performance which are due to failure to understand instruction from failures due to competence factors. This is particularly crucial in experimental work with deaf children. Pollack concluded "Perhaps we must embark upon a theory of tasks before we can embark on a theory of behavior."

DISCUSSION: PERCEPTUAL AND COGNITIVE STRATEGIES

In opening the discussion Pollack pointed out that the difficulty of distinguishing among sensory capabilities, perceptual strategies and cognitive function is underlined when we begin to devise tests of performance. An open set speech intelligibility test requires a higher level of function than evoked response or heart-rate audiometry. He suggested that the deaf child has an important role to play in adding to the understanding of sensory and perceptual processes, or problems such as the link between auditory and articulatory theories of speech perception. Pollack felt that any arbitrary intellectual transformation can be set up as a perceptual processing task if the subject learns to process the information rapidly by means of a natural code or as a result of sufficient practice in handling an arbitrary code.

Tests of performance

Watson then discussed methodology of sensory and perceptual experiments. He stated that the most primitive distinction of all is that between aspects of sensory processing that a scientist can deal with objectively, and those that are out of reach of his methods. In dealing with behavioral measures Watson proposed that the major concerns of psychophysics are what we are capable of doing with our senses on the one hand and what we actually do with them on the other. He referred to the first as "sensory capability" and to the other as "response proclivity." He then elaborated this idea in some detail by suggesting experimental methods for each and citing an illustrative experiment by Divenyi and Hirsh on the perception of temporal

Methodology of psychophysical testing

order in normal-hearing adults, and pointing up possible misinterpretations of data from previous experiments.

Watson described an attempt of his own to use methods in presenting complex stimuli, in such a way as to improve our understanding of the capability to deal with these stimuli, and ultimately, with speech. Forty-msec tone bursts were programmed to resemble words in duration and in frequency range of the higher formants. Patterns and instructions to subjects were varied. Watson's results led him to state that we should be cautious in drawing premature conclusions that fine grained perception of complex sounds is restricted to speech sounds.

Responses to complex auditory stimuli

Ling reported an experiment conducted by his wife (A.H. Ling) in which recall of temporal sequences of speech and nonspeech stimuli were compared. The sounds used were (1) five CV syllables differing in initial consonant, (2) five CV syllables differing in final vowel, and (3) five nonverbal sounds such as the bark of a dog and the hoot of a horn. For the syllables the response was repetition, for the environmental sounds it was pointing to pictures. In general, for the syllable sequences the hearing-impaired were less often correct than the normal-hearing children, whereas on an identification task utilizing environmental sound sequences, with which none of the children had any experience, the hearing-impaired children did about as well as the normal-hearing children. Liberman suggested that in responding to phonetic elements, where the average element duration would be much lower than for syllable sequences, the superiority of the normal-hearing children would be more impressive. Watson suggested more precise feedback and training to distinguish capability from proclivity. Hirsh suggested that studies of processing of musical sequences might be helpful in finding out just how great the difference between processing of verbal and nonverbal material really is.

Responses to speechlike stimuli

Pickett described an experiment in which two groups of college-age hearing-impaired adults with moderate to severe bilateral sensorineural hearing losses participated. One group had flat and the other group had sloping audiograms. The subjects were asked to say on which of three synthetically produced vowels they detected a second formant transition. The flat loss subjects showed consistently better discrimination on this task than the sloping loss subjects. In addition, the results suggested masking of the second formant transition by the first formant, especially if the first formant had a transition. Basic psychoacoustic experiments have shown that backward masking occurs in normal-hearing subjects when masking stimuli are presented at the high levels at which many hearing-impaired subjects listen. If vowels do produce backward and forward masking, this might help to explain some of the speech discrimination problems associated with sensorineural hearing loss.

Denes thought that the effects of recruitment upon second formant discrimination should be considered. House felt that Pickett's experiments could not be compared directly with psychophysical experiments employing sequences of pure tones, however complex. Rather than discriminating F2 transitions, subjects might be demonstrating their perceptual boundaries for phonemes.

House then suggested that the concept of F1 masking was merely the concept of pre-emphasis of speech in another guise. Denes pointed out that the acoustics of speech production will necessarily make the intensity of F2 of vowels lower than that of F1. Pre-emphasis is merely a matter of equalizing intensity level across the frequency range, but is the speechlike character of the sounds affected? Pickett felt that the Harvard studies in the 1940's, which showed better discrimination by listeners with sensorineural loss when amplification with a low-frequency roll-off was used, should be repeated with greater precision using new equipment and methods.

Implications for hearing aid design

Gengel (observer) reported studies of consonant and vowel discrimination as a function of gain and his results seemed to reinforce House's suggestion with respect to pre-emphasis. Frequently, the hearing-impaired subject sets a signal-to-noise level for listening to speech with respect to the vowels. Since the consonants are on the average 13 dB lower in intensity, pre-emphasis would improve their reception.

Miller summarized the views of himself, Niemoller, and Pascoe. He discussed the field-to-eardrum transfer function, and the 18 dB increase between 2 KHz and 4 KHz due to the resonance of the ear canal and to head diffraction. The Harvard Report recommended a frequency response out to 3 KHz at about a 6 to 7 dB per octave boost beginning at 300 Hz. In actual fact, according to Miller, the circumaural cushions worn by the subjects of the Harvard experiments added about 10 dB between 2 KHz and 3 KHz resulting in a total high-frequency emphasis in this region of 18 to 20 dB. Thus, the investigators were reproducing almost exactly the natural listening condition provided by the acoustics of the external ear. These facts have caused Miller and his colleagues to take as their design goal the reproduction for the hearing-impaired listener of the normal field-to-eardrum transfer function plus a constant. They were experimenting intensively with a presbycusic adult who understood speech more easily in noise and in quiet when these requirements were met. Miller also noted the adverse effect on speech reception by this patient when vocal effort was increased. An exchange among Denes, House and Weiss (observer) on this point led to Weiss' comment on two effects of shouted speech which work in opposition to one another, an unfavorable change in vowel-consonant ratio, and emphasis on F2 in vowels as vocal effort increases.

Blesser maintained that in the design of prostheses and in the choice of

Use of perceptual and cognitive strategies in speech reception

codes, two things were being confused, namely the ability to learn speech and the ability to perceive speech. Someone who has language competence can understand speech very well even when it is severely degraded. Blesser was convinced that cognitive processes are sufficiently flexible and powerful to dig meaning out of a speech signal provided that the whole framework is there. In the case of the hearing-impaired children he felt that the concept of language was not secure and there was little confidence in redundancy. The choice of code should be based on these criteria, not simply on supplying features which are missing from the input. The child must acquire confidence using prosodic features and patterning to replace missing phonetic features or vice versa. Boothroyd cautioned against such a global approach. His experience at Clarke School indicated that deaf children tend to rely on small pieces of the signal and develop a one-word cue strategy which may work well at first but not as the demands of communication increase. Failure to emerge from this stage resulted in some children being regarded as poor lip-readers.

Blesser then described an experiment in which he tried to simulate certain kinds of deafness in normal-hearing mature adults with language competence. He developed some simple electronics which would invert the speech spectrum in real time. The subjects were isolated from each other in acoustic chambers and were instructed to converse with one another using any strategy they found practical to establish communication, except that they were not to use a code which circumvented use of the transformed signal such as the Morse Code. Discrimination and identification testing was interposed.

Blesser expected the subjects to learn spectral rotation, that is, to rotate everything back perceptually in a manner analogous to the subject reinverting visual images which have been inverted by special lenses. This did not happen. Instead, the subjects began to ignore certain features and to place a higher reliance on others.

In general, source features and consonant manner features were unaffected by spectral transformation, as were prosodic features of pitch, stress, and temporal ordering. Tense and lax vowels were confused at first and quickly relearned, but sets of lax vowels and place features for consonants were never discriminated.

Among the implications of his experiment, according to Blesser, was that speech abilities did not form any kind of sequence. Identification for monosyllabic words was essentially zero. Discrimination scores and phoneme and single word identification scores were not correlated with one another or with the ability to converse. Performance on additional conversational tasks requiring advanced cognitive skills seemed to support Blesser's thesis. Subjects reversed their cognitive strategy. They abstracted the prosodic features first to gain some feeling for the context and then performed a phonetic match on the features that were intact. Blesser also suggested that personality factors could be predictive. The person who was not upset by failure to get every word, a "synthetic generalist," would do better than a compulsive "analyst." This notion could apply to deaf subjects. Silverman commented that he had speculated about the relationship with lipreading of the kind of personality variables described by Blesser and his experience supported Blesser's point.

The ensuing discussion revolved around such points as subject interaction between sessions, rehearsal of strategies, progress along stages of cognitive difficulty and previous familiarity among subjects. Watson felt that the question of learning spectral information should be pursued by giving the subject systematic training with feedback as to correctness of perception and also having him participate in the kind of interactive situation Blesser had studied. Levitt and Watson suggested experiments in which all spectral cues would be removed and temporal prosodic features retained, using speech-modulated noise. Blesser objected since pitch features and prosodic information in the spectrum would be absent. Other suggestions were made to deal with the confounding of spectral and prosodic cues.

Relative importance of prosodic and phonetic features of speech

Pickett thought that Blesser's findings offered encouragement to those who lose hearing in adult life but were not too applicable to the deaf born who do not develop language competence. The deaf person could not acquire language without having access to phonetic detail which was needed to resolve ambiguities. Liberman pointed out that deaf children did not seem to acquire language through reading. If speech and its phonetic detail were merely ancillary to language, syntactic and semantic constraints could be learned through the printed word. Blesser insisted that speech and syntactic and semantic constraints should be described separately. In the continuing exchange between Blesser and Liberman, they differed in their estimates of the relative contributions of redundancy and phonetic information to various kinds of conversation. Ling said it would be foolhardy to deprive a young deaf child of information about phonetic units since it was difficult to predict the child's responses to a natural language approach. Hirsh commented that length of unit used in teaching was not as important as the style of communication, e.g., corrective teaching versus the necessity for real communication.

Eisenberg asserted that Blesser's subjects were more like people learning a second language than deaf subjects. Given the knowledge and experience of certain rules of language, these rules could be applied to a distorted code. Blesser disagreed and cited experiments with speech scramblers which almost destroyed spectral information and in which reconstruction was accomplished in what Blesser thought was in reverse order from that which is usually proposed, from a framework to function words to content, rather than from phonetic features to syllables, and so on, to sentences. Menyuk commented that the ability of subjects to pick out function words in rotated speech, which Blesser had reported, was clearly related to their knowledge of prosody, of pause and juncture and those changes in fundamental frequency found in phrasal pauses in English. The situation in the acquisition of language was different. Blesser conceded that this was true but prosodic features are available to the hearing-impaired child and he would start out teaching them with this in mind building confidence as he went along.

Design of nonauditory aids

Miller said the discussion suggested further questions as to the features which must be emphasized in presenting the speech signal. If, in designing an aid for a hearing-impaired adult who has language competence, it is possible to present only a limited number of cues, which cues is it important to select? Is this same set of cues or a different set important in the case of the child who is still in the process of acquiring language?

State-of-the-art report

SECTION III: LANGUAGE PROCESSING

Liberman's main thesis was that "grammatical recoding serves to reshape information so as to enable the speaker-listener to move it efficiently between a nonlinguistic intellect, which has facilities for the processing and long-term storage of ideas, and a transmission system, where sounds are produced and perceived." Liberman believed that capacity for grammatical processing evolved as a kind of interface, matching the output of the intellect to the vocal tract and the ear. He suggested that by appropriately interfacing mismatched structures of intellect and transmission, grammar makes possible the efficient communication of ideas from one person to another, the kind of advantage conferred on us by mathematics.

Speaking of the human intellect as though it were in no sense linguistic leaves out of account the possibility that in the evolution of language the intellect and the transmission system themselves underwent alterations that tended to reduce the mismatch. In the case of the vocal tract there is evidence that such an accommodation did occur.

Liberman then considered the function of phonetic representation in the interconversion between ideas and sounds. There is a need for a buffer in which the shorter segments of language can be held until the meaning of the longer segments has been extracted. Liberman suspected that the universal phonetic features became specialized in the evolution of language as appropriate physiological units for storage and processing in that short-term buffer. Speech is not an alphabet or simple substitution cipher on the phonetic representation but rather a complex and grammatical code that enables the system to work efficiently. At the rate at which phonetic segments are communicated a simple cipher would far exceed the temporal resolving power of the ear. The complex code enables the normal listener to get around the problem of temporal resolution and the difficulty of identifying the order of the segments. This is accomplished at the cost of a very complex relation between phonetic message and acoustic signal. We do not realize the complexity because the decoding is ordinarily done by an appropriately complex decoder that speech has easy access to. Unfortunately for the deaf child the decoder is connected to the auditory system.

What are the consequences for grammar when deafness prevents the use of the normal transmission system? If speech is bypassed, as in the case of natural sign, must the child use a grammar different from the grammar of spoken languages? If so, what are the differences and how far "up" the system do they extend? Can the signer adapt the grammar of spoken language? Must he contrive a more suitable grammar? Does it work and at what cost in effort?

Since the substitution of sign for speech does not remove the need to spread ideas in time, how well is the need for short-term storage met? What happens in the case of finger spelling if these substitute signals do not engage the phonetic features? If we avoid the sound by representing the phonetic message directly (as in finger spelling) or if we try to present the acoustic signal to the deaf child, to the eye or the skin, we encounter the problem that arises from the nature of the relation between sound and the phonetic message.

Liberman believed that human beings come equipped with the capacity to develop grammars, including the grammar of speech that connects the phonetic message to the acoustic signal. To the extent that we force these processes into unnatural channels we can expect to encounter difficulties. The inability of people to learn to read spectrograms illustrates this.

Liberman thought that we should want, if possible, to develop in the deaf child a reasonable approximation to standard, spoken language. Because the greatest number of natural grammatical processes is then used, the fullest possible development of language becomes a relatively easy matter, and there is the least risk of crippling the kinds of cognitive processes that normal grammatical processes ordinarily serve. This may be done by transmission of the undecoded speech signal through an auditory or nonauditory modality, or by transmission of the decoded speech signal. It should be emphasized that there is an aspect of the speech signal that has, in principle, nothing to do with encodedness but that can make speech hard to deal with, especially for the deaf. Speech is, from an engineering standpoint, a very poor signal. The important linguistic information is not where the acoustic energy is concentrated and rapid frequency swings, e.g., in formant transitions, are physically indeterminate. Since linguistically important cues are poorly represented perhaps we can help the deaf by altering speech so as to make it a better signal.

To get the undecoded speech signal in by ear and evade the condition of deafness the simplest and most common alteration is obviously amplification, but amplification does not always solve the problem. Complicated alterations take advantage of techniques that enable us to manipulate cues in convenient and flexible ways. Liberman suggested appropriately tailored synthetic speech since he felt it is beyond our present technological capabilities to process real speech in such a way as to produce those patterns that are likely to be most effective. Another possibility derives from the experiments of Rand, who found that when higher and lower frequency regions of a speech signal are presented dichotically, the second and third formants are to a significant extent released from the masking effects of the first formant.

The difficulties of getting the undecoded signal in through a nonauditory modality such as the eye or the skin have been reviewed elsewhere. The difficulty reflects the complexly encoded nature of the relation between the acoustic signal and the phonetic message. Liberman expressed pessimism about the possibility that the eye or the skin can ever be a wholly adequate substitute for the ear, as a pathway for speech sounds or even as an alternative entry to the speech decoder. However, some useful information may be transmitted through nonauditory channels particularly about those transparent stretches of speech not in need of complex decoding. We need to continue our efforts to apply what we know and what we may still learn about the speech code as we tackle the problem of design of prosthetic aids.

In presenting language to the eye of the deaf child we might suppose it would be better not to offer the raw speech signal, which requires decoding, but rather an already decoded alphabetic representation. After all, while people have not learned to read spectrograms they have learned to read language in an alphabetically written form. However, it is not that simple. There is evidence that reading is a secondary linguistic activity in the sense that it is grafted on to a spoken language base. Reading came late in the history of the race. We find that congenitally deaf children, having little or no opportunity to master the primary spoken language, have difficulty acquiring a secondary, written form of it. It surely is important to recognize that reading is significantly harder for those who do not speak—that it is, in effect, difficult to acquire language by eye. With respect to lipreading, Liberman pointed out that although the decoding is not complete, the mouth gestures we see are, contrasted with the acoustic signal, more simply related to the phonetic message.

Liberman commented that, for the language of sign, the transmission system is very different and involves neither the vocal tract nor the ear. We should ask whether the grammar of sign is different from that of any spoken language, and if so, exactly how different? The answer should be of interest to students of language because it tells us something about how far up the grammatical interface the effects of the transmission system extend. If the grammar of sign is very different, is there a price to be paid, either in effort or in efficiency, for not being able to use those grammatical processes that presumably evolved with language and are now a part of our physiology?

DISCUSSION: LANGUAGE PROCESSES AND THE HEARING-IMPAIRED CHILD

Furth presented a model which dealt with the symbolic behavior of the deaf child coming into an educational program at the age of four years (Figure 3.1). Essentially, the deaf child is normal at certain of the levels discussed by Liberman. Intellect and long-term memory are intact and the capacity for symbol formation begins to develop. Unlike that case of the hearing child whose symbols take the form of spoken language, the deaf child has symbols which derive from kinesthetic and visual input. The deaf child's intellect develops rather normally without the acoustic input. Language simply has no place in his development and he has no need of it. He has no motivation to make use of acoustic or visual cues to acquire language. The deaf child at this age has nonverbal symbols, he has grammar, and he does not need verbal language for cognitive and personality development. He organizes his world, he memorizes the world, he stores his experiences, he can recall them. Furth did not wish to convey the idea that language is unimportant to the operations mentioned previously once it is acquired, but what is really important is the underlying capacity which allows us to make use of language and the deaf child has this.

Symbol formation and language in the deaf child

Furth criticized studies on short-term memory of deaf children because the items used in testing were not motivating for them. The deaf child has the capacities that all human beings have. His difficulties are related only to his lack of motivation for learning linguistic cues which are quite meaningless to him.

Eisenberg objected that the deaf child did not develop or organize his world in the same way as the hearing child. A child who has input from four sources is not going to be the same organism as one who has input from five sources. She could not agree that the deaf child was like a hearing child, in that the same rules or concepts could be applied in thinking about him. Furth maintained that characteristically human intelligence is not bound to any particular sensory input. What really counts in human life is the human intelligence and personality. Hirsh agreed with Furth that all human beings have the capacity for language but he felt it would be more profitable to talk about how the deaf child could be brought into a language community which extends to the majority of human beings, than to indulge in metaphysical debate.

In reply, Liberman pointed out that what a person does with his biologically given intellect might depend on the extent to which he can gain access to the grammatical system. Grammatical recoding was necessary for communicating with oneself. If grammatical processes contributed to the ability to move ideas around in our heads, then the consequences for the effectiveness of the intellect could be great.

Boothroyd pointed out that the deaf child causes changes in his linguistic environment just as the environment causes changes in him. The motivation of the child to adapt to the language of a larger community is reduced as the community adapts to his language.

Normal language acquisition

Menyuk thought it would be useful to relate what was known about normal language acquisition and language acquisition in the deaf child. She discussed the one-word stage of development and particularly the influence of context which consists of what is present in the environment plus the behavioral repertoire of the mother and of the child, that is, pointing, gesture, and facial expression. In terms of verbalization, the child seems to be selecting both particular phonetic features to use in talking and particular semantic relations to talk about. Menyuk elaborated these points as they related to the views expressed by Liberman and Furth. She emphasized the importance of considering how mothers talk to their children. She also pointed out the need to analyze form and meaning features for sensory input and to carry this over to training in communication between mother and infant. The progression from the one-word stage to the string of content words without syntax and subsequently to use of syntax was touched upon.

Language acquisition in the deaf child

Ling then presented some data on ways in which mothers communicated with normal-hearing and with hearing-impaired children. These data described the verbal aspects and the nonverbal aspects of communication that Menyuk had referred to. The nonverbal aspects are used by the child to arrive at the speaker's meaning, which he then maps onto verbal symbols used by the speaker. It is interesting that Ling did not observe the use of expansions of the child's utterances on the part of the mother with anything like the frequency (30%) reported in the literature. He felt that this was extremely important in view of the fact that, in the effort to model training of the deaf child upon normal mother-infant interaction, teachers attempt to use expansions.

Sign language and finger spelling

Sign language was not discussed. Not enough expertise was represented to do justice to the topic. Ling mentioned that until recently the lexicon of sign language amounted to about 2500 words and raised the classical question of its range of subtlety as compared with a language such as English. The work on aspects of varying adaptations of signs, concept-gesture and language-gesture relationships needs to be carefully studied. Ling felt that the use of finger spelling did not have the same limitations. He reported an experiment to find out if lipreading and finger spelling would supplement one another as he varied the length of verbal materials presented from syllables to words and phrases. The reader is referred to the data in the body of the proceedings.

Pickett stated that he and his colleagues had been investigating one type of processing of the undecoded signal, namely dichotic presentation of the first and of the second formant of vowels. Their aim was to find out in hearing-impaired listeners (1) if dichotic presentation of speech would reduce the amount of upward spread of masking from F1 to F2, and (2) if this improved discrimination. These data suggest that high- and low-pass hearing aids placed on opposite ears might be of benefit to some hearing-impaired individuals. One needs to be cautious about a mismatch due to unequal amounts of distortion in the two ears. Levitt said he had used a comb filter to extract narrow (third octave) bands from the speech signal, presenting one set of bands to the right ear and a set of intervening bands to the left ear with six deaf children. A small but fairly significant improvement in speech reception was found with the comb filter type hearing aid. Liberman felt that the question of filter width should be studied further.

Getting the undecoded signal in by ear

Ling described a study carried out by his wife in which digits were presented both monotically and dichotically to hearing-impaired and normal children. The responses of the hearing-impaired children were inferior to those of normal children for both types of presentation. On the dichotic task, normal-hearing children showed a small right ear superiority while the hearing-impaired did not. Some individual hearing-impaired children showed a large right or left ear superiority, but the most striking feature of their performance was their tendency to respond to one ear only, suppressing the stimulus to the other ear.

The discussion then focused on the merits of current attempts to present supplementary speech information to the visual and tactile senses by means of specially designed devices. Erber felt that essentially the profoundly deaf subject showed the same degree of improvement when receiving vibrotactile time/intensity cues from his hearing aid. Recent attempts to analyze the signal in some way before presenting it to the visual or tactile sense were more ambitious.

Getting the undecoded signal in by a nonauditory modality

The form of display of the undecoded speech signal which is to be presented to a nonauditory modality is a fundamental question. Among those presently available are (1) the vocoder, which performs a filtered spectral analysis and presents the output to the skin or the eye, (2) a feature extractor, which makes decisions about the presence or absence of features such as nasality, plosion, and frication presented to the eye or skin, and (3) a traveling wave display. Whether the deaf child can extract important features presented to the eye or skin by vocoder or traveling wave is open to question.

Sherrick felt there was merit in tactile devices based on cochlear analogs and that the problem of frequency transposition in real time was not insurmountable. Denes said he was not clear what basic principle of information processing was inherent in the Bekesy model which would facilitate speech learning. In what way would it be an improvement over available devices that give visual or tactile transforms of the acoustic speech signal? Denes maintained that the eye was a better substitute for the ear than skin. For example, we learn to read the written word. Hirsh commented that the skin in handling complicated vibratory patterns responds in a time-associated sense modality and is more like the ear than the eye. The eye responds to a spatial display of information over time as in a spectrogram but cannot read the information with ease. Liberman cited two possible reasons for the difficulty in reading spectrograms. First, the spectrographic signal is a poor one since the acoustic energy is not concentrated where the important linguistic information is, e.g., in rapidly changing formant transitions. From this point of view the skin might provide a more efficient input channel than the eye. Second, it is conceivable that there are special devices in our auditory system which have the ability to deal with linguistically important information. Even then, because a "cleaned up" signal is a code and not a cipher, decoding will remain a problem whenever the acoustic information of speech is presented to a nonauditory sensory modality. Liberman questioned whether the decoder can in fact be hooked up to any sensory modality other than hearing.

Hirsh agreed, if the statement were restricted to the acoustics of speech, but felt that pre-phonetic categories of articulatory gestures of which lipreading was an example might be easier to process. Ling stated that sensory aids should supplement lipreading and should operate in real time. He described an experiment in feature extraction in which a tactile aid displayed frication and nonfrication. The results of training were promising.

Miller commented on the optimism/pessimism issue with respect to nonauditory aids. Some profoundly deaf children who have essentially no usable hearing have the sensory ability to learn language including speech. Perhaps with the aid of special devices others could also. The experimental evidence thus far shows that nonauditory aids improve the speech recognition of deaf children to some extent, consistently and reliably. However, the spectrogram is hard to use in this way and Denes and Liberman provided a valuable service in making this clear. In general, he felt, there was room for mild optimism.

Transmission of the decoded signal

The participants raised questions as to whether learning to speak would facilitate reading, or conversely, if learning to read would facilitate speaking. Menyuk felt that these questions were premature and grossly oversimplified. Nevertheless, the participants discussed means for more rapid transmission of the decoded signal, e.g., a computer operated typescript prosthesis, with or without an accompanying visual or auditory display of the message in synthetic speech.

Levitt considered nonauditory systems where the rates of transfer of speech information were close to those for normal speech. These included touch shorthand, speech-reading (lipreading), and reading by means of tactual coding, e.g., with the aid of the Optacon device. House felt that short forms in some nonspeech systems, and the type of recoding that takes place in reading and speech recognition, might be very different. He wished to concentrate on the effects of communication solely by typewritten means. Ling objected that a message could not be related to everyday events, actions or objects, if the receiver were attending to a typescript or other visual display. He believed that children needed to explore relations by combining words before they could learn to read. Only when they could define words in terms of other words were they ready to read on their own.

Blesser felt that speech and written language were not interchangeable. It is true that both involve cognitive activity but written language as the child experienced it was socially passive, introspective, without emotional responsiveness or motivation for contact. These features were related directly to questions of motivation for learning. If there were written forms of the language which had the characteristics of speech, namely social and emotional responsiveness, extroversion, and contact, then the linguistic contrast between them might disappear.

Watson then developed some speculation about the possible role of extra-curricular reading for deaf children and emphasized that the intellect and personality in civilized man continued to develop and change after puberty. He questioned, among other assumptions by investigators, that language abilities are fully acquired in the developmental era of birth to puberty. House commented that there were two channels of research that ought to be exploited more fully than at present: the use of reading per se and the use of a typescript prosthesis. Should education be putting more emphasis on reading as a way of teaching language skills? Is reading a more practical and profoundly important way of getting language in a deaf population? Miller cautioned against this approach. Without a strong base in spoken language, the child might learn destructive reading strategies, like guessing from nouns and pictures. Ling again emphasized that spoken language should come first. Conditions conducive to spoken language acquisition should be engineered prior to those for reading. The conditions he observed in many schools mitigated against intellectual and language growth, speaking and reading. He seconded Miller's thoughts on destructive habits. Watson pointed out that he was not proposing self-motivated reading as a substitute for, but as a supplement to, a curriculum.

Rosenstein thought that cued speech should also be taken into consideration as a phonetically based system which should facilitate reading. In this system hand gestures are used to disambiguate all gestures which look alike on the lips. The gestures have the important property that they cannot be read in the absence of speech gestures at the mouth; they only supplement the information of speech gestures.

In thinking of ways to engineer proper conditions for learning Miller suggested reinforcement to modify behavior. He cited recent work classifying learning situations in three categories: (1) those for which the animal is prepared, (2) those for which he is unprepared, and (3) those for which he is contra-prepared. Since animals differ with respect to these categories, we cannot think of laws of learning as universal. This has implications. for training human subjects. Miller suggested that a human is prepared to learn auditory tasks in a social situation but unprepared to learn tactile tasks in this way. This is not to say that he cannot learn such tasks, but that he would have great difficulty in doing so.

This discussion continued up to the scheduled time for closing the conference. In deference to the discussion the oral summary was omitted. Nevertheless, this summarizer, Chairman of the Conference, cannot resist the opportunity to express in writing his appreciation for the contributions of all participants, to Dr. John Bordley for his hospitality, to Mrs. Lyda Sanford, secretary for arrangements, and finally and importantly to Dr. Rachel E. Stark for her compilation and organization of the manuscript and for the efficient and gracious manner in which she fulfilled the many responsibilities placed upon her in connection with the Conference. I am encouraged by the interest of so many able people from allied fields in problems of deaf children. This interest is, indeed, welcome at a time when rational approaches are needed to the many controversies current in the field. I trust that in the future the problems of deaf children will continue to appeal to the curious minds and the humanitarian impulses of all of our participants and their co-workers.

11

Looking to the Future:
Overview and Preview

Rachel E. Stark, Ph.D.
Johns Hopkins University School of Medicine

The aim of this Conference was to bring together investigators from a number of fields so that they might consider the problems of deaf children. It was hoped that, as they exchanged their views they would generate fresh concepts with respect to the habilitation of deaf children, concepts based upon the child's needs and capabilities as well as upon the technology presently available. Some of the information deriving from research over the last decade, which was already available to the participants, was not discussed, partly because it was known and thus was a given aspect of the discussion; partly because of time limitation. In this section, I shall attempt to relate the issues raised in discussion and the research aims which were identified to this background material.

The participants occupied themselves largely with questions about teaching a standard, spoken language to the deaf child. Most participants took the point of view that success in this endeavor was important because it would give the child access to a larger community, and to the shared experience of that community in the form of ideas, expression of opinion, news, and all aspects of its culture. Furth (1971) has shown that the deaf child's performance on certain tasks reflects linguistic and thus cultural deprivation. The endeavor would also facilitate the deaf child's academic progress and possibly even his ability to handle concepts and ideas (Liberman, p. 132). The participants did not necessarily believe that manual communication skills should not be taught under any circumstances, either solely or in combination with spoken language. This question was not addressed in depth. Readers interested in recent concepts with respect to manual communication might wish to consult Kavanagh and Cutting (1973).

ACQUISITION OF STANDARD, SPOKEN LANGUAGE

Relation of speech skills to measures of hearing

First of all, the participants reviewed current information about the relationship between residual hearing, as reflected in the audiometric configuration, and speech skills, i.e., speech perception and production skills. Several of the participants (Boothroyd, p. 36; Levitt, p. 42; Erber, p. 46) had recently re-established the finding that both perception and production skills are highly correlated with average pure-tone thresholds in the frequency ranges most important for speech. The relation held when perceptual capabilities were measured in terms of phoneme recognition (Smith, 1973) or of word recognition (Erber, 1972); and when production was measured in terms of overall speech intelligibility or percentage of phonemes judged to be correctly produced (Boothroyd, 1972; Smith, 1973). Measures of these speech perception and production skills were also highly correlated with one another (Smith, 1973). The slope of the audiometric configuration was also identified as an important factor in speech acquisition (see also Wedenberg, 1954; Risberg and Martony, 1972; and Martony et al., 1972). However, the role of perception and production of prosodic features of speech and their relationship with one another was less clear (Levitt, unpublished data).

A more recent concept was that of a bimodal distribution in the population of deaf children based on the presence or absence of residual hearing (Risberg, 1968a; Erber, 1972). Some subjects with total loss of hearing give responses to pure tones in the lower frequencies when these tones are of sufficient intensity to give rise to vibrotactile sensation. However, these subjects can receive only time and intensity information about the speech waveform from vibrotactile input and their scores on speech production and speech perception tasks are correspondingly depressed.

The effect of level and slope of audiometric configuration can be understood in terms of the acoustic structure of speech. For example, the vowels are recognized by means of the peaks in their spectra, i.e., their formant structure. Deaf children are better able to identify back vowels (e.g., /u/ as in 'do'), whose first and second formants are in a low frequency region, than front vowels (e.g., /i/ as in 'see'), whose second formant is high (Smith, 1973) as would be predicted from the responses of deaf adults (Pickett et al., 1972). Normal-hearing subjects respond in a similar way when listening to vowels in which the higher formant structure is masked by noise (Pickett, 1957). In addition, the lower frequencies in speech are higher in intensity than the higher frequencies, and thus tend to mask the higher frequencies, especially when the speech signal is presented at levels above those of conversational speech (Martin and Pickett, 1970; Danaher et al., 1973). Pickett and Danaher (1973) have shown that, in amplified synthetic speech, the more intense first formant (F1) of the vowel has a backward masking effect, i.e., it can mask the weaker F2 even when the onset of F1 is delayed with respect to F2 by as much as 150 msec. This effect disappears when the two formants are presented dichotically, i.e., F1 to one ear and F2 to the other.

The transition, or movement over time across a portion of the frequency scale, of the second formant (F2) of a vowel sound provides important cues not only to the identity of a steady-state vowel sound but also for identification of consonant sounds adjacent to that vowel, especially with respect to place of articulation of these sounds. Children with little residual hearing in the frequency regions above 500 Hz have difficulty in hearing F2 transitions and thus in recognizing the place of articulation of consonants. In addition, consonant sounds are less intense than vowel sounds (Fletcher, 1929).

Presenting the undecoded signal to the auditory system

These findings have implications for hearing aid design. The overall gain of the aid must be sufficient to make consonant sounds audible (p. 108); high-frequency emphasis deserves special attention (Miller, p. 109; Thomas and Sparks, 1971); low-frequency emphasis, although helpful to some children listening in quiet (Ling, 1969) may be detrimental in noisy settings (Martin and Pickett, 1971; Sung, Sung and Angelelli, 1971); and the transposition of higher frequencies to lower frequency regions may be of benefit to a few deaf children (Johansson, 1966; Ling, 1968; Foust and Gengel, 1973). The strategy of dividing the frequency range of speech sounds into bands and presenting certain bands to one ear and the remaining bands to the other ear should be explored further (Franklin, 1970; Rosenthal et al., 1972).

If dichotic presentation of this kind were to be tried with children, however, special training in attending to the information arriving at both ears might be necessary. A.H. Ling's (1971) finding, that school-age hearing-impaired children attend predominantly to the right ear or the left ear in dichotic listening (p. 166), did not appear to be related to hearing levels at the two ears. The same phenomenon is observed in normal-hearing preschool children (Yeni-Komshian, personal communication); it is possible that its persistence in hearing-impaired children is related to linguistic immaturity.

A further suggestion was that synthetic speech might be used in training the deaf child in speech perception (Liberman, p. 136). Important cues in the speech spectrum could be presented clearly and precisely by this means. Once familiar with these cues, the deaf child might be better able to abstract them from the noise and imprecision of the real speech signal.

Auditory perceptual skills

Some disquiet was expressed (Sherrick, p. 62) that tests of speech production and perception were being used to infer auditory perceptual capabilities in hearing-impaired children. Others, e.g., Eisenberg (p. 18), felt that we should approach the problems of deaf children by studying the basic capabilities of the deafened auditory system. Techniques developed in studying both normal and impaired systems with respect to these capabilities, e.g., temporal resolving power (Smiarowski, 1970; Perrott and Williams, 1971; Patterson and Green, 1970; Ronken, 1970; Resnick, 1973), temporal integration (Watson and Gengel, 1969; Gengel and Watson, 1971), ability to order acoustic events temporally (Hirsh, 1959; Hirsh and Sherrick, 1961; and Gengel, 1972b), and difference limens for frequency (Pickett and Martony, 1970; Gengel, 1969) and duration (Abel, 1972) could be applied to the study of hearing-impaired children. Ability to perceive features of synthetic speechlike stimuli, e.g., the amount of change in a sweep tone necessary for recognition of a frequency transition (Martin et al., 1972), was also thought to be important. The findings of such studies might cause us to revise our concepts of training or our approaches to sensory aids. Elliot (observer) added the comment, contributed after the workshop, that although basic information concerning the capacity of the deafened human system to process sensory information will be needed and sought for many years, the pressing, urgent need is for research and development which examines communication competency among the hearing-impaired and which seeks to improve those competencies. Statistically significant differences between sets of laboratory administered treatments may be dissolved by the realities of a lifelike situation and, too often, the question of generalization, e.g., to other stimuli or other settings, is never raised. The problem is analogous to the gulf between establishing curves of serial learning and the difficulty of teaching certain children to read.

Nonauditory perceptual skills

It was also felt that too little was known about the nonauditory perceptual skills of deaf children (Bordley, p. 62). The results of some tests of such skills, e.g., of oral sterognosis and short-term memory for phonemes, appeared to reflect the level of the deaf child's skill in speaking (Bishop et al., 1973; Conrad, 1973). The relationship might indicate that in the absence of these skills speech is less likely to develop; or alternatively, that these skills are not developed if, by reason of extent of hearing loss, lack of motivation or inadequate instruction, the child does not learn to speak. Knowledge of nonauditory perceptual skills becomes particularly important when the decision is made to use nonauditory input in training.

Specially tailored amplification probably will not be as useful to children with hearing below 500 Hz only, or to children with no residual hearing at all. In their cases, it was suggested (Sherrick, p. 13; Liberman, p. 137) that information from another sensory modality be provided as a supplement to, or substitute for, hearing. The supplementary information with which we are most familiar derives from lipreading. Skill in lipreading is itself not well understood (Franks and Oyer, 1967; Neyhus, 1969; Hardick et al., 1970; Berger et al., 1970). It has been shown that lipreading and hearing or vibrotactile input do supplement one another in speech reception (Erber, 1972). However, the two forms of input combined do not always yield a perfect score, even under favorable lighting and speaker conditions. Certain kinds of information, e.g., information about pitch contour, voicing, and nasality, may still be absent or ambiguous in the case of the child with no residual hearing. Errors made in lipreading because of the absence of these cues are reflected in speech production, i.e., sound contrasts poorly discriminated in lipreading are poorly discriminated in speech production (Levitt, p. 62).

Additional forms of nonauditory input may be used in prosthetic devices to supplement hearing and/or lipreading. Their use gives rise to further problems which have to do with the fact that speech is not a cipher, with a direct, invariant relationship between acoustic pattern and phoneme, but a code (Liberman et al., 1967). Briefly, this means that one small stretch of the acoustic speech stream carries information about more than one phoneme element. This multidimensionality makes the speech code a highly efficient one, with the possibility of rapid transmission rates (Nye, 1963). As a corollary of their multidimensionality, however, the patterns yielding perception of certain phonemes, e.g., stops and glides, vary from one speech context to another (Liberman et al., 1967; Klatt and Stevens, 1971). Patterns will also vary with stress, and with the age and sex of the speaker. It is not clear how we recover these varying phoneme elements from the speech stream; but it has been suggested that the capability is inherent in the auditory system and that, in this system, the speech signal is processed differently from the nonspeech signal (Hirsh, p. 4; Liberman, 1970). In the view of these investigators, the special speech processing capability cannot be made to handle acoustic speech signals delivered to another sensory modality, i.e., by visual or tactile input. Lipreading is an exception because it utilizes visual information about articulatory gestures directly, rather than acoustic information.

Sensory capability and response proclivity in speech reception

Two basic aspects of perception were proposed in the course of the workshop (Watson, pp. 86–91), in terms of which we may consider the special ability of normal-hearing adults to decode speech. These aspects were sensory capability, i.e., what we are capable of doing with our senses, and response proclivity, i.e., what we actually do with our senses. For example, although we can be trained to discriminate differences in the ordering of very brief tones in 3-element sequences (Divenyi and Hirsh, 1973) and to discriminate 10-tone sequences which differ only in the frequency of one of their 40-msec. elements (Watson, p. 91), we more often exercise such fine discrimination skills in our response to speech. This response proclivity may be determined by the natural affinity of the auditory system for the speech signal, by our continuous exposure to speech, or both of these factors. On the one hand, our ability to perceive speech may be attributable to the evolution of special detectors and integrative processes in the auditory system (Liberman, p. 169), just as our versatility in speech production can be attributed in part to evolutionary changes in vocal tract configuration (Lieberman et al., 1972). Perhaps these special properties are engaged only by signals identified as speech at some pre-processing stage. On the other hand, perhaps we can be trained to utilize them in processing any complex auditory signal, given a sufficient number of trials with feedback, i.e., immediate indication to the subject about the correctness of his response.

Relationship of speech reception and speech production

Our receptive processing of speech reflects the special relation between speech perception and speech production. We not only monitor our own output and receive input from others in terms of the same set of features, we may also receive input from others in terms of our own output. This idea has been developed in analysis-by-synthesis models for speech perception (Stevens and Halle, 1967; Stevens and House, 1972). In its most recent form, this model includes peripheral auditory analysis (e.g., feature detection) and preliminary analysis (derivation of phonemes which are not context-dependent) (Stevens, 1972). These components of the model have to be borne in mind when considering the development of speech perception and production (see p. 112, p. 148). The correspondence of perceptual and productive processes does not obtain for many complex acoustic signals other than those of speech, and in some cases of music. It is consciously applied by the deaf subject attempting to match an articulatory model with the aid of tactile or visual speech input. The latter experience has until now been provided on an experimental basis and has therefore been of relatively short duration. It is noteworthy that older school-age subjects have been reported as more successful in such matching tasks than younger school-age subjects (Levitt, 1972b; Boothroyd, 1972). The kind of learning the older subjects demonstrate is likely to be quite different from that which we see in preschool children acquiring spoken language. None of these older subjects has learned to read speech with any degree of success, utilizing visual or tactile input. We do not know whether preschool profoundly deaf children are likely to acquire speech as a result of continuous, long term exposure to such input or not. Before undertaking a project designed to test the effects of such exposure, it was agreed that we need to know more about (1) the relative importance of different speech production errors for the intelligibility of the speech of deaf children (Levitt, 1972a); (2) the ways in which normal-hearing children acquire speech perception and speech production skills (Menyuk, p. 148); and (3) those aspects of nonauditory sensory modalities, i.e., vision and taction, which would dictate the design and format of the display device (Sherrick, p. 13, p. 168; Eisenberg, p. 18; Denes, p. 169).

Speech production errors of deaf children

In the 1930's and 1940's, Hudgins and Numbers described many of the speech errors of deaf children and attempted to assess the correlation of different types of errors with speech intelligibility. A number of studies have been carried out more recently with a similar aim (Calvert, 1961; Martony, 1966; Lafon et al., 1967; Markides, 1970; Smith, 1973). These have agreed in finding (1) the average speech intelligibility score for tape recorded speech of deaf children is about 19% (for naive listeners) and (2) that both phonemic and prosodic errors contribute to this failure of intelligibility. Those studies employing techniques of acoustic analysis (Calvert, 1961; Martony, 1966; Levitt, 1972a) indicate that errors in timing result in both phonemic and prosodic errors. Phonemic errors are also related to lack of formant structure of vowel sounds and lack of vowel transitions.

Brannon (1964) tracked tongue movement during speech with the aid of a glossal transducer and found not only that tongue movements of deaf children were slower than normal but also that additional unnecessary tongue movements were added. Huntingdon et al. (1968) obtained electromyographic data for the speech of three young deaf adults. Speech patterns varied a great deal from subject to subject but showed a high degree of within-subject consistency.

Speech reception skills in normal-hearing children

Eimas et al. (1971), Eisenberg (p. 20), Moffit (1971), Morse (1972), and Trehub and Rabinovich (1972) have found that, very early in life, infants show remarkable speech discrimination capabilities. Even in the first week of life Eisenberg (personal communication) has recorded different EEG patterns in response to the vowels /a/ and /ae/. Using measures of heart rate and nonnutritive sucking, other investigators cited above have shown that, in the first months of life, infants discriminate voiced and voiceless stops, e.g., /ba/ from /pa/, voiced stops produced at different places in the vocal tract, e.g., /ba/ from /ga/, and a falling and rising intonation on a single stop-vowel syllable. These findings have cast doubt upon statements by earlier investigators (Lewis, 1951; Fry, 1966; Weir, 1966; Lieberman, 1967a) that intonation and other suprasegmental features are distinguished earlier by the infant than segmental or phonemic features (Morse, 1972).

In a more recent paper, however, Morse (1973) has suggested that, although the features of place, voicing, and intonation are linguistically relevant and the specific voicing cues discriminated by infants are those used by adults in categorical perception of speech sounds, the infant responds to these cues by virtue of low-level auditory processing. The cues are not linguistically relevant for him. Ability to extract unencoded phonemes (the preliminary analysis stage in Stevens' analysis-by-synthesis model) and encoded phonemes which are relevant to his language has still to be acquired. In this process, the infant may show developmental changes in his mode of transferring information from a preperceptual store to an auditory and phonetic short-term store (Massaro, 1972; Pisoni, 1971), a processing sequence referred to by Morse as microgenetic coding. At the same time the infant must acquire linguistic coding capabilities; these are determined by his knowledge of the grammars of speech and language (Liberman, 1970) at any particular time.

Similarly, the infant must learn to utilize prosodic features in speech perception and production. Kaplan (1969), for example, has found that infants do not discriminate a rising and a falling intonation contour on the final word of a short sentence, 'See the cat,' until eight months of age, and then only if the final word is stressed. This finding suggests that infants acquire the ability to discriminate differences of intonation contour in long speech sequences (sentences) later than in short speech sequences (syllables). The ability to utilize and interpret different patterns of intonation, rhythm, and stress may, in turn, be related to increasing skill in recognizing phonemes, and increasing knowledge of phonological rules. At one stage, for example, the infant may respond to stress and intonation as indications of the emotional state of the speaker (Buhler, 1930); at another he may utilize stress and intonation to locate the key words of an utterance (Macnamara, 1971; Brown, 1973) while at a third stage, he may utilize these features as an aid to arriving at the syntactic structure of a sentence (Lieberman, 1967b; McNeill, 1970). It is tempting to think of this development as cyclical in nature, in that learning to handle phonemes and phoneme sequences at progressive levels of difficulty might alternate with learning to utilize suprasegmental features in increasingly complex ways. Whether or not this is true, it seems that the speech addressed to infants is characterized by exaggerations of stress and intonation contour and possibly also of articulation, which might facilitate the infant's ability to recognize and use these features in speech reception (Snow, 1973; Phillips, 1970).

Acquisition of speech production skills in normal-hearing children

In the acquisition of speech production skills, the elaboration of smaller segments and of the larger framework within which the segments occur may also be taking place alternately rather than one being completed before the other is undertaken. For example, as the class of stop consonants undergoes modification, its members begin to be produced within increasingly complex prosodic patterns. When initial stops first appear at 25 to 35 weeks of age, they are voiced (Preston et al., 1969) and are used in single stop-vowel syllables, or strings of identical syllables. Each string is initiated by a vowel sound, and a silence is interposed between each one of its members (e.g., ə dæ dæ dæ) (Stark et al., in preparation). During the second year of life initial stops at all three places of articulation, labial, apical, and velar, begin to be produced in jargonlike utterances in which segmental and suprasegmental features appear in combinations of great variety. Similar elaborations of the stop-vowel segments and of the prosodic framework in which they occur may be observed later during spoken language acquisition. As stops are successively used in patterns of (1) single-word utterances (Greenfield et al., 1973), (2) two-word utterances (Bloom, 1970), (3) so-called telegraphic utterances (Bellugi, 1972), and (4) well-formed sentences (Menyuk, 1969; McNeill, 1970; Brown, 1973), greater control over the voiced-voiceless distinction for stops is being acquired (Port and Preston, 1972; Zlatin, 1972).

Prosodic features in speech reception and production

As the result of learning and experience, the adult speaker-listener is able to make running predictions as to the structure and meaning of an utterance addressed to him. In doing so, he probably makes heavy use of prosodic features, e.g., intonation, timing and stress (Blesser, 1972). If his predictions are correct, as in the case of stereotyped exchange or conversation about highly familiar matters, he may be able to recover the intent of an utterance using higher level linguistic units only, i.e., syllables and words (Fodor and Bever, 1965; Garrett et al., 1966; Neisser, 1967). When the speech material is less familiar, he may have to process utterances addressed to him with reference to lower level units, i.e., phonemes and possibly phonetic features. This use of lower level units appears to be more time consuming (Savin and Bever, 1970), and may involve cognitive rather than perceptual processing (see Pollack, p. 80).

The importance of prosodic features of speech and in particular its rhythmic structure has been stressed by J. Martin (1972). Martin proposes that rhythmic structure, i.e., temporal patterning of speech, is central to the problems of serial ordering in its production (Lashley, 1951) and provides a link between perception and production of speech. Also, the temporal patterning of speech implies a hierarchical structure with respect to the sound elements of which it is comprised. This structure must be observed in the motor control of speech production; it may at some stage in the generative process be imposed upon the neural commands specifying positional targets in the vocal tract (MacNeilage, 1970). It may also be used in speech perception. By means of the temporal patterning of speech, the adult may be able to predict the locus of the next accented syllable, i.e., the next highly informative unit of an utterance. Thus, his attention may be focused upon segmental feature analysis of earlier parts of the utterance during low information intervals (J. Martin, 1972, p. 503).

Deaf child's use of prosodic features

Blesser proposed that we should help the deaf child to better speech by teaching him to rely more upon the prosodic framework available to him. The ability of congenitally deaf children with severe to profound losses to utilize prosodic features in speech perception appears to be very limited (Smith, 1973), although these features are present in low-frequency regions of the speech signal and are thus available to most deaf children. Many profoundly deaf children have difficulty in discriminating productions of a single sentence in which different patterns of timing, intonation, and stress are used (Levitt, 1973). Similarly, profoundly deaf children do not reflect the prosodic patterns used by others in their attempt to speak (Hudgins and Numbers, 1942; John and Howarth, 1965; Lafon et al., 1967).

This failure to use prosodic features may result from the deaf child's difficulty in receiving and producing segmental features. Thus, the segmental features are never inserted into the prosodic framework, in perception or production, and the framework retains little value for him. This lack of use of the framework may, in part, result from too heavy an emphasis on phoneme production or reception, and too little on prosodic features in speech instruction; or from a failure to learn their relation to one another at successive levels of organization. As a result, the deaf child may have difficulty in recovering linguistic units at different hierarchical levels in receiving speech or in reading. Boothroyd (p. 114) points out, for example, that many deaf children tend to use strategies in both reading and lipreading which reflect a concatenative rather than a hierarchical model of language. These children search for single words and subsequently assign relationships to these words by virtue of guesswork which they base upon pictures or contextual features. In addition, the written output of many profoundly deaf children is limited to the use of either strings of simple noun and pronoun words or to simple subject-predicate sentences in which stereotyped verb forms, e.g., the present participle, appear (Levitt, 1973). These features of their written output may reflect teaching methods which fail to present a model of language which is hierarchical with respect to its grammatical structure.

Display format for nonauditory aids

In planning for the use of nonauditory aids we must take into account not only the deaf child's knowledge of language, but also the special nature of the modality to be used and thus, the most suitable format for presenting speech signals by means of that modality. Two strategies have been employed in designing nonauditory displays. One is to present an uncomplicated signal providing information about prosodic or articulatory features which are not easily received through lipreading (Upton, 1968; Martony, 1968, 1972; Risberg, 1968b; Goldberg, 1972; Willemain and Lee, 1972; Gengel et al., 1973; Cornett, 1973; Houde, 1973). These displays are less useful in a noisy situation such as a cocktail party or a classroom. Another strategy is to present a highly complex but integrated display conveying the undecoded acoustic information in the speech signal. Such displays have proved useful in training speech production skills (Stark, Cullen, and Chase, 1968; Stark, 1972), but, in spite of early optimism, have not been very useful as aids to speech perception (Potter, Kopp, and Green, 1947; House et al., 1968; Pickett and Pickett, 1963; Kringlebotn, 1968).

In the case of the visual sense, we must observe the limitations imposed by poor temporal resolution. We may take advantage of the eye's superior spatial resolution by presenting vocoded speech information spread out spatially and stored over time, as in the speech spectrogram. The resulting signal is a complex one which even normal speakers have great difficulty in reading (Liberman et al., 1968). Perhaps the difficulty would be less if pitch and stress patterns were presented simultaneously with segmental and timing information, i.e., by means of color or emphasis upon three dimensional depth; and if the patterns were presented sufficiently often in a real speech context to allow the subject to detect phonologic, semantic, and syntactic regularities.

With respect to both temporal and spatial resolution, the skin's power falls somewhere between that of the eye and of the ear. Major problems which have been encountered in presenting speech to the skin, at least by means of a tactual vocoder, have to do with the poor frequency response of the skin and the slow rate at which a sensation reaches its full value and with which it disappears after the stimulus is withdrawn (Bekesy, 1959). Also the spatial separation of stimulators in a tactual vocoder does not prevent simultaneous masking of one point by another (Sherrick, 1964; Geldard, 1968). This strategy further limits the amount of information transmitted. A quite different approach has been suggested by the work of White et al. (1970), and of Linvill and Bliss (1966), who have found that spatio-temporal stimulation of a large number of points in a manner that permits coherent perceptual organization of input will provide optimal utilization of the skin sense, at least for the purpose of reading print. Perceptual organization requires not only that the patterns should be moved over the cutaneous surface as in the case of the subject reading braille, but also that there should be a high degree of correlation between one set of stimulus points and the next (Kirman, 1973). These requirements are met in the most recent use of basilar membrane models for skin stimulation and could be met in the presentation of a vocoded signal. In the case of speech, patterns representing rhythm and pitch should probably be preserved simultaneously with patterns representing phonemic units. Research along these lines is presently being undertaken (Magrisso, 1972; Kirman, 1973; Keidel, 1973).

Reading as a first language input

It was also suggested in the course of the workshop (p. 138) that a decoded signal, e.g., finger spelling or some form of typescript, might be used as a primary means of teaching the deaf child language (Department of Education and Science Report, 1968; Morkovin, 1962; Lenneberg, 1967). The major problem with such systems is that of transmission rate. Also, it would probably be difficult for young children to attend to these forms of visual input and to lipreading at the same time. Ling's (p. 162) work further suggests that the sequential presentation of letters as in finger spelling makes it difficult to achieve chunking, i.e., to organize the input into higher level linguistic units. The same is true in the case of sequential presentation of printed letter forms (Nye, 1963; Taenzer, 1970).

Typed messages might be transmitted with sufficient rapidity for mother-child or teacher-child interaction if touch shorthand were used. Emphasis and the emotional content of the message could in such situations be conveyed by gesture and facial expression. The question is, could this form of communication be used as the primary or even the sole form of communication with deaf children? We know of only one attempt to teach deaf children to communicate primarily by means of written language, and this attempt has been made with multiply-handicapped deaf children (Kirsch and Preston, in preparation). These investigators have taught at least two deaf, retarded children, who had not succeeded in acquiring oral or manual communication skills, to read and to write. During planned lesson periods with one instructor, the children used reading and writing of words communicatively. One child, by means of the Fitzgerald Language Key, was taught to respond to simple subject-predicate sentences and to express himself in previously learned sentences. He did not generalize the use of language forms in his own output nor expand his knowledge of words beyond the restricted set used in the classroom. These limitations might, however, be a function of his cognitive deficit.

Normally intelligent deaf children can be made to demonstrate logical thinking based upon picture symbols conveying concepts of classes and logical connectives (Furth, 1966). They are less likely to succeed in a symbol discovery task in which they must use initiative to arrive at the meaning of pictured symbols (Youniss and Furth, 1964). Learning to read English, however, might be a more difficult task than responding to picture sequences, since the unit of written English is the grapheme. It is necessary to learn only a small stock of graphemes but the correspondence of these graphemes to the phonemes of English has then to be acquired. Many normal-hearing children have trouble with the grapheme-phoneme correspondence, which demands a high level of linguistic awareness (Mattingly, 1972). Some of these children are better able to read Chinese characters (Rozin, Poritsky and Sotsky, 1971). There are many thousands of these characters, each one quite complex and composed of separate parts (S.E. Martin, 1972). They correspond to morphemes of the language rather than phonemes. Thus, verbal skills are still involved in the learning of these characters.

Intermediate use of phonemic coding may not be essential to reading in the normal-hearing adult (Baron, 1973), but may be important in early stages of learning to read. However, there is evidence that deaf children learn to recognize grapheme patterns (e.g., blong vs. nblog) as allowable in English or not (Gibson et al., 1970). They acquire this recognition skill even when they cannot produce the units represented and thus use their knowledge of pronounceableness in making the judgment. It has also been shown that some deaf children encode letters visually, i.e., by shape, rather than auditorially, i.e., by letter name (Conrad, 1970, 1972). It is believed that the short persistence of memory traces for visual stimuli (Neisser, 1967) might make purely visual coding less efficient than auditory coding. However, Paivio (1971) suggests that visual imagery, if linked to a symbolic motor response, might provide an effective code for serial processing and storage in short-term memory. If this is true, then deaf children may well be able to use visual imagery linked with a symbolic motor response. The motor response pattern in that case could be that of typing a particular set of keys or of finger spelling (Locke and Locke, 1971), and could be evoked at higher levels in the nervous system rather than at the periphery.

DIRECTIONS FOR FUTURE RESEARCH

In this final section, I shall attempt to summarize the views expressed during the Conference as to the direction which future research might take. Some of the participants urged that more basic research should be undertaken while others argued for more applied research. Silverman in a comment contributed after the Conference expressed the view that a compromise between these two types of studies should be maintained. As our knowledge increases, the gap between them should diminish.

Areas in which it was indicated that continued or renewed efforts might be most profitable are outlined below. In some cases, the outline may reflect my own biases.

Early detection of hearing loss

Economical and reliable methods of objective assessment of hearing in young infants should be developed. These methods might utilize heart rate measures as proposed by Eisenberg, or evoked response audiometry, as proposed by Davis and his colleagues at CID. Recommendations with respect to such procedures, and also parent and physician education, are dealt with in Miller (1972, pps. 12–13). However, early identification will be of value only if suitable amplification and training are provided.

Development of prostheses

Research attention should be given to the design of hearing aids, especially those prescribed for young children. This topic was also dealt with in a previous conference (Miller, 1972). A new suggestion was that different frequency bands should be presented to the right and to the left ear. This might reduce masking of higher frequencies by the more intense lower frequencies of speech. Dichotic presentation might require that child users be trained to pay attention to information from both ears (see p. 137). Its use might underscore a need for studies of binaural phenomena in general in young normal-hearing and deaf children. In addition, it was suggested that some classic studies of transfer functions and frequency response of hearing aids should be repeated with modern techniques and instrumentation (Pickett, p. 108; Miller, p. 109).

For the child with little or no residual hearing, nonauditory prostheses should be developed. These might have as their aims (1) supplementation of the time-intensity cues and lipreading information which these children already receive and (2) provision of input intended to substitute for hearing. Both approaches involve the difficult task of developing on-line speech analyses.

A feature extraction device would fulfill the first aim. Prosodic and/or phonemic features presented to the eye or the skin should supplement lipreading and residual hearing (see p. 52). The device would be very useful in training school-age deaf children. It is not yet clear whether the signals should be based upon the cued speech system which was designed to disambiguate lipreading or whether they should be made to represent articulatory gestures directly. These approaches need not be mutually exclusive. For example, voicing could be signaled by an arbitrary signal or by a light flashing on the lower part of a pair of spectacles, just at the level of the larynx as it is viewed by the deaf child.

The use of another modality to substitute for hearing is more demanding than supplementation of lipreading from an engineering point of view. It would be necessary to fabricate a wearable device for use by young children (see p. 18) and to determine by psycholphysical experimentation what types of display might permit the young deaf child to extract sufficient information to understand speech. If this could be done, it might be very successful with the preschool deaf child who is still in the most plastic stage of central nervous system maturation and in the most active period of natural language acquisition. It is possible that, in this period, children can learn to decode a speech signal presented to a nonauditory modality. Some preliminary work at least should be done to find out.

Studies of development of speech production and speech perception in normal infants

In order to use prostheses effectively, it is important for us to find out (1) how speech sounds are processed by normal-hearing infants and young children, and (2) what changes in this processing take place as children begin to understand speech. It may be necessary as part of this endeavor to learn more about the supra-threshold functioning of the normal and of the impaired auditory system (Eisenberg, p. 18). EEG and behavioral indices might both be used to find out, for example, whether distinctive features of phonemes are utilized by young children in decoding speech, how prosodic information is utilized and how the two kinds of information interact in the decoding process (Blesser, p. 118).

The development of speech production skills should also be studied in normal-hearing infants. Recent work suggests that this development is lawful and constitutes an essential prerequisite to language development (Kaplan and Kaplan, 1971). It may prove possible to find out how one skill is built upon another in speech development and to identify specific stages with respect to it. The possibility that speech production has an effect upon speech perception should be considered.

Studies of development of speech perception and production skills should be related to observations of nonverbal communication in infants (see Menyuk, pp. 148–149). Nonverbal behaviors and contextual cues which form an integral part of the situation in which an infant is vocalizing or listening to speech should be documented. Ethological approaches of this kind have been used by Ling in studying the development of deaf infants (pp. 152–157).

Information deriving from these studies would enable us to assess the effects of auditory amplification or of a nonauditory prosthesis upon the development of speech skills in deaf infants within a short period of time. At the present time, assessment is made much later in terms of scholastic achievement. Treatment procedures might also be based upon this information.

Studies of development of spoken language in school-age deaf children

Speech and language skills of many younger school-age deaf children are so limited that it is not possible to apply standard language achievement tests with these children (see pp. 151–152). It is important to find out which speech errors are most detrimental to intelligibility (Levitt, 1972a). Also, few attempts have been made to apply a transformational grammar approach to a corpus of spoken language obtained from young deaf children. Theories of language development in normal-hearing preschool children have not been applied to the language development of young deaf children. Thus we do not know to what extent their language is delayed and to what extent it is quite aberrant. Information of this kind would aid us in developing assessment and treatment procedures for use with school-age children.

Reading and writing in first language learning

It was suggested by House (p. 174) and Watson (p. 178) that reading and writing should be employed more extensively in teaching deaf children. Efforts should be made to develop a typescript prosthesis which should have transmission rates as high as those of speech. This would permit reading and typing to be socially interactive (see p. 177), and would provide immediate reference to the situational context (see p. 176). It was proposed that typed language forms might be tried out as a primary language input to the deaf child.

In all of such studies, it would be necessary to consider the population to which the experimental results might be generalized. Elliott (in a comment contributed after the Conference) suggested that this requires a definitive list of the variables pertinent for generalization. However, many would agree that the same variables pertinent for all children, e.g., "general intelligence," amount and kind of environmental stimulation, physical and health characteristics and specific individual differences, should be included along with type and degree of hearing impairment and age of onset of hearing impairment. Among the places where research facilities are proximal to sources of deaf subjects, many are likely to draw samples nonrepresentative of the universe of deaf children. Therefore, results of such experiments should be viewed in the context of the appropriate subpopulation. Better yet, it should be replicated with samples drawn from other subpopulations. Although researchers cannot expect to resolve the conflicts among various factions of deaf educators, they are expected to contribute an objective information base applicable to the total population of deaf children.

Finally, concern was expressed by many participants over the styles of communication adopted in the teaching of deaf children. In some cases, it was believed the teaching tended to be didactic, based upon set curricula, and lacking in spontaneity and naturalness. Silverman felt that teachers tended, for example, to teach what they have materials for and not what children need. In other words, the deaf child was treated as deviant and as having to make up for his deficiencies by hard work. It is just such a social climate that may contribute to failure to learn to read in normally-hearing children (Halle, 1972; Entwistle, 1973). As Furth has pointed out (p. 145), it certainly reduces the motivation of the deaf child to learn to speak. It also makes the classroom a less rewarding place for the teacher. Such social and cultural factors may be responsible in large part for the schisms which presently deplete the energies of deaf educators. Perhaps, as new techniques become available, they will be found by both teachers and deaf children to be useful and fun to use and will enable the deaf child to realize his own potential as a human being.

BIBLIOGRAPHY

Abel, S.M.: Discrimination of temporal gaps, J. Acoust. Soc. Amer. 52:519–524, 1972.

Baron, J.: Phonemic stage not necessary for reading, Quart. J. Exp. Psychol. 25:241–246, 1973.

Bekesy, G. von: Similarities between hearing and skin sensations, Psychol. Rev. 66:1–22, 1959.

Bellugi, U.: Development of language: the normal child, In: McLean, J.E.; Yoder, D.E., and Schiefelbush, R.L. (eds.): Language Intervention with the Retarded, Baltimore, University Park Press, 1972.

Berger, K.; Martin, J., and Sakoff, R.: The effect of visual distractions on speechreading performance, Teacher Deaf 68:384–387, 1970.

Bishop, M.E.; Ringel, R.L., and House, A.S.: Orosensory perception, speech production, and deafness, J. Speech Hear. Res. 16:257–266, 1973.

Blesser, B.: Speech perception under conditions of spectral transformation: I. Phonetic characteristics, J. Speech Hear. Res. 15(1):5–41, 1972.

Bloom, L.: Language Development: Form and Function in Emerging Grammars, Cambridge, M.I.T. Press, 1970.

Brannon, J.B., Jr.: Visual feedback of glossal motions and its influence on the speech of deaf children, Doctoral dissertation, Northwestern University, 1964.

Boothroyd, A.: Some experiments on the control of voice in the profoundly deaf using a pitch extractor and storage oscilloscope display, In: Smith, C.P. (ed.): Conference on Speech Communication and Processing, AFCRL-72-0120, Special Report No. 131, 1972.

Brown, R.: A First Language: The Early Stages, Cambridge, Harvard University Press, 1973.

Buhler, C.: The First Year of Life, New York: Day, 1930.

Calvert, D.R.: Some acoustic characteristics of the speech of profoundly deaf individuals, Doctoral dissertation, Stanford University, 1961.

Conrad, R.: Short-term memory processes in the deaf, Brit. J. Psychol. 61:179–195, 1970.

Conrad, R.: Short-term memory in the deaf: A test for speech coding, Brit. J. Psychol. 63:173–180, 1972.

Conrad, R.: Some correlates of speech coding in the short-term memory of the deaf, J. Speech Hear. Res. 16:375–384, 1973.

Cornett, O.: Study of the possibility of developing a speech analyzing hearing aid, Contract NINDS-73-13, 1973.

Danaher, E.M.; Osberger, M.J., and Pickett, J.M.: Discrimination of formant frequency transitions in synthetic vowels, J. Speech Hear. Res. 16:439–451, 1973.

Department of Education and Science Report: The education of deaf children: The possible place of fingerspelling and signing, London, Her Majesty's Stationery Office, 1968.

Divenyi, P.L., and Hirsh, I.J.: Identification of the temporal order of three tones, J. Acoust. Soc. Amer. 54:315A, 1973.

Eimas, P.D.; Siqueland, E.R., Jusczyk, P., et al.: Speech perception in infants, Science 171:303–306, 1971.

Entwistle, D.R.: Socialization of language: Educability and expectations, In: Maehr, M., and Stallings, W. (eds.): Culture, Child and School, In press.

Erber, N.P.: Auditory, visual, auditory-visual recognition of consonants by children with normal and impaired hearing, J. Speech Hear. Res. 15:413–422, 1972.

Fletcher, H.: Speech and Hearing, New York, Van Nostrand, 1929.

Fodor, J.A., and Bever, T.G.: The psychological reality of linguistic segments, J. Verb. Learn. Verb. Behav. 4:414–420, 1965.

Foust, K.O., and Gengel, R.W.: Speech discrimination by sensorineural hearing-impaired persons using a transposer hearing aid, Scan. Audiol. 2:161–170, 1973.

Franklin, B.: The effect on consonant discrimination of combining a low-frequency passband in one ear and a high-frequency passband in the other ear, J. Aud. Res. 9:365–378, 1970.

Franks, J.R., and Oyer, H.J.: Factors influencing the identification of English sounds in lipreading, J. Speech Hear. Res. 10:757–767, 1967.

Fry, D.B.: The development of the phonological system in the normal and in the deaf child, In: Smith, F., and Muller, G.A. (eds.): The Genesis of Language, Cambridge, M.I.T. Press, 1966.

Furth, H.G.: Thinking Without Language, New York, Free Press, 1966.

Furth, H.G.: Linguistic deficiency and thinking: Research with deaf subjects, Psychol. Bull. 76:58–72, 1971.

Garrett, M.; Bever, T.G., and Fodor, J.: The active use of grammar in speech perception, Percept. Psychophys. 1:30–32, 1966.

Geldard, F.A.: Pattern perception by the skin, In: Kenshalo, D.R. (ed.): The Skin Senses, Springfield, Charles C Thomas, 1968.

Gengel, R.W.: Practice effects in frequency discrimination by hearing-impaired children, J. Speech Hear. Res. 12:847–855, 1969.

Gengel, R.W.: Auditory temporal integration at relatively high masked threshold levels, J. Acoust. Soc. Amer. 51:1849–1851, 1972a.

Gengel, R.W.: Recognition of auditory temporal onset patterns by hearing impaired persons and by persons with normal sensitivity, Paper presented at the ASHA Convention, San Francisco, 1972b.

Gengel, R.W., and Watson, C.S.: Temporal integration: I. Clinical implications of a laboratory study. II. Additional data from hearing-impaired subjects, J. Speech Hear. Dis. 36:213–224, 1971.

Gengel, R.W.; Foust, F.O., Upton, H.W., et al.: Upton's wearable eyeglass speech reading aid: A preliminary evaluation, Paper presented at the ASHA Convention, Detroit, 1973.

Gibson, E.J.; Shurcliff, A., and Yonas, A.: Utilization of spelling patterns by deaf and hearing subjects, In: Levin, H., and Williams, J.P. (eds.): Basic Studies on Reading, New York, Basic Books, 1970.

Goldberg, A.J.: A visual feature indicator for the severely hard of hearing, IEEE Trans. Audio Electroacoust. AU-20, 16–22, 1972.

Green, D.M.: Temporal auditory acuity, Psychol. Rev. 78:540–551, 1971.

Greenfield, P.M.; Smith, J.H., and Laufer, B.: Communication and the Beginnings of Language, New York, Academic Press, 1973.

Halle, M.: On a parallel between conventions of versification and orthography; and on literacy among the Cherokee, In: Kavanagh, J.F., and Mattingly, I.G. (eds.): Language by Ear and by Eye: The Relationship between Speech and Reading, Cambridge, M.I.T. Press, 1972.

Harbert, F.; Young, I.M., and Wenner, C.H.: Auditory flutter fusion and envelope of signal, J. Acoust. Soc. Amer. 44:803—806, 1968.

Hardick, E.J.; Oyer, H.J., and Irion, P.E.: Lipreading performance as related to measurements of vision, J. Speech Hear. Res. 13:92—100, 1970.

Hirsh, I.J.: Auditory perception of temporal order, J. Acoust. Soc. Amer. 31:759—767, 1959.

Hirsh, I.J., and Sherrick, C.E.: Perceived order in different sense modalities, J. Exp. Psychol. 62:423—432, 1961.

Houde, R.A.: Instantaneous visual feedback in speech training for the deaf, Paper presented at ASHA Convention, Detroit, 1973.

House, A.S.; Goldstein, D.P., and Hughes, G.W.: Perception of visual transforms of speech stimuli: Learning simple syllables, Amer. Ann. Deaf 113:215—221, 1968.

Hudgins, C.V., and Numbers, F.C.: An investigation of the intelligibility of the speech of the deaf, Genetic Psychol. Monog. 25:289—392, 1942.

Huntingdon, D.A.; Harris, K.S., Shankweiler, D.P., et al.: Some observations on monosyllable production by deaf speakers and dysarthric speakers, Amer. Ann. Deaf 113:134—146, 1968.

Johansson, B.: The use of the transposer for the management of the deaf child, Int. Audiol. 5:362—371, 1966.

John, J.E., and Howarth, J.N.: The effect of time distortion on the intelligibility of deaf children's speech, Lang. Speech 8:127—134, 1965.

Kaplan, E.L.: The role of intonation in the acquisition of language, Doctoral dissertation, Cornell University, 1969.

Kaplan, E., and Kaplan, G.: The prelinguistic child, In: Eliot, J. (ed.): Human Development and Cognitive Processes, New York, Holt, Rinehart and Winston, 1971.

Kavanagh, J.F., and Cutting, J. (eds.): Communication without speech for the deaf, Fifth Conference on Communicating by Language, National Institute of Child Health and Human Development, M.I.T. Press, 1973.

Keidel, W.D.: The cochlear model in skin stimulation, Paper given at the Conference on Cutaneous Communication Systems and Devices, Monterey, California, April, 1973.

Kirman, J.H.: Tactile communication of speech: A review and analysis, Psychol. Bull. 80:54—74, 1973.

Kirsh, I., and Preston, M.S.: The Deaf Mentally Retarded Child: A Statement, In preparation.

Klatt, D.H., and Stevens, K.N.: Strategies for recognition of spoken sentences by visual examination of spectrograms, Report No. 2154, Bolt Beranek and Newman, Inc., Cambridge, 1971.

Kringlebotn, M.: Experiments with some visual-vibrotactile aids for the deaf, Amer. Ann. Deaf 113:311—317, 1968.

Lafon, J.C.; Dulac, A.M., Lacroix, F., et al.: La melodie de la parole et la surdite, Rev. Laryng., Otol., Rhin. 88:179—187, 1967.

Lashley, K.S.: The problem of serial order in behavior, In: Jeffress, L.A. (ed.): Cerebral Mechanisms in Behavior, New York, Wiley, 1951.

Lenneberg, E.H.: Biological Foundations of Language, New York, Wiley, 1967.

Levitt, H.: Analysis of acoustic characteristics of deaf speech, Progress Report, Grant 09252, NINDS, 1972a.

Levitt, H.: Sensory aids for the deaf: An overview, In: Smith, C.P. (ed.): Conference on Speech Communication and Processing, AFCRL-72-0120. Special Report No. 131, 1972b.

Levitt, H.: Language Disorders in Deaf Children, First Annual Report, Grant No. EQ73-001 DC, New York State Department of Education, 1973.

Lewis, M.M.: Infant Speech, London, Rantledge and Kegan Paul, 1951.

Liberman, A.M.: The grammars of speech and language, Cognitive Psychol. 1:301–323, 1970.

Liberman, A.M.; Cooper, F.S., Shankweiler, D.P., et al.: Perception of the speech code, Psychol. Rev. 74:431–461, 1967.

Liberman, A.M.; Cooper, F.S., Shankweiler, D.P., et al.: Why are spectrograms hard to read? Amer. Ann. Deaf 113:127–133, 1968.

Lieberman, P.: Intonation, Perception, and Language, Cambridge, M.I.T. Press, Research Monograph 38, 1967a.

Lieberman, P.: Intonation and the syntactic processing of speech, In: Walthen-Dunn, W. (ed.): Models for the Perception of Speech and Visual Form, Cambridge, M.I.T. Press, 1967b.

Lieberman, P.; Crelin, E.S., and Klatt, D.H.: Phonetic ability and related anatomy of the newborn and adult, Neanderthal man, and chimpanzee, Amer. Anthrop. 74:287–307, 1972.

Ling, A.H.: Dichotic listening in hearing-impaired children, J. Speech Hear. Res. 14:793–803, 1971.

Ling, D.: Three experiments on frequency transposition, Amer. Ann. Deaf 113:283–294, 1968.

Ling, D.: Speech discrimination by profoundly deaf children using linear and coding amplifiers, IEEE Trans. Audio Electroacoust. AU-17, 298–303, 1969.

Ling, D.: Comment on "Sensorineural loss and upward spread of masking", J. Speech Hear. Res. 14:222–223, 1971.

Linvill, J.G., and Bliss, J.C.: A direct translation aid for the blind, Proc. IEEE 54:40–51, 1966.

Locke, J.L., and Locke, V.L.: Deaf children's phonetic, visual and dactylic coding in a grapheme recall task, J. Exp. Psychol. 89:142–146, 1971.

Macnamara, J.: Cognitive basis of language learning in infants, Psychol. Rev. 79:1–13, 1972.

MacNeilage, P.F.: Motor control of serial ordering of speech, Psychol. Rev. 77:182–196, 1970.

Magrisso, R.: Patterned electrical stimulation of the skin senses, Master's thesis, The Johns Hopkins University, 1972.

Markides, A.: The speech of deaf and partially hearing children with special reference to factors affecting intelligibility, Brit. J. Disorders of Comm. 5:126–140, 1970.

Martin, E.S., and Pickett, J.M.: Sensorineural hearing loss and upward spread of masking, J. Speech Hear. Res. 13:426–437, 1970.

Martin, E.S., and Pickett, J.M.: Re: Sensorineural hearing loss and upward spread of masking, J. Speech Hear. Res. 14:223–224, 1971.

Martin, E.S.: Pickett, J.M., and Colten, S.: Discrimination of vowel formant transitions by listeners with severe sensorineural hearing loss, In: Fant, G. (ed.): International Symposium on Speech Communication Ability and Profound Deafness, Washington, D.C., Alexander G. Bell Assoc., 1972.

Martin, J.G.: Rhythmic (hierarchial) versus serial structure in speech and other behavior, Psychol. Rev. 79:487–509, 1972.

Martin, S.E.: Nonalphabetic writing systems. Some observations, In: Kavanagh, J.F., and Mattingly, I.G. (eds.): Language by Ear and by Eye: The Relationship between Speech and Reading, Cambridge, M.I.T. Press, 1972.

Martony, J.: Studies on the speech of the deaf, Quart. Prog. Report, Speech Transmission Laboratory, Royal Inst. of Techn., Stockholm, 1966.

Martony, J.: On the correction of voice pitch level for severely hard of hearing subjects, Amer. Ann. Deaf 113:195–202, 1968.

Martony, J.: Visual aids for speech correction, In: Fant, G. (ed.): International Symposium on Speech Communication Ability and Profound Deafness, Washington, D.C., Alexander G. Bell Assoc., 1972.

Martony, J.; Risberg, A., Spens, K.-E., et al.: Results of a rhyme-test for speech audiometry, In: Fant, G. (ed.): International Symposium on Speech Communication Ability and Profound Deafness, Washington, D.C., Alexander G. Bell Assoc., 1972.

Massaro, D.W.: Preperceptual images, processing time and perceptual units in auditory perception, Psychol. Rev. 79:124–145, 1972.

Mattingly, I.G.: Reading, the linguistic process, and linguistic awareness, In: Kavanagh, J.F., and Mattingly, I.G. (eds.): Language by Ear and by Eye: The Relationship between Speech and Reading, Cambridge, M.I.T. Press, 1972.

McNeill, D.: The Acquisition of Language, New York, Harper and Row, 1970.

Menyuk, P.: Sentences Children Use, Cambridge, M.I.T. Press, Research Monograph 52, 1969.

Miller, J.D.: Directions for research to improve hearing aids and services for the hearing-impaired, A Report of Working Group 65, NAS-NCR Committee on Hearing, Bioacoustics, and Biomechanics, Washington, D.C., 1972.

Moffitt, A.R.: Consonant cue perception by twenty- to twenty-four week old infants, Child Develop. 42:717–731, 1971.

Morkovin, B.: Experiment in teaching deaf preschool children in the Soviet Union, Volta Rev. 62:260–268, 1962.

Morse, P.A.: The discrimination of speech and nonspeech stimuli in early infancy, J. Exp. Child Psychol. 14:477–492, 1972.

Morse, P.A.: Infant speech perception: A preliminary model and review of the literature, Paper presented at Conference on Language Intervention with the Mentally Retarded, Wisconsin Dells, Wisconsin, June, 1973.

Neisser, U.: Cognitive Psychology, New York, Appleton-Century-Crofts, 1967.

Neyhus, A.I.: Speechreading failure in deaf children, Department of H.E.W., Office of Education, Washington, D.C., 1969.

Nye, P.W.: Psychological factors limiting the rate of acceptance of audio stimuli, In: Clark, L.L. (ed.): Proceedings of the International Congress on Technology and Blindness, Vol. 2, New York, American Foundation for the Blind, 1963.

Nye, P.W.: Reading aids for blind people: A survey of progress with the technological and human problems, Medical, Electronics, and Biomed. Engin. 32:247–264, 1964.

Paivo, A.: Imagery and Verbal Processes, New York, Holt, Rinehart, and Winston, 1971.

Patterson, J.H., and Green, D.M.: Discrimination of transient signals having identical energy spectra, J. Acoust. Soc. Amer. 48:894–905, 1970.

Patterson, J.H., and Green, D.M.: Masking of transient signals having identical energy spectra, Audiology 10:85–96, 1971.

Perrot, D.R., and Williams, K.N.: Auditory temporal resolutions: gap detection as a function of interpulse frequency disparity, Psychonomic Sci. 25:73–74, 1971.

Phillips, J.R.: Formal characteristics of speech which mothers address to their young children, Doctoral dissertation, The Johns Hopkins University, 1970.

Pickett, J.M.: Perception of vowels heard in noises of various spectra, J. Acoust. Soc. Amer. 29:613–620, 1957.

Pickett, J.M., and Danaher, E.M.: On discrimination of formant transitions by persons with severe sensorineural hearing loss, Paper presented at a Symposium on Auditory Analysis and Perception of Speech, Leningrad, August, 1973.

Pickett, J.M., and Gengel, R.W.: Research on frequency transposition for hearing aids, Final Report, Grant No. OEG-2-7-070070-1522, Sensory Communication Research Laboratory, 1972.

Pickett, J.M.; Martin, E.S., Johnson, D., et al.: On patterns of speech feature reception by deaf listeners, In: Fant, G. (ed.): International Symposium on Speech Communication Ability and Profound Deafness, Washington, D.C., Alexander G. Bell Assoc., 1972.

Pickett, J.M., and Martony, J.: Low-frequency vowel formant discrimination in hearing-impaired listeners, J. Speech Hear. Res. 13:347–359, 1970.

Pickett, J.M., and Pickett, B.H.: Communication of speech sounds by a tactual vocoder, J. Speech Hear. Res. 6:207–222, 1963.

Pisoni, D.B.: On the nature of categorical perception of speech sounds, Doctoral dissertation, University of Michigan, 1971.

Port, D.K., and Preston, M.S.: Early apical stop production: A voice onset time analysis, Status Report on Speech Research, Haskins Laboratories, 29130, 125–152, 1972.

Potter, R.K.; Kopp, G.A., and Green, H.C.: Visible Speech, New York, Van Nostrand, 1947.

Preston, M.S.; Yeni-Komshian, G., Stark, R.E., et al.: Certain aspects of the development of speech production and perception in children, J. Acoust. Soc. Amer. 46:A102, 1969.

Resnick, S.B.: Discriminability of time-reversed click pairs: Intensity effects, Doctoral dissertation, University of Oklahoma, 1973.

Risberg, A.: Periodic-nonperiodic test of hearing capacity, Quart. Prog. Report, 2–3, Speech Transmission Laboratory, Stockholm, 1968a.

Risberg, A.: Visual aids for speech correction, Amer. Ann. Deaf 113:178–194, 1968b.

Risberg, A.: A critical review of work on speech analyzing hearing aids, IEEE Trans. Audio Electroacoust. AU-17, 290–297, 1969.

Risberg, A., and Martony, J.: A method for the classification of audiograms, In: Fant, G. (ed.): International Symposium on Speech Communication Ability and Profound Deafness, Washington, D.C., Alexander G. Bell Assoc., 1972.

Ronken, D.A.: Monaural detection of a phase difference between clicks, J. Acoust. Soc. Amer. 47:1091–1099, 1970.

Rosenthal, R.D.; Lang, J.K., and Levitt, H.: Effects of low-frequency speech bands on intelligibility, Communications Sciences Laboratory Report No. 3, City University of New York Graduate School, 1972.

Rozin, P.; Poritsky, S., and Sotsky, R.: American children with reading problems can easily learn to read English represented by Chinese characters, Science 171:1264–1266, 1971.

Savin, H.B., and Bever, T.G.: The nonperceptual reality of the phoneme, J. Verb. Learn. Verb. Behav. 9:295–302, 1970.

Sherrick, C.E.: Effects of double simultaneous stimulation of the skin, Amer. J. Psychol. 77:42–53, 1964.

Smiarowski, R.A.: Relations among temporal resolution, forward masking and simultaneous masking, Doctoral dissertation, Northwestern University, 1970.

Smith, C.: Residual hearing and speech production in deaf children, Communicative Sciences Laboratory Report #4, CUNY Graduate Center, New York, 1973.

Snow, C.E.: Mother's speech to children learning language, Child Develop. 43:549–565, 1973.

Stark, R.E.: Teaching /ba/ and /pa/ to deaf children using real-time spectral displays, Lang. and Speech 15:14–29, 1972.

Stark, R.E.; Rose, S.N., and Maclagan, M.: Features of infant vocalization, In preparation.

Stark, R.E.; Cullen, J.K., and Chase, R.A.: Preliminary work with the new Bell Telephone Visible Speech Translator, Amer. Ann. Deaf 113:205–214, 1968.

Stevens, K.N.: Segments, features and analysis by synthesis, In: Kavanagh, J.F., and Mattingly, I.G. (eds.): Language by Ear and by Eye: The Relationship between Speech and Reading, Cambridge, M.I.T. Press, 1972.

Stevens, K.N., and Halle, M.: Remarks on analysis by synthesis and distinctive features, In: Wathen-Dunn, W. (ed.): Models for the Perception of Speech and Visible Form, Cambridge, M.I.T. Press, 1967.

Stevens, K.N., and House, A.S.: Speech perception, In: Tobias, J. (ed.): Foundations of Modern Auditory Theory, Vol. 2., New York, Academic Press, 1972.

Sung, G.S.; Sung, R.J., and Angelelli, R.M.: Effect of frequency transposition characteristics of hearing aids on speech intelligibility in noise, J. Aud. Res. 11:318–321, 1971.

Taenzer, J.C.: Visual word reading, IEEE Trans. Man-Machine Systems, MMS-11, 44–53, 1970.

Thomas, I.B., and Sparks, D.S.: Discrimination of filtered/clipped speech by hearing-impaired subjects, J. Acoust. Soc. Amer. 49:1881–1887, 1971.

Trehub, S.E., and Rabinovitch, M.S.: Auditory-linguistic sensitivity in early infancy, Develop. Psychol. 6:74–77, 1972.

Upton, H.W.: Wearable eyeglass speechreading aid, Amer. Ann. Deaf 113:222–229, 1968.

Watson, C.S., and Gengel, R.W.: Signal duration and signal frequency in relation to auditory sensitivity, J. Acoust. Soc. Amer. 46:989–997, 1969.

Wedenberg, E.: Auditory training of severely hard of hearing preschool children, Acta Oto-Laryng. Supplement 110, 1954.

Weir, R.H.: Some questions on the child's learning of phonology, In: Smith, F., and Muller, G.A. (eds.): The Genesis of Language, Cambridge, M.I.T. Press, 1966.

White, B.W.; Saunders, F.A., Scadden, L., et al.: Seeing with the skin, Percept. Psychophys. 7:23–27, 1970.

Willemain, T.R., and Lee, F.F.: Tactile pitch displays for the deaf, IEEE Trans. Audio Electroacoust. AU-20, 9–16, 1972.

Youniss, R., and Furth, H.G.: Attainment and transfer of logical connectives in children, J. Educ. Psychol. 55:357–361, 1964.

Zlatin, M.: Development of the voicing contrast: A psychoacoustic study of voice onset time, Doctoral dissertation, Northwestern University, 1972.

Subject Index

Author Index